# I BELIEVE IN SATAN'S DOWNFALL

# I Believe in
# Satan's Downfall

Michael Green

Hodder & Stoughton

LONDON SYDNEY AUCKLAND

First published in Great Britain 1981. Second edition 1988.
Third edition 1995.

10  9  8  7  6  5  4  3  2  1

British Library Cataloguing in Publication Data
A record for this book is available from the British Library

ISBN 0 340 63034 5

Printed and bound in Great Britain by
Cox and Wyman Ltd, Reading, Berkshire

Hodder and Stoughton Ltd
A Division of Hodder Headline PLC
338 Euston Road
London NW1 3BH

For
the Faculty and Members
of Regent College
in the University of British Columbia
Vancouver
at whose Summer School
part of this book was written

The seventy returned with joy, saying,
"Lord, even the demons are subject to us in your name!"
And Jesus said to them,
"I saw Satan fall like lightning from heaven."

Luke 10:17,18

The reason the Son of God appeared
was to destroy the works of the devil.

1 John 3:8

## Foreword to the Third Edition

HIGH AMONG the list of Christian doctrines that have fallen into disrepute is belief in the devil. The theologian in his study and the ordinary churchgoer in the pew are, for once, agreed. It is ridiculous to believe in Satan in this enlightened age. Such credulity went out at the beginning of the scientific revolution.

Nevertheless a remarkable thing has happened. At the very time when legislation against witchcraft was being removed from the Statute Book in the mid-1950s, the biggest explosion of the occult for three centuries was beginning to take off. Satan worship, black and white magic, cultic abuse, horoscopes, seances, astrology and tarot cards have now become commonplace. Ouija boards and levitation are to be found in many schools. Despite our professed sophistication there is today in the West a greater interest in and practice of magic than there has been for generations. God may be in decline in Western hearts, but his Satanic Adversary is very much in the ascendent.

At the same time, humankind seems to be gripped by forces far greater than the individual, national or international community can cope with. Never has our technological competence been greater, but never has there been so much fear and gloom about the future of *homo sapiens* on this planet as there is today. The mad frenzy of insensate wars and the constant oppression of the poor by the rich are but two of the expressions of corporate evil which we seem incapable of handling. In every big city in the world crime and abuse, corruption and murder hold centre stage.

There is a further paradox. Despite our professed scepticism and proud scientific outlook, our world is falling back into a naïve acceptance of any new religion which comes along. There is a massive revival of paganism in our countries. Monotheism gives way to its ancient foe, pantheism – the oldest of heresies. Faith is replaced by superstition. At the intellectual level postmodernism and deconstructionism have encouraged a profound dissatisfaction with our simplistic acceptance of science as the only source of knowledge. Crystals and channelling, ancient lore and nostrums jostle together in the New Age thinking which has made such inroads into our culture. It does not pretend to be rational: indeed it glories in the irrational. But deeply entwined in its roots is an openness to dark Satanic forces which are as lethal today as they were in the second and third centuries AD when they nearly destroyed Christianity altogether.

For these reasons I felt it might be useful to take a fresh look at the biblical account of evil, and the possibility of its defeat. This book arose partly out of the factors I have just outlined, partly out of the suggestion of a friend, and partly out of personal experience of naked evil which I had not been trained to expect. I have seen this ravaging many lives in recent years, and have also seen it being triumphantly routed by the power of Jesus Christ. It is therefore out of much more than academic interest that this book has arisen. It constitutes a call to Christians to take seriously the spiritual battle in which followers of Christ are necessarily engaged, and to recognise both the strength of the devil and the far greater strength of the living God. It revels in the truth that "he who is in you is greater than he who is in the world".

This book makes no attempt to examine in detail the different faces of evil in the world. It is designed, rather, to explore the nature and extent of Christ's victory over the very fount of evil, and to see how that victory can be applied in the realm of contemporary discipleship, both corporate and individual.

Frankly, I found this a difficult book to write. I gather C.S. Lewis felt very much the same when he wrote *The Screwtape Letters*. It brought unwelcome and unusual pressures on myself and my family: the master of disguise is not best pleased to have his disguises stripped from him. But I am confident that Christ has won the supreme victory over evil in every shape and form, and that the culmination of all history will demonstrate as much.

This book was written more than a decade ago, but there has remained a steady demand for it on both sides of the Atlantic and in other parts of the world. Attention has focused more than I would wish on chapter five, "The Fascination of the Occult". I suppose that is inevitable — considering the current prevalence of the occult. People are interested to see something of its origins and how to discover in their experience the victory of Christ. But I hope this new edition will lead many to concentrate on the other chapters of this book which, though less exciting, are probably more important. Holiness of life, opposition to structural evil, and the recognition of false religion are crucial for any Christians who hope to have a confident and credible impact on society in the last years of this millennium.

I decided not to contribute a bibliography to the first edition because I had little to add to the extensive bibliographies in John Richards *But Deliver Us From Evil* (DLT, 1978) and Kent Philpott *Demonology and the Occult* (Zondervan, 1973), although a good deal has been written since then. But the more I looked into the subject the more grateful I became to Jesus Christ my Lord, whose life, death and exaltation spelled Satan's downfall.

MICHAEL GREEN
ADVENT 1994

# Contents

# CHAPTER 1

## *Satan? That I Can't Believe!*

IN THE 1940s in the midst of the most titanic struggle between two world powers, Dr. Rudolf Bultmann, arguably the most distinguished New Testament scholar in the world at that time, made his celebrated plea that we should demythologise the New Testament. It is impossible, he maintained, at the same time to believe in the world of angels and devils, and to make use of aeroplanes and electric light. The scientific age in which we now live has made it impossible for us to hold these naïve views about incarnation, the demonic and the rest which our forefathers took for granted. Bultmann's essay set off a furious debate, but has proved extremely influential in scholarly circles.

So much so that when, in the early 1970s, the Bishop of Exeter in England chaired a serious Report on Exorcism, and when public attention was caught by a disastrous death after failure to administer exorcism properly, a large number of theologians were invited to sign an open letter deploring the credulity of those who thought that demons still existed or were foolish enough to believe in a personal devil. Although I was asked to sign that letter, I declined. It seemed to me that the naïveté might possibly lie with those who wished so summarily to dispose of His Infernal Eminence.

But there is no doubt that those theologians spoke for a wide section of Christian opinion, for whom the idea of a devil with horns and cloven hoof is utterly ridiculous. How bygone ages could have believed it is a mystery to them. At any rate all sensible modern Christians will want to jettison so bizarre a notion.

But who does think of Satan as a being with horns and cloven hoof? This is a cartoon figure, and has no right to be taken seriously. The Scriptures give no countenance to it, but they do very seriously warn us of a malign power of evil

15

standing behind the pressures of a godless world without and a fallen nature within the Christian. The world, the flesh and the devil have formed a crucial part of Christian teaching from the very beginning. More, they have been embodied in the baptismal vows of renunciation and repentance. At the very moment of visible incorporation into Christ almost all liturgies have a specific act of repudiating the devil. Belief in the devil, therefore, is very much in the lifeblood of the Christian tradition. We are bound to ask what justification there may be for believing not in some cardboard figure of devilish fun, but in a person (or personification?) so utterly ghastly and wicked, so totally opposed to our race, that he stands behind all other types of evil, be they physical, corporate, moral or spiritual. Is it possible to believe in a unified centre and focus of evil? I believe it is, for a number of reasons.

## A Personal Devil?

### Prolegomena

Before we glance at the reasons which dispose some of us to believe in the existence of Satan, there are two preliminary points which are worth noting.

If there is a devil, whose aim is to rebel against God and embroil the whole cosmos in his rebellion, then nothing would please him better than the current ridicule in which he is held. As we shall see in the course of this study, the New Testament makes it abundantly clear that Satan is a defeated foe, who received his death-blow on Calvary, although he is taking an unconscionably long time about dying! If that New Testament emphasis is true, there are two opposite attitudes that would equally suit him. The first is that of excessive preoccupation with the Prince of evil. The second is that of excessive scepticism about his very existence.

For the majority of the past two thousand years, men have veered towards the former extreme. The overtones of Dante's *Inferno* have echoed down the centuries. For many ages Satan has occupied too prominent a place in men's thoughts, and many things have been ascribed to his agency

16

which we now know belong to natural causes and processes. Satan has been only too vividly recalled, but the fact of his crushing defeat by Christ has often been soft-pedalled or forgotten. If the devil does exist, this course of action (which, curiously enough, seems to be coming about again in the current preoccupation with the occult) is bound to please him.

But equally, if he exists, he is bound to be glad when men forget all about him, when they ridicule him, when they dismiss him as a satyr-like figure appropriate for myths and legends but not for the cold light of twentieth-century day. Like any general who can persuade the opposition to underestimate him, Satan (supposing him to exist) must be enchanted at the present state of affairs which leaves him free to operate with the maximum of ease and efficiency, confident that nobody takes him seriously. The more he can do to encourage this doubt of his existence, the better. The more he can blind people's minds to the true state of affairs, the better his aims are furthered. The very doubt of his existence becomes evidence for it.

The other interesting point is this. Doubt about the existence of a malign focus of evil is to be found, by and large, only in Christian lands. It is only where the victory of Christ is so well known, only where the defeat of the devil is so celebrated, that doubts are expressed. If he exists, it must please him mightily to have his existence denied by the only people who know his inherent weakness, and are aware of the act of Christ on Calvary that spelt his doom. Were he better known he would be more hated, more resisted, more defeated in the lives of Christians. So it suits him admirably for them to slumber in the bland assurance that he does not exist.

In non-Christian lands it is not so. There you find the most vital awareness of the reality and personality of evil forces, focused in the great adversary himself. Animism, Islam, Hinduism are under no illusions about the great Enemy. There he is known, dreaded and often slavishly worshipped. The grip, the fear, the squalor of demon worship and Satan worship either in this country or overseas is something which nobody who has witnessed it can readily forget. I found in Ghana, for instance, and not least among the best educated members of society, two deep convictions. One was belief in the existence of God; the other, belief in the existence of Satan. It would be broadly true to say that disbelief in the devil is a characteristic only of materialistic Western Christendom.

## Seven Considerations

So much for the prolegomena: now for the reasons which lead me, at all events, to believe in Satan. I shall mention seven, in what may be seen as ascending order of importance.

### Philosophy

First, there is a philosophical point to consider. There is no power in our world without personality. To be sure, there are plenty of manifestations of power in society without personalities being at all obvious. But they are there all the same. There cannot be power apart from an originating intelligence, planning it, calling it into being, using it. Owen Whitehouse, in his careful article on 'Satan' in Hastings *Dictionary of the Bible*, is prepared to make massive allowances both for the cultural climate in which biblical writers operated and for the limitations imposed on Jesus and his beliefs by the incarnation. He maintains (which I would question) that the demonology of the Bible was "the latest phase of that animistic interpretation of the universe which was destined to survive for centuries until the gradual growth of our inductive methods has substituted for demonology (as formerly understood) a rationally co-ordinated nexus of physical causality and law". But he goes on to maintain most robustly that science never can overturn the fundamental truth of demonology, namely that "behind and beyond the physical nexus of interrelations there must lie personality".

We certainly live our lives, complex and influenced by varied non-personal factors as they are, on the assumption that there is such a thing as volition and free will, and that we do in fact influence others by the exercise of them. It is

18

impossible to imagine the universe in which we live as subsisting without reason and will. This is the surd in the atheist's position. In the name of reason he rejects the supreme Reason, God. Instead, he assumes that we all spring from mindless plankton, and therefore he is unable to resist the riposte that his mind, which reaches this atheistic conclusion, is equally the product of randomness and hence has no claim to be rational.

It is simply flying in the face of evidence if we reject either mind or matter, two ineluctable strands in the universe. Eastern mysticism in its rejection of matter is no more convincing than Western materialism in its rejection of mind. By far the most reasonable assumption is that behind our intelligible and moral sphere there lies a supreme intelligence and will. The name we give to it is God. But as we observe the variety of forms in which evil, no less than good, shows itself, are we not to suppose that there is an organising spirit of supreme evil and malignity? The name we give to it is Satan. Belief in a great transcendent power of evil adds nothing whatever to the difficulties imposed by belief in a transcendent power of good. Indeed, it eases them somewhat. For if there were no Satan, it would be hard to resist the conclusion that God is a fiend both because of what he does, in nature, and what he allows, in human wickedness.

## Theology

Closely allied with this philosophical point there is a theological consideration which is worth a moment's pause. Despite temporary aberrations such as the 'Death of God' school in the 1960s, belief in a good, personal, transcendent God has remained unshaken as the foundation for all Christian thought over two thousand years. Some of the reasons which have led to and supported this belief are the marks of design in our world; the existence of moral qualities such as beauty, truth and goodness; and the uniformity of nature, which suggests the care of a beneficent Creator and Sustainer. But do not similar considerations lead us to infer the existence of Satan? Are there no marks of design in the forces of evil which form so large a part of our daily news coverage? Does not the persistence with which these forces continue to show themselves with ever increasing horror as the years go by (so much so that some of the most sensitive thinkers today believe that this generation may well be the last) point in the same direction? And does not the existence of wicked characteristics which are the very opposite of beauty, truth and goodness point beyond our world to an evil source for these things?

It is impossible to prove an argument like this. But consider where the probabilities lie. If we allow the existence of a God who is personal but whom we cannot see, is the existence of a great Counterfeiter so utterly incredible? Do we not see in every generation men who seem to be the very embodiment of evil – monsters in their time? It is very hard to believe of them that wickedness is merely the absence of good. No, it is a mighty force, a poisonous miasma emanating from them and affecting all within their range. Is it so improbable that they are the instruments of Satan, a supernatural centre and embodiment of evil who fouls all he touches? This is not to add any dimension to the problem of evil. It assists in understanding it. After all, if Christians believe in the Holy Spirit, why should they be so averse to giving credence to an Unholy Spirit, particularly when the evidence for his handiwork is just as obvious as that of his celestial counterpart? So long as we do not relapse into dualism (and that the Bible is careful to avoid) I can see no theological reason whatever for believing in the one and deeming the other incredible.

Indeed, I would go further. I believe the Christian doctrines of God, of man and of salvation are utterly untenable without the existence of Satan. You simply cannot write him out of the human story and then imagine that the story is basically unchanged. At the beginning, at the mid-point of time and at the end, the devil has an indelible place in Christian theology. The fallen nature of man and of everything he does, the self-destructive tendencies of every civilisation history has known, the prevalence of disease and natural disasters, together with "nature, red in tooth and claw" unite to point to a great outside Enemy. I would like to ask theologians who are sceptical about the devil how they can give a satisfactory account of God if Satan is a figment of the imagination. Without the devil's existence, the doctrine of God, a God who could have made such a world and allowed such horrors as take place daily within it, is utterly monstrous. Such a God would be no loving Father. He would be a pitiless tyrant.

## Environment

The third consideration is environmental. Ronald Higgins, a governor of the London School of Economics, taught sociology at Oxford, and then for twelve years was a member of the British Diplomatic Service before joining the staff of *The Observer* newspaper. He has recently written an overview of the world environmental situation which is neither hysterical nor complacent. Based as it is on experience rather than cynicism, his book *The Seventh Enemy* may well prove to be the most formidable assessment yet made of the way the world is likely to go in the next twenty years or so. Higgins lists six immense, impersonal threats to our world. They are overpopulation, famine on a massive scale, the shortage of non-renewable resources, the rapid destruction of our environment, the terrifying and growing nuclear threat, and technology racing out of control.

It is, as he points out in this sober but frightening book, the human factor which causes him the greatest anxiety. Theoretically it would be possible for us to cope with the six massive threats he outlines, but given the chaotic way in which diplomacy is carried out throughout the world (and remember, he has had first-hand experience of it), given the pressures upon governments to think only about tomorrow because there is no time to think about the day after, and given the human apathy and smugness that assumes something is bound to turn up to alleviate the gloom – given all this, the Seventh Enemy (man's inertia and blindness) is the greatest threat of all. Higgins explores not only the moral basis of power in our world, but the spiritual basis that is necessary for morality. And although it is not written from any Christian presuppositions, this remarkable book gives enormous reinforcement to the Christian belief that behind the evil in the world and in man there is an organising genius, a focus of horror far greater than man himself, a power which can only be overcome by allowing spiritual considerations to change our lifestyle and policies. If anyone wishes to see a contemporary exhibition of what St. Paul called the "god of this world" at work, "blinding the minds of unbelievers" Richard Higgins has provided it. A careful look at the world around us points strongly to an organising force to evil, to Satan in fact.

## Experience

The fourth consideration comes from experience. It is the fact of temptation. Every man, woman and child on this earth is tempted. That is to say, he is exposed to inducements, some of them exceedingly delectable, to do what he knows is wrong. The desire from within and the pressures from society do not seem sufficient to explain the force of this strange phenomenon. You have only to try to break with habits formed by giving way to temptation, and you will find yourself gripped by a power much bigger than you. You will soon discover that you have got a real fight on your hands. If this were only the experience of modern man, or of Western man, one might be inclined to minimise it. But it is the experience of every man, unless he has so made a practice of surrendering to temptation that he has forgotten what it is to fight. But anyone who has genuinely tried to overcome his failings as and when he becomes aware of them, discovers how persistent, how cunning and how subtle are the bonds which encircle him. He finds himself acknowledging with the Roman poet Ovid, "I see the better course, and I approve it . . . but I follow the worse." That has been the experience of mankind down the ages. And the more upright the man is, the more vividly is he aware of the battle and of the strength of the opposition. Experience teaches me that Satan is a reality.

## Occult

Fifth, there is the dark area of the occult. I shall deal with this more extensively in chapter five. Here it is enough to

22

say that in our own day and in our own country there are plenty of people who are worshipping Satan direct, and by the exercise of black magic are discovering the reality of spiritual forces to which they were previously complete strangers. A few years ago this might have sounded wild exaggeration. Now, anyone who is aware of tendencies in society will know that it is an understatement. When men and women deliberately seek occult powers, they very quickly discover that these powers are both real and terrible. But involvement can come in a more tentative way. Many get sucked in through playing with ouija boards, reading tarot cards, experimenting with levitation or going to séances. Charms and horoscopes have, to my certain knowledge, brought dangerous and damaging exposure to the reality of evil forces. Although much in this realm is sheer chicanery, much is not. And that resisduum is nakedly evil. It does not prove the existence of a personal devil. But it does show the existence of a concentrated power of evil to which men's lives can become prey. Paul talks of enabling men to "escape from the devil's snare after being captured alive by God to do his will" (2 Tim. 2:25). Anyone who has seen the astounding contrast between a person possessed by an occult force and that same person set free by Christ fully and completely – it may be only an hour later – will not need any persuading that man has a mighty, hateful enemy in Satan.

## Scripture

The sixth factor which convinces me that Satan is a reality to be reckoned with, and cannot be satisfactorily disposed of by neglect or ridicule, is the witness of the Bible. This witness is particularly widespread and explicit. From Genesis to Revelation we are confronted by an anti-God force of great power and cunning. He is arrogant and determined, the implacable foe of God and man, who is out to spoil and mar all that is good and lovely. We find him in the Garden of Eden at the beginning of the story. We find him in the lake of fire at the Bible's end. We find him tempting David, tempting Saul, tempting the Israelities, tempting Job. We find a major concentration on him in the Gospels, and there can be no doubt whatever that the apostles made recognition of Satan's reality and enlistment against him a crucial part of their ethical teaching. Not only have we whole chapters given over to this, such as the Temptation stories in Matthew 4 and Luke 4, together with 2 Thessalonians 2 and Ephesians 6, but scholars have given good reason to believe that "Stand", or "Withstand the devil" was a prominent feature in primitive Christian catechisms within the apostolic period. You have only to sit down with a concordance and look up the words "Satan" and "devil" to see what a great deal is directed this way in the Bible. Moreover, far from it being a primitive anthropomorphism which fades away as the fuller light of Christ dawns on the scene, there is more in the Gospels about Satan than anywhere else in the Bible, as if the appearance of the Prince of heaven challenged the Prince of hell to frenzied activity.

It is sometimes suggested that the Hebrews did not believe in a devil until after the Exile had exposed them to the influences of Persian dualism. It is true that the name "Satan" does not occur until after that, but then there are only three references in the Old Testament anyway to Satan as a proper name. It may well be the case that the Exile sharpened Hebrew perception. But it would be a great mistake to attribute their belief in the devil to Iranian origins. For one thing, Judaism never succumbed to the dualism which characterised Persian thought. Israel never imagined God and the devil as equal and opposite forces: such a thing would be unthinkable for such passionate monotheists. For another thing, there are indications that they were well aware of a powerful force of evil long before the Exile.

If we assume that the classic passage in Genesis 3 was written after the Exile, at all events in its present form (as most scholars do) we are still left with a good deal of earlier material. The most obvious is a group of passages where an "evil spirit" comes upon a man, possesses him, and drives him to actions against the will of God (1 Sam. 16:14, Judges 9:23, 1 Kings 22:21f are all highly significant).

24

Centuries before the Exile we find allusions to the primal dragon of evil, Leviathan, Rahab or Tannin. It was the slimy chaos-monster, subdued by God at the dawn of creation. Passages like Job 7:12, 9:13, 26:12f., Ps. 74:13f, 98:9f, Isaiah 27:1, 30:7, 51:9 are among the many Old Testament allusions to this force of utter evil seen in the imagery of a mythical beast. There is something very similar in the Babylonian Creation Epic, where Tiâmat, the dragon monster of the great abyss, is defeated by Marduk, god of light. Similarly in the Iranian myth, Azhi Dahaka, the poisonous serpent, was defeated at the dawn of time by Thraetaona and kept captive in the bowels of the earth, until, after a prescribed time, he breaks loose again and is finally conquered by Keresapa.

Or we might look at Gen. 6:1-4, a passage of immemorial origins, where supernatural causes are assigned for the growing corruption of the human race. It is all opaque; we do not know much about these "sons of god" who united with the daughters of men and bred a race of *nephilim*, giants – though this became a happy hunting ground for all sorts of speculation in the inter-testamental period, particularly in the Book of Enoch, leaving strong traces in the New Testament, the Fathers and the rabbinic writings. But we have seen enough to be sure that the anti-God principle was there in the earliest Hebrew writings. In no way can it be ascribed to post-exilic speculation. What is interesting is the way in which all over the Middle East you find a profound conviction of the cosmic struggle, the existence of an utterly malign force, with an army of evil spirits at his bidding. Only in the religion of Israel do you find a firm and unflinching conviction that "the Lord God omnipotent is reigning", yes, even over the forces of evil.

Belief in a personal devil was, then, firmly ensconced in Hebrew religion long before the time of Jesus. Satan is the tempter of men and the accuser of the brethren. He is powerful but not omnipotent. He is a force to be reckoned with. And this view is shared by all alike in New Testament times. It is there in all the evangelists, Acts, Paul, Peter, John, James, Jude, Hebrews and the Book of Revelation. If any subject is taught with clarity and persistence throughout the Bible and supremely in the New Testament it is the existence of the personalised source of evil, Satan or the devil. Whatever strand one looks at in Scripture, it is prominent. I do not see how anybody who regards the Scriptures as at all normative for belief or behaviour can possibly avoid the conclusion that this is the firm and unwavering teaching of the Bible, and that therefore any simple rejection of such uniform and decisive teaching needs a great deal of justification. It simply will not do to say, "Oh, we can't believe that these days." Since when has any of the biblical revelation fitted neatly into what could be believed these days? If unaided reason were enough to disclose God to us, the Almighty might have spared himself the trouble both of revelation and of incarnation.

### Jesus

The final and to my mind conclusive reason for believing in the reality of Satan is simply this. Jesus believed it. He has more to say about Satan than anyone else in the Bible. He has no doubt whatever of his reality. Satan is the one who tempted him so skilfully and fiercely, and who kept coming back at him with devious suggestions all through his ministry (Matt. 4:1–11). It is the devil who snatches away the message of the good news from those who listen to it half-heartedly, or who sows tares in the field of God's wheat (Mk. 4:15, Matt. 13:39). "Deliver us from the evil one" is a crucial petition he taught his disciples to pray (Matt. 6:13). Accused of being possessed by Beelzebul (apparently a synonym for Satan) he pointed out the folly of the charge: "How can Satan cast out Satan?" He went on to liken Satan to a marauding baron holding his possessions in peace until a stronger than he comes and casts him out (Mk. 3:22–26). He himself was that stronger one: but he had no illusions about the magnitude of the task. Jesus knows that the devil has usurped God's place of leadership in this world: it does lie in his hand to bestow "all the kingdoms of the world and the glory of them" (Matt. 4:8), and Jesus does not deny it. But rather than compromise with this subtle and evil force, Jesus knows that he must oppose him to the bitter end. Hence the way of the cross.

That was to sound the death knell for the usurper prince of this age. It was as he spoke of the cross that Jesus cried, "Now is the judgement of this world. Now shall the ruler of this world be cast out. And I, when I am lifted up from the earth, will draw all men to myself" (John 12:31f). As the premonition of the cross grew upon Jesus on the last night of his life, his mind turned again to Satan. "The ruler of this world is coming. He has no power over me – I do as the Father has commanded. Rise, let's go to meet him!" (John 14:31). The battle, the last and greatest battle was joined. But it was appallingly real to Jesus: no mythological imagery, but a life and death struggle in which nothing short of utter and complete obedience to the Father, over-coming where the First Man fell, would suffice to win the day.

That is just a small part of the teaching of Jesus about Satan. Nor is teaching all. The Gospels are full of his actual conflict with Satan, which reached its climax on the cross. There is no suggestion that Jesus adopted some of the grosser speculations about the forces of evil such as we find in the *Testaments* and the *Book of Enoch*, but on the central matter of the existence of Satan, his power, his utter opposition to good and to God, there can be no doubt whatever. Like the Old Testament and the rabbinic Judaism which preceded him, like the Jews of his day and of a subsequent day as recorded in the *Mishnah*, like the apostles whom he commissioned, and like the Christian church almost from that day to this, Jesus believed in the devil. One would have thought that the teaching and behaviour of Jesus on this important subject was sufficient to settle the matter for Christians.

**Was Jesus mistaken?**
There are two ways in which the force of this argument can be evaded. The first is to maintain, as many since Beyschlag have done, that Jesus did not really mean what he said. He couched his teaching in poetic form, but would have been horrified to be taken literally.

However, if Jesus did not mean what he said in this matter, on which he spoke so often and so specifically, it is hard to see how we can trust him on any other. He saw the whole of his ministry as a conflict with Satan. He saw his death as the supreme battle with the evil one. If you are to play around with language in this fashion, why should you not treat all Jesus' teaching about a personal loving Father as a pleasing myth to be eliminated at will? No, that expedient will not do. If language means anything, then it is certain that Jesus' repeated teachings and warnings about Satan are to be taken with the utmost seriousness and not evaporated into metaphor.

The other way of evading the force of Jesus' teaching on the subject is to suppose that Jesus was so much a child of his age that he took over uncritically all its presuppositions, in particular this belief in a personal devil.

This view is unsatisfactory, but it draws attention to one important point. Jesus was not God walking around this earth dressed up as man. His deity shines through his humanity, and was veiled and limited during the period of his earthly life by those very conditions of being mortal which he unwillingly undertook for us. Nevertheless, three things must be said.

First, Jesus did not take over uncritically the views of his day. On almost every front we find his radical freshness cutting through centuries of tradition. His teaching on the Kingdom, on discipleship, on money, on the sabbath, on the new covenant, on forgiveness – all of these fly in the face of the presuppositions of the time. Why should he have been more pusillanimous, more traditionalist in this area of the demonic?

Second, we have to give full weight to the tremendous moral earnestness of his teaching and living in this whole area of the satanic. His teaching is bound up with it. His healing is bound up with it. His exorcisms are bound up with it. His death is bound up with it. At all the major points in his life and ministry the conflict with Satan is of cardinal importance. I find it almost as difficult to believe that Jesus was mistaken in this central area of his whole mission as I do to suppose that he was consciously (as some hold) adapting his superior knowledge to the ignorance of his benighted disciples who, poor things, still believed in the demonic. Neither view does sufficient justice to the centrality and intensity of the subject.

The third objection to the extreme form of this kenotic theory which robs Jesus of accurate knowledge on the subject, because he was still a child of his age, is this. If Jesus was mistaken on a matter as vital as whether or not there is a great Adversary to God and man, why should we take him as our teacher on anything else? Perhaps his belief in the free forgiveness of God is equally culturally conditioned – is there not some talk of free acceptance before God in the Hymns of the Qumran covenanters?

This kenotic theory if applied to Jesus' understanding of Satan, proves much too much if it proves anything at all. It will not do simply to take those areas of the teaching of Jesus which we like and regard them as coming from God, while rejecting those areas of his acknowledged teaching which do not appeal to us. Such eclecticism is academically indefensible, and is not a proper option for those who call him Lord and set out to be his learners, or disciples. The fact that Jesus taught so clearly the existence of Satan is the most powerful reason for his followers to take the same stance and act accordingly.

### Personality or Personification?

Personality is a difficult word. We know, more or less, what we mean by it when we apply it to a human being. But whenever we extend the word and its attribution, we run into problems. You have only to contend for a personal God, and you will find this sort of response in many people: "If God is like my old man, you can count me out!" When we attribute personality to God like this, it is an extension of the word almost beyond the boundaries of language. What we mean is that we cannot conceive of human individuality coming from a source which is less than personal. As C. S. Lewis has immortalised in a famous phrase, God is beyond personality. All we claim by calling him personal is that he is at least personal, whatever else he may be.

How do we know that? Partly because we, his creatures

29

are personal – and a river cannot flow higher than its source. But supremely because of the incarnation. God has showed himself to be one of us. He came to share our conditions as man. It happened at a thoroughly precise and well-documented time in history, nineteen centuries ago.

But what do we mean by saying that Satan is a personal devil? What most people mean by that is to claim that Satan is an organising intellect, a single focus and fount of evil inspiration. That seems to me to be a very proper inference to draw from the teaching of the Bible. But it is doubtful if we can call him "personal" in any other sense. To be sure he is brought before us with the masculine article in Greek – but that could be because of the gender of the word "devil". Scripture depicts him as a spirit; as a fallen angel; as a ruler of this world; but not, so far as I can see, as "personal" in any meaningful sense. Unlike Jesus, Satan has not become incarnate, though there have been many people down history who have so sold their soul to him that they have almost become living embodiments of his beastliness. Satan has never been one of us. He has not shared our human condition. Counterfeiter to the last, he even counterfeits personality. "Satan" stands as the personification for God and man's spiritual adversary, utterly devoid of compassion, of caring, of all the qualities that make us personal. He is, rather, a personification of the implacable evil against which we are called to contend. An intelligence, a power of concentrated and hateful wickedness: that is how we are to think of him. If the pronoun "he" predominates in English as in Greek (and it will in this book), that may be entirely proper so long as we neither underestimate Satan as an insubstantial figure of fun nor glorify him with the feelings and understanding of human personality. The great "It" is in every way the pale imitation of the ultimate "He".

### Does it matter?

In an age when a great majority of our citizens have little more than the vaguest of beliefs (if that) in the supernatural at all, is it worth writing a book on the subject of the devil? Does it matter whether or not we believe in him? Dr.

Martyn Lloyd-Jones has written two massive volumes on *The Christian Warfare*, (Ephesians 6:10–13). He gives reasons for his conviction that to regain and restate this belief is one of the most important contributions the contemporary church can make to the disturbed times in which we live. Instead of making somewhat jejeune social and political utterances the church is the one body that has the means, through God's revelation to us, of penetrating to the heart of the human problem. It is foolish to medicate symptoms whilst failing to recognise the disease. If, as modern secularists are prone to do, we reject the whole idea of the devil, we are reduced to an evolutionary optimism coupled with widespread education as the twin bases for any hope that man's lot will improve. Lloyd-Jones remarks robustly:

> It is to me almost beyond understanding that anybody who looks at the modern world and reads a newspaper can still go on believing such theories. Indeed, if they never even read a newspaper how can anybody who has ever known an educated, cultured, reasonable man, who nevertheless fails drastically in his own personal life, possibly believe such things? How can they believe that wisdom and knowledge and learning, and the ability to reason and to use logic, is the solution of the problem, when what is to be seen daily in the lives of men and women proves the exact opposite? It is amazing!

> (*The Christian Warfare*, p. 47)

Much hangs on the judgement we make about the devil. It is logical for an atheist to reject belief in the devil, just as he rejects belief in God. He is perfectly consistent, though he is, I believe, quite mistaken, and can give no profoundly satisfying explanation of the concentrated evil in the world and in human affairs. His world view is shallow, but consistent.

What is totally inconsistent is to accept one part of the spiritual realm, God, and to reject the other. The existence of a devil is a necessary part of consistent theism. Many who

31

call themselves Christians will want to protest at that, but let them ask themselves if they are not in danger of reducing Christianity to a system of morals. Can they continue to accept the idea of revelation whilst rejecting the devil of whom it speaks? Can they listen to Jesus Christ whilst rejecting the devil to whom he bears witness? What satisfactory account can they give of the chaos in God's world if there is not destructive force of evil at work? How can they make sense of the atonement if there is no devil? They cannot have any cool perspective on the chaos of world affairs, and paradoxically, they cannot have any clearly based hope for the future without belief in the personal devil – and his defeat – of which the Bible speaks so firmly. Dr. Lloyd-Jones is right when he concludes:

> The modern world, and especially the history of the present century, can only be understood in terms of the unusual activity of the devil and the "principalities and powers" of darkness.
> Indeed, I suggest that belief in a personal devil and demon activities is the touchstone by which one can most easily test any profession of Christian faith today.
> In a world of collapsing institutions, moral chaos, and increasing violence, never was it more important to trace the hand of "the prince of the power of the air". If we cannot discern the chief cause of our ills, how can we hope to cure them?
> (*The Christian Warfare*, p. 6)

## CHAPTER 2

### *The Devil and All His Works*

WHAT ARE WE actually talking about when we speak of the devil? There is a good deal of reserve on the subject in the Bible, and it is easy to see why. Scripture is not a book of speculative theology. It is written "that he who runs may read". There are, therefore, many gaps in our knowledge: we are only given enough to go along with, and in Satan's case, enough to fight with. Moreover, the Enemy is expert at covering his traces.

### *The Origin of Satan*

How comes it that in the perfect world which God claims to have made, the devil should ever have emerged? There are really only three possible answers.

The first is the one commonly adopted in critical circles. We have already glanced obliquely at it in the first chapter. It maintains that the idea of Satan is an aetiological tale. That is to say, it is a mythical or poetic story to explain a perplexing phenomenon, the existence of evil, disease and death in God's world. We have seen reason in chapter one to dissent from this view. Satan is no mere explanatory tale: he is a menacing reality. He was for the Old Testament heroes: he was for Jesus: he was for the apostles, the saints and martyrs: and he is for us. Even if this view were true, it would still leave the origin of evil unexplained.

The second possibility is that the devil existed all the time. He is, so to speak, the Opposition Party in God's Parliament, with as old if not as distinguished a history as the Government itself. This is a view which many ancient religions held. It perfectly explains the opposition between good and evil of which we are all aware. It is, however, utterly at odds with the teaching of the Bible. When the

Hebrews came to understand that there was but one God for all the nations of the world, they were driven also to the conclusion that in some mysterious way, even disease, death, sin and the devil must be under his ultimate sovereignty. So we find no dualism in the Bible: no hint of equal and opposite forces headed up by God and Satan.

The third possibility is that the devil was one of God's creatures – a spirit of great ability, who became consumed by pride, rebelled, lost his position, and set up in opposition and in implacable hatred against God, the source of his existence. That is the picture, broadly speaking, with which the Bible operates. Satan is God's creature: for everything springs from God in the first instance. That is why Isaiah can say in God's name, "I am the Lord. There is no other. I form light and create darkness, I make weal and create woe, I am the Lord who do all these things" (45:6f). Amos is equally bold in his monotheism, "Does evil befall a city unless the Lord has done it?" (3:6). Nothing happens without the permissive will of God: he permits even what he does not will, and he does so confident that in the end the pattern will emerge beautiful if intricate. Satan, then, is God's devil, and nowhere is this more clearly brought out than in the story of Job. In the picturesque language of this poetic book Satan is imagined as one of the "sons of God" presenting themselves from time to time before the Lord, as if to receive their orders. Satan is free to slander Job before God (1:9). Satan is free to afflict Job, first in his possessions and later in his person (1:12, 2:5,6). "Behold, all that he has is in your power: only upon himself do not put forth your hand" says God, exercising his restraining power. Again, "Behold, he is in your power, only spare his life." Whatever the problems that a passage like this brings up, it makes one point with enormous simplicity and power. His power, though great, is limited by God's *fiat*. He is a creature and is ultimately subject to God's authority. The rub lies in the "ultimately" . . .

**In the Gospels**

How did this great spirit fall? We do not know in full. However there are a few clues which may facilitate an intelligent guess, and they all point in the same direction. One of the most evocative and perplexing is that exclamation of Jesus, "I saw Satan fall like lightning from heaven" (Luke 10:18). What did he mean? The context helps us to some extent. Jesus has just sent out the seventy to go ahead of him as messengers of the Kingdom. He sends them out with his authority. And they return, triumphant, finding that even the demons are subject to them in his name. Then comes his great exclamation, along with the gift of authority over all the power of the Enemy, and the reminder that the supreme cause for their joy should be that their names are written in heaven.

Was the "I saw Satan fall" a quasi-historical statement? Did Jesus mean that in some great cosmic battle back in the mists of pre-history, he saw Satan fall? Or was it a prophetic past tense, as often in Hebrew, where the event which will assuredly come in the future is spoken of as if it has already taken place? In this case Jesus would be looking to the final defeat of Satan at the end of time. Or was it what he saw then and there, in a vision, as the seventy returned in triumph? Did he see in them, their message, their mission and their authority (derived from himself) a preview of the history of the church? And was the ultimate conclusion of the whole scenario anticipated in that vivid sketch of the fall of Satan from heaven?

We cannot be certain which of these possible explanations is right: we have no access to the inner thoughts of Jesus. But the verse in its context makes several things plain. It indicates that Satan's home was in heaven with God. It tells us that Satan fell from that happy estate. It reveals that there is a war on. It asserts that God's people have power over the Enemy. It affirms that their names are written in the very heaven from whence he fell. It is a highly illuminating sentence.

Three other passages in Scripture help to fill out the picture a little.

## In the Apocalypse

The first comes in Revelation chapter 12. This is a highly apocalyptic picture of the persecuted first-century Christians. We shall return to it, for it is a key passage, but at the moment it will suffice to glance at verse seven and following. "Now war arose in heaven, Michael and his angels fighting against the dragon: and the dragon and his angels fought, but they were defeated and there was no longer any place for them in heaven. And the great dragon was thrown down, that ancient serpent, who is called the Devil and Satan, the deceiver of the whole world, he was thrown down to the earth and his angels were thrown down with him."

The main purpose of that chapter is to encourage Christians in the face of seduction or persecution by the current world power, Rome. But the incidental light it sheds on the origin of Satan is considerable. He had been a denizen of heaven, one of the angelic spirits, and for some undisclosed reason, he rebelled. Michael (who is like God?), seen as the leader of the hosts of God, succeeds in casting the dragon out of heaven, but he sweeps a third of the stars of heaven with him down to earth (12:4): his angels were thrown down with him. As this chapter relates, earth is now the sphere of his operations, and behind the pressures upon Christians as a church and as individual believers we are to see the dragon at work, along with his two henchmen, the beast from the sea and the beast from the earth. To these we will return. But a very plain hint has been given of the fall of Satan from his original state as one of the angels of God. What accounts for that fall?

## In Ezekiel

We come to the next of these evocative glimpses which Scripture gives of Satan's origin in Ezekiel. Like the passage in Revelation, it needs to be treated with due caution. The language is poetic and the subject mysterious, but the main outline is as astonishing as it is clear. Ezekiel has been prophesying the doom of Tyre for three whole chapters (26–28). Tyre was an island kingdom lying north west of Israel. It belonged to the Phoenicians, and was without doubt one of the richest, most luxurious, most powerful and most arrogant of the great kingdoms of the day. The prophecy is very remarkable, as has been well pointed out by S. D. Gordon years ago in his devotional book *Quiet Talks about the Tempter*. The first ten verses of chapter 28 speak of the prince of Tyre, while the next nine verses speak of the king of Tyre. The first ten verses contain a message to the prince. The second part consists of a lamentation over the king. The language used of the prince of Tyre is such as is appropriate to a man: indeed he is called a "man". The language used of the king of Tyre is highly inappropriate to any man: indeed, it could not be used of any human being. But, as Gordon notices, exactly the same spirit dominates the prince as the king. Both have tremendous beauty, wisdom and power: both defy the living God. The prince is the understudy of the king: he is dominated by the spirit of the ultimate ruler of Tyre, Satan himself.

Does that seem extreme? Then consider what is written of king and prince respectively. "Son of man, raise a lamentation over the king of Tyre, and say to him

Thus says the Lord God:
You were the signet of perfection,
Full of wisdom and perfect in beauty.
You were in Eden, the garden of God.
Every precious stone was your covering,
Carnelian, topaz and jasper,
Chrysolite, beryl and onyx,
Sapphire, carbuncle, and emerald;
And wrought in gold were your settings and engravings.
On the day that you were created they were prepared.
With an anointed guardian cherub I placed you;
You were on the holy mountain of God.
In the midst of the stones of fire you walked.
You were blameless in your ways
From the day that you were created
Till iniquity was found in you.
In the abundance of your trade
You were filled with violence, and you sinned;

37

So I cast you out as a profane thing from the mountain
   of God,
And the guardian cherub drove you out
From the midst of the stones of fire.
Your heart was proud because of your beauty;
You corrupted your wisdom for the sake of your splendour.
I cast you to the ground . . ."

(Ezek. 28:11–17)

Such is the portrait of the one designated as king of Tyre.
Now for his lieutenant.

Son of man, say to the prince of Tyre, "Thus says the
   Lord God:
Because your heart is proud
and you have said 'I am a god,
I sit in the seat of the gods, in the heart of the seas'
Yet you are but a man and no god,
Though you consider yourself as wise as a god –
You are indeed wiser than Daniel: no secret is hidden
   from you;
By your wisdom and understanding you have gotten
   wealth for yourself
And have gathered gold and silver into your treasuries;
By your great wisdom in trade you have increased
   your wealth
And your heart has become proud in your wealth –
Therefore thus says the Lord God:
Because you consider yourself as wise as a god,
Therefore, behold, I will bring strangers upon you
The most terrible of the nations;
And they shall draw their swords against the beauty of
   your wisdom
And defile your splendour.
They shall thrust you down into the pit
And you shall die the death of the slain in the heart of
   the seas.
Will you still say 'I am a god'
In the presence of those who slay you,
Though you are but a man, and no god,

In the hands of those who wound you?
You shall die the death of the uncircumcised,
By the hand of foreigners;
For I have spoken, says the Lord God"
(Ezek. 28:1–10)

The parallels are obvious. The charming, able, wealthy, prosperous prince of Tyre, so proud of himself, his achievements and his wisdom, will perish utterly: as a matter of fact he did. But behind the prince stood the king of Tyre, and the characteristics of the two of them are much the same. What concerns us here is the picture of the king.

He was originally in close intimacy with God. He dwelt on the holy mountain of God: he was placed with an anointed cherub. He was blameless in all his ways, splendid in wisdom, skilful in operation, perfect in beauty, the very signet of perfection. Such was God's assessment of this magnificent creature – and note that he was a creature: "on the day that you were created they were prepared."

But he fell. "I cast you out." "I cast you to the ground." "I cast you as a profane thing from the mountain of God." "The guardian cherub drove you out from the midst of the stones of fire." And why this eviction?

"Because iniquity was found in you." In what way? "Your heart was proud because of your beauty" . . . "You corrupted your wisdom for the sake of your splendour" . . . "You were filled with violence." That was it. This superb angel allowed his wisdom to corrupt him. Pride took over: pride of intellect, pride of beauty, pride of status. And Satan fell. He involved others in his fall: he did not go quietly: "you were filled with violence." His outlook is precisely mirrored in his underling, the prince of Tyre: "You consider yourself as wise as a god . . . you have said your heart is proud and you have said 'I am a god, I sit in the seat of the gods, in the heart of the seas.' . . . Will you still say 'I am a god'?"

## In Isaiah
The final passage is no less allusive. It comes in Isaiah 14, where the prophet is depicting a taunt that will be used

39

against the king of Babylon. This proud monarch will be laid low. His oppressive rule will be broken. His strength will be cut off like the dead. "All of them will speak and say to you: 'You too have become as weak as we! You have become like us! Your pomp is brought down to Sheol, the sound of your harps; maggots are the bed beneath you, and worms your covering" (v.10f).

Isaiah continues the taunt. And it may seem that he continues to address the king of Babylon. But as with Ezekiel's king of Tyre, another and more sinister figure is to be seen lying behind the king of Babylon.* The words that follow do not it would seem apply primarily to the king but to his Master. They could scarcely be ascribed to any man. Listen:

How you are fallen from heaven, Lucifer, son of the
    dawn!
How you are cut down to the ground,
You who laid the nations low!
You said in your heart
"I will ascend to heaven; above the stars of God
I will set my throne on high;
I will sit on the mount of assembly in the far north;
I will climb above the heights of the clouds,
I will make myself like the Most High."

* "These descriptions, though primarily perhaps meant to apply to Tyre and to Babylon, are generally agreed to have a much wider meaning. That is something which is quite customary in prophecy. You start with the immediate but it is also a foreshadowing of something bigger which is to come. This happens with regard to good as well as evil. There are many prophecies in the Psalms which appear to relate to Kind David alone, but obviously they go beyond David and point to the Messiah. There are promises made to the Children of Israel which primarily refer clearly to their coming back from the captivity of Babylon; but they are too big for that alone, they are at the same time pictures of the Christian salvation. It is exactly the same in regard to this matter of evil. In describing the fall of Tyre and Babylon the prophets were inspired to suggest something bigger. Tyre and Babylon are not merely earthly powers that are opposed to God; they are also symbols, as it were, of the power of the devil and his forces."

(D. M. Lloyd-Jones *The Christian Warfare*, p. 70f)

Such are the claims, such the ambitions and insensate pride of Lucifer, son of the dawn. But his doom is the archetype which the king of Babylon is to follow. God humbles the proud and brings them low. And to this fivefold "I will!" of Satan, God gives his response:

> But you are brought down to Sheol,
> To the depths of the Pit.
> Those who see you will stare at you and ponder over
>     you,
> "Is this the man who made the earth tremble,
> Can this be the one that shook the earth,
> Who shook kingdoms,
> Who made the world like a desert
> And overthrew its cities?"

Pride was the trouble; not content to be God's lieutenant, Satan had to be God. That is why he fell. And the Fathers like Tertullian believed that Jesus' words about Satan's fall from heaven were a direct allusion to Is. 14:12. Jude's reference to "the angels which did not keep their own position but abandoned their proper dwelling" (v. 6) and Paul's warning in 1 Tim. 3:6 not to promote a new convert "or he may be puffed up with conceit and fall into the condemnation of the devil" (i.e. the condemnation pronounced on the devil) both point in the same direction. The archetypal spirit turned from good to evil and from God to self through pride. Through Satan's instigation men have been giving way to pride ever since. "The proper devilishness of sin is this," says Luther, "that it *thus* modifies the first words of the Decalogue: I am *my* Lord and *my* God." Not surprisingly, therefore, we read that pride is the number one thing that God hates (Prov. 6:17, 8:13). It is the very antithesis of the dependence on him and companionship with him that all God's creation was made to enjoy.

Such are the hints in Scripture of how this noble angelic spirit became the archetypal fount of evil. These hints are not extensive; they do not answer half our questions; but they have proved deeply satisfying to believers down the ages, particularly those who like Milton and Tolkien are used to thinking pictorially rather than analytically.

## The Names of Satan

An astonishing number of names are used of Satan in Scripture. They will provide a useful starting-point for examining his characteristics. For to the Hebrew mind a name is not just a label; it depicts character. Despite the variety of names, however, and the many centuries over which Scripture was written, there is a remarkable uniformity in the way in which the great Enemy is regarded.

### Son of God
Before we look even at the most basic name, Satan, there is an astounding title occasionally used, which ties up with his origin. He is numbered among the "sons of God" in Job 1:6: "Now there was a day when the sons of God came to present themselves before the Lord, and Satan came also among them." "Sons of God" generally refers to angels in the Old Testament, and here we are told that when the sons of God came to the heavenly court, Satan was one of them. A mysterious concept indeed: we shall look at it more closely in chapter four. It is sufficient at present to see it as alluding to Satan's origin; he was originally God's creation, and he remains God's devil, subject to God's ultimate control.

### Satan
The word "satan" means "accuser" or "slanderer". It is a Hebrew word, and is rendered in Greek by *daibolos* from which the French derive *diable* and the English *devil*. "Accuser" is at first sight a curious root meaning for one we have come to regard as the arch-enemy of man. But it arose very simply. Satan is the one who accuses us before God, the one who maintains we cannot be acceptable. The name is applied to human beings in the sense of "accusers" (e.g. 1 Sam. 29:4, 1 King's 11:14) and in later intertestamental writings a variety of evil spirits are called "satans" (see

42

Enoch 40:7, 69:4,6). But in three Old Testament passages we find it applied to the devil.

In the prologue to the Book of Job "the satan" appears as both the accuser of Job and his tormenter (chapters 1 and 2).

In Zech. 3:1ff "the satan", crowing over the devastation of Jerusalem, seeks to calumniate Joshua, who was high priest at the time of the restoration after the Babylonian captivity. "And the Lord said to Satan, 'The Lord rebuke you, O Satan! The Lord who has chosen Jerusalem rebuke you! Is not this a brand plucked from the fire?'" At once Joshua's filthy garments were stripped away, with the words, "Behold, I have taken your iniquity away from you, and I will clothe you with rich apparel", and he is promised rule within the household of God if he keeps God's commands. The Christian will see a deeper significance in this ancient story from the sixth century B.C. It hints at another Joshua, another assault of Satan, another vindication, another rule. But here, in this early appearance, we see a cameo of the persistent role – and ultimate failure – of the Accuser of the brethren who accuses them day and night before God (Rev. 12:10).

The third passage comes from 1 Chron. 21:1, where Satan tempts David to number the people and exult in his military might. Whereas in the two previous passages "satan" is an appellative with the definite article, now the article is dropped; Satan is firmly enshrined as a proper name.

It has often been observed that in the parallel and pre-Exilic passage, 2 Sam. 24:1ff, God himself is said to encourage David to number the people. This looks like a straight contradiction. Actually it is nothing of the kind. The whole context in 2 Samuel 24 makes it plain that David was wrong to number Israel in this self-glorifying way. We read that "the anger of the Lord was kindled against Israel and he incited David against them, saying 'Go, number Israel'" (24:1). We read that Joab, his army commander, tried in vain to dissuade David from this pointless exercise in sabre-rattling (24:3). We read that David realised his guilty arrogance (24:10) and that God sent a fearsome judgement (24:15). So there is no doubt in either account that David's action was wrong. In the days when 2 Samuel was written, a good spirit and an evil spirit were both ascribed in origin to the Lord, the sovereign source of all, just like the two spirits within a man (the *yetzer ha tob* or "evil inclination" and the *yetzer ha ra* or "good inclination". See, e.g. 1 Sam. 16:14, 16, 23, 18:10, 19:9). By the time Chronicles was written the experiences of the Exile had brought the personality of this evil force, Satan, into sharper focus.

## Tempter
Satan is often, of course, called "the Tempter" (e.g. Matt. 4:3, 1 Thess. 3:5). The meaning is obvious and we need not stay on it. The Tempter seeks to embroil men in the same alienation from God which he has willingly chosen for himself. We find him in this role throughout the Bible. The cases of Job in the Old Testament and Jesus in the New show him at his work.

## Dragon and serpent
His skills and power as tempter are underlined by the title "that old serpent" (Rev. 12:9), with obvious allusion to Genesis 3. The identification of Satan and the serpent or dragon is very frequent. In the Apocrypha they are identified in Wisdom 2:24, Psalms of Solomon 4:9 etc, and of course in the New Testament this is quite common (1 Tim. 2:13ff, Rom. 16:20, Rev. 12:9, 20:2). Many ancient religions saw the dragon as the pristine foe of all that is good, and we have already seen the links with the mythical Babylonian figure of Tiâmat. It was one of the traditional ways of conceiving of the spirit of evil throughout the near East; a monstrous beast, wreaking havoc and destruction on the earth, and devouring man. This comes out very clearly in Revelation 12:3, "a great red dragon, with seven heads and ten horns, and seven diadems upon his heads". John is picking up the monstrous apocalyptic beast of Daniel's prophecy (7:7ff) and showing how the archetypal enemy of God is the destructive ("red") chaos-monster ("dragon"), with perfectly multiform expression ("seven

44

heads"), immense though limited power ("ten horns"),
and widespread authority ("seven diadems upon his
heads").

## Destroyer
This destructive aspect of the devil's character is brought
out by the title Apollyon (Rev. 9:11). The word literally
means "the Destroyer". Once again the allusion takes us
back to Genesis 3, where sin and death both enter the world
through the Fall which the Enemy contrives. That is why
Jesus calls him a "murderer from the beginning" (John
8:44). This does not mean that Satan is free to kill indis-
criminately: he can do so only if God permits him (Job 2:6).
But it does point to the tyranny Satan exercises over man
through the fear of death. He is a killer by instinct and
appetite. In Paul's vivid phrase "the prince of the power
of the air" has already rendered his captives spiritually
"dead through trespasses and sins" (Eph. 2:1f) and is
enthusiastic to seal their state by physical death, which is an
integral part of God's curse on sin. That is why it is called
"the last enemy", and along with all the other works of
the destroyer, it will finally be destroyed by Christ (1 John
3:8).

And then shall come to pass the saying that is written:

> Death is swallowed up in victory.
> O death, where is your victory?
> O death, where is your sting?
> (1 Cor. 15:54f)

## Prince of the power of the air
Satan is called "prince of the power of the air" (Eph. 2:2), a
curious title which caused some of the pious to oppose
aviation in its earliest days! To be sure, it presupposes a
cosmogony different from ours. We tend to think of hell as
"down". This is not a geographical statement, of course,
but a value judgement. The ancients tended to see "the
abyss" as the final destination of Satan and his angels (Lk.
8:31, Rev. 20:2) but the air, the area between earth and

45

heaven, as the sphere of his present activities. In Ephesians 6:12 he is seen as head of "the world rulers of this present darkness, spiritual hosts of wickedness in the heavenly places". The symbolism indicates Satan's "in between" position, a rebel banished from the throne of God but all the same a mighty force to be reckoned with, far more powerful than man. He has an empire: did not Jesus acknowledge this with his rhetorical question, "If Satan be divided against himself how shall his kingdom stand?" He has servants: the hosts of evil spirits whom he drew with him from heaven (cf. Rev. 12:4, 9). He has world rulers: the position aspired to by Alexander and Napoleon and Hitler is actually enjoyed by the usurper prince of evil and his allies. He controls the power of darkness. It is not surprising that in the late first-century A.D. Epistle of Barnabas (4:9) Satan is called *ho melas* "the Black One". He rules the darkness of this world, and his aim is to keep men incarcerated within it.

### Beliar and Beelzebub

There is an interesting passage in The Testament of Levi, 3, which says, "He who fears God and loves his neighbours cannot be smitten by the spirit of the air, Beliar." Beliar is another name we find once attributed to the devil by Paul in 2 Cor. 6:15, and its precise meaning is both obscure and contested. Possibly it may be the same as Belial, the common intertestamental name for Satan, meaning "the Worthless One" – a very precise evaluation. Similar doubt hangs over the name "Beelzebub" or "Beelzebul" (Matt. 10:25, 12:26, Lk. 11:15, etc.). It may mean derisively, "Lord of the flies" or "Lord of filth" but probably means "Lord of the dwelling". On any showing it refers to the devil – Beelzebub is specifically called "prince of the demons", and the name draws attention to the grip that Satan gets of a life once entry is effected. He becomes Lord of the dwelling, however much men may ridicule him as Lord of the flies or hate him as Lord of filth. He exercises a terrible grip.

## Ruler of this world

That grip is referred to in the title "ruler of this world" which comes three times in St. John (12:31, 14:30, 16:11). It is also alluded to in Eph. 6:12 where Paul speaks of "the world rulers of this present darkness". John, in his first letter, says bluntly, "the whole world lies in the arms of [literally 'in'] the wicked one" (5:19) and Paul calls him "the god of this world" (2 Cor. 4:4). These references all make the same point, a point underlined during the Temptations of Jesus. Satan has a particular relation to this world. That may be only as a result of his rebellion, but is it possible that he was assigned some special task of oversight of the world by God in the beginning before his fall? Was he originally God's angelic administrator of our earth? And did the rightful prince turn through rebellion into the usurper prince? That must remain sheer speculation, but it might account for the strong links between Satan and our world, and would lend particular point to the cry in Revelation after Satan's fall from heaven: "Rejoice then, O heaven, and you that dwell therein! But woe to you, O earth and sea, for the devil has come down to you in great wrath, because he knows his time is short." (Rev. 12:12).

As Professor Torrance has put it:

> It is precisely because the Devil and all his minions have been so utterly defeated that the earth is thrown into such turmoil and trouble. That decisive defeat becomes apparent as all the powers of spiritual evil, dislodged by the Cross, fall upon the earth and gather, by subtle deception, the prides and passions and lusts of men, and direct them against the Kingdom of God as it is being enacted in history.
>
> (T. F. Torrance, *Apocalypse Today*, p. 95)

## The Evil One

Rebel that he is, it is not surprising to find Satan called the Antichrist, the embodiment of opposition to our Lord. Here again there was a great deal of speculation in late Judaism about what form the Antichrist might be expected to take. John short-circuits tedious discussion by affirming that the early gnosticising heresy which he has to deal within his First Letter is itself one of the manifestations of the Antichrist without being in the least exhaustive (1 John 4:1ff). For Satan is the implacable "enemy" of mankind (e.g. Lk. 10:19). He is the "plaintiff" (*ho antidikos*, 1 Peter 5:8) determined to bring us to book, especially when we have the effrontery to "turn from darkness to light, from the power of Satan to God" (Acts 26:18). He is set for our downfall, and will come at us either as the king of the jungle, the "roaring lion seeking whom he may devour" (1 Peter 5:8) or else seductively, as the "angel of light" (2 Cor. 10:14) seeking whom he may deceive. He is the archetypal "evil one" (Matt. 19:38, 13:19, 38, 2 Thess. 3:3), and the most probable translation of the climactic petition in Matthew's version of the Lord's Prayer is, "Deliver us from the Evil One." The phrase *rhusai hemas apo tou ponerou* may simply mean "deliver us from evil" but the whole thrust of the request and the definite article before *ponerou* make it very probable that Jesus is personalising the petition. Deliver us not merely from evil, but from every test (*peirasmon*) that the Evil One brings upon us.

The titles of Satan, the great Accuser, give us some clue to his character. Subtle as the serpent, violent as the dragon, ruthless as the lion, deceptive as the angel of light, he is the Destroyer, the Enemy, the murderer of men's spirits. He is the usurper prince of this world, and his writ runs over it; but he is the worthless one, the evil one, the Antichrist.

Titles can only get us so far. What else has Scripture to tell us about his characteristics? To be forewarned is to be forearmed.

### The Characteristics of Satan

One of the principles of warfare is to study the enemy. Thousands of millions of pounds are spent annually by world governments in studying *potential* enemies. And yet Christians give very little thought to the nature and characteristics of the *actual* Enemy they face.

Perhaps the most important factor to realise is this.

## Satan is bound

He has no rightful authority over men: he is simply a usurper. We must not acquiesce in his proud claim to the kingdoms of this world; that would be treason to Christ. Satan has lain under judgement since Eden. The judgement was implemented on Calvary. The sentence passed on Satan in Genesis 3 has been executed. Strong man that he is, he has been dispossessed and bound by the Stronger than the strong, Jesus himself (Mark 3:27). We see him bound in the preservation of Jesus from murderous assaults at his birth and throughout his life, bound in the Temptations, bound in the healings and exorcisms, and supremely bound by the cross, resurrection, coming of the Spirit and spread of the church. The most probable interpretation of the "thousand years" of Satan's binding in Revelation 20 is not, to my mind, some future period before or after the return of Christ, as premillennialists and postmillennialists dispute. It is the extensive though limited period between the Advents, the age of the church and the Spirit and the gospel. It is now, in this age, that Satan is bound; his power is curbed. He cannot prevent, though he can hinder the spread of the gospel. He cannot prevent, though he can hinder the ultimate victory of God. We read that not only is the devil, but so are his demons chained (Rev. 20:2, Jude 6). They may not appear to be, but such is the case. John Bunyan understood this well. In *Pilgrim's Progress* he recounts Christian's fear when he saw two lions in the way – a sight which sufficed to make Timorous and Mistrust turn back from their pilgrimage. "The lions were chained", wrote Bunyan, "but he saw not the chains."

It is possible, then, to overestimate the power of Satan. He is not omniscient, omnipotent or omnipresent. He is a defeated foe and he cannot ultimately prevail. Nevertheless we run much the greater danger of underestimating him. The Bible makes it very clear to us what a formidable foe he remains.

## Satan is mighty

A man lies under the power of Satan if he does not turn to God (Acts 26:18). Satan assails mankind assiduously: "the

serpent was more subtle than all the beasts of the field"
(Gen. 3:1). Satan attacks the minds of men with doubts,
fears and propaganda. Satan assails the spirits of men with
lust, pride and hatred. Satan assaults the bodies of men
with disease, torture and death. Satan assails the institutions of men (which he seeks to impregnate) with
structural evil. In the Bible itself we find him manipulating
nations (Daniel 10), city councils (1 Thess. 2:18), rioting
mobs (John 8:44, 59) and the very elements themselves
(Mark 4:39). Satan is immensely powerful. It is unwise to
underestimate him. He can be resisted and overcome in the
name of Jesus, but other names he can and does brush aside.

**Satan is violent**
He loves bitterness and hatred, war and revenge. Both of
the passages in Ezekiel and Revelation which give us a
glimpse of his origin stress his violence. The same holds
good for certain Gospel accounts of the demon-possessed
(Mk. 5:3, Lk. 4:35). Violence is a very noticeable feature of
the demon-possessed today: a slight woman will often have
the strength of several men. Revelation 2:10 shows Satan
casting men into prison: Matthew 11:12 shows him storm-
ing the very gates of Christ's kingdom. It is very noticeable
politically that when a State has given itself over to evil
structures violence becomes a normal feature of life.

**Satan is highly intelligent**
His intelligence lacks originality: he travels along God's
pathways. He does not create a situation: he corrupts it. He
has well been called "the ape of God". But, though not
original, his mental powers are massive. He is uncannily
crafty, subtle and cunning. Think of him tempting the first
Adam in the Garden. Think of him tempting the second
Adam in the desert. It is hardly surprising that Paul insists
that if we are to withstand the wiles of the devil we shall
need nothing less than the whole armour of God. For Satan
is quick to gain an advantage over us. He is apt at catching
us like birds in his net (2 Cor. 2:11, 2 Tim. 2:26, 1 Tim. 3:7).
It is little comfort that his intelligence may be strictly
second class: the same is true of our own.

## Satan is a liar

He lies at his first appearance in the Garden, when he says, "You shall not surely die!" Jesus calls him "the father of lies" (Jn. 8:44). He is the master of misrepresentation. He has to be, otherwise nobody would fall for his propaganda and choose to sin. For in the end sin does not satisfy: "its end is the way to death" (Prov. 14:12). This is the reality that his lies must at all costs mask. Two of his most effective lies are these. First, that he himself does not exist. Second, that man is at his most free when in pursuit of "free thought", "free expression", and "free love". But his deceptions take other forms. Pretended signs and wonders are attributed to Satan and his human embodiment in 2 Thess. 2:9. And here it might be worth mentioning that imitation healings are part of his stock in trade. They figure widely in magic of all sorts. They stand out graphically in the wonders achieved by Pharaoh's magicians. They are alluded to drily in the Apocalypse (13:12–15). The power of the witch doctor is not totally illusory. Some of it is real: it comes direct from the Enemy, who is all for healing if he can thereby keep men in greater thraldom to himself. I have myself seen men converted to Christianity who had effected cures by demonic agency in their pre-Christian days. Faced with an Enemy as mendacious as this, it is no surprise that the Christian is often confronted with false teaching, false apostles and false brethren in the church (2 Pet. 2:1, 2 Cor. 11:13, Gal. 2:4). Jesus himself warned that "false Christs and false prophets will arise and show great signs and wonders, so as to lead astray, if possible, even the elect" (Matt. 24:24). History has provided abundant evidence of siren voices in the church down the centuries teaching a message very different from that of Jesus and the New Testament. The master of subterfuge is behind it.

## Satan can enter a man

He entered into Judas Iscariot, as both Luke and John tell us (Lk. 22:3, John 13:27). He cannot do this without a man's free will (Eph. 4:27). But deliberate sin opens up the gates in his entry. In the case of Judas, it was his determination to betray Jesus that gave the devil access. Indeed, the

51

devil can so control a man that he becomes "Beelzebul", master of the house. As Peter recognised in Ananias, "Satan has filled your heart" (Acts 5:3) and when this happens a man can fitly be described as "a child of Satan" (Acts 13:10).

## Satan can dominate

Satan can be so dominant in a situation that he can be said to be enthroned. There is that mysterious reference in the letter to the church at Pergamum, "I know where you dwell, where Satan's throne is" (Rev. 2:13). This may refer to the imperial cult, which upon pain of death demanded that all should acclaim Caesar as Lord: it would be hard to resist in Pergamum, where the imperial governor had his headquarters. It may refer to one of the many pagan temples in the city. It may refer to the atmosphere of corruption and compromise which dominated public life: people were plumbing "the deep things of Satan, as they call them" (2:24). And when dominant in such a way, Satan can have a field day: disease, oppression and disaster can readily follow. This seems to have been the case at Corinth where gross disorders at the eucharist allowed the devil to capture the situation: "that is why many of you are weak and ill, and some have died," said the apostle (1 Cor. 11:30).

## Satan is persistent

We see this in the temptations of Jesus. Foiled in each of three attempts to make Jesus misjudge his messianic calling, Satan departed from him, we read, *achri kairou*: this could mean "for a while" or, more decisively, "until an opportune moment". On any showing it points to his persistence. He tempted Jesus right through the ministry, not giving up even on the cross, as the seductive cry went up from the bystanders, "Save yourself and come down from the cross" (Mk. 15:30). Satan shows that same persistence in his attack on the people of Jesus. In Revelation 12 this point is made abundantly plain. The dragon tries first to devour the man-child when the woman gives birth: but her child was caught up to God and his throne. So the dragon

52

turns his attention to the woman, that is to say the church, and her offspring, the individual Christians who are faithful to their Lord. For sheer persistence he wins high marks.

## Satan is cowardly

He fears the name of his conqueror, Jesus Christ. And he fears those who stand up to him in this name. "Resist the devil and he will flee from you" (James 4:7). It only takes trust in the Lord and obedience to him to make the devil turn tail. That is why such a note of confidence in facing Satan runs through the New Testament. He is a defeated foe, and faced with resolute courage in the name of Jesus he will run.

These, then, are some of the characteristics of the Enemy of man. None of us is a match for a foe of this cunning, intelligence, power and hatred. He can deceive us. He can overcome us. He can enter us. He can murder us. Left to our own resources we would not have a hope. It is well that we are not required to rely on our own strength. Instead we have the victory of Calvary to celebrate, and as often as he is faced with that, the devil slinks away.

### The Allies of Satan

The classic trinity of evil, counterfeiting the Holy Trinity, consists of the world, the flesh and the devil. The devil operates primarily through the world and the flesh. He is essentially an undercover agent.

## The world

"The world" in this connexion does not mean the planet on which we live. It means society which leaves God out of account. A very great deal of temptation comes to man through this milieu. We are all placed in situations where we are influenced by other people. That influence, particularly the power of the peer group, the gang, the work mates, the boardroom, the media, is very strong. "Do not love the world or the things in the world. If any one loves the world, love for the Father is not in him," says John (1 John 2:15f). He makes it clear that he is using "the world"

53

in this special sense of godless society, for he continues, "for all that is in the world, the lust of the flesh, the lust of the eyes, and the pride of life, is not of the Father but is of the world. And the world passes away, and the lust of it. But he who does the will of God abides for ever." John is very firm in what he has to say about the world. It "lies in the power of the wicked one", under his thraldom (1 John 5:19). There is – or should be – a clear distinction between children of the heavenly Father and children of the world. "See what love the Father has given us that we should be called children of God: and so we are. The reason why the world does not know us is that is did not know him" (1 John 3:1). Anti-Christian teaching springs from the world. "They are of the world, therefore what they say is of the world, and the world listens to them. We are of God . . ." (I John 4:4). Our faith, or more precisely the Spirit of the Lord within us, is a force greater than the world and can preserve us from its downward pull (1 John 5:4, 4:4). But that is the only way of coping with a power so all-pervasive and insidious. The devil, we are reminded, endeavours to get us to "walk according to the course of this world" (Eph. 2:2). He is, after all, the "god of this world" (2 Cor. 4:4).

**The flesh**
"The flesh" is as misleading a term at first sight as is "the world". It does not in the New Testament normally mean our physical bodies. It is a technical term to denote man in his frailty and sin. It can denote our bodies but, particularly in Paul's writings, this more sinister sense of flesh prevails.

The flesh battles against the Spirit in our lives, and we are all aware of the war that is on (Gal. 5:17). The flesh is the seat of our lusts (Eph. 2:3). It is a mighty power, treacherous as can be, within each person: always liable to give in to evil impulse, and to side with the world. So compromised has the flesh become that in a moment of despair Paul can cry out in his famous chapter on the inner battle, Romans 7, "I know that nothing good lives in me, that is in my flesh" (7:18) and he ruefully has to admit that although he serves the law of God with his mind, with his flesh he serves the law of sin (7:25).

No wonder, therefore, that he writes so feelingly of the need to keep that flesh in the place where Jesus drew its poison, on the cross. "Those who are Christ's have crucified the flesh with its passions and desires," he writes (Gal. 5:24). And he warns Christians sharply against allowing their liberty in Christ to turn to an occasion for the flesh to rear its ugly head (Gal. 5:13). He urges us to "put on the Lord Jesus Christ and make no provision for the flesh to gratify its desires" (Rom. 13:4). Unless we do that, we shall remain in the ambiguous and defeated state of Romans chapter 7. For the flesh within us is as fickle as the world without. Both, though neutral in themselves, have become untrustworthy and potentially dangerous. Such, then, is the traditional picture of the Satanic trinity, the devil, the world and the flesh. What is not so often recognised is another dimension of allies which the devil commands. I mean the demonic.

**The demonic**
It is an interesting fact that modern society uses the word "demonic" a great deal in an allegorical way. For the West, Communism can be demonic. For the Communists, "reactionary capitalists" are no less demonic. The destruction of six million Jews in concentration camps, the embroilment of America in the Vietnam war, the grip of the Pentagon, the Watergate scandal are all described as demonic. And the Bible would not disagree. But it would not leave the matter there.

For the teaching of Scripture is uniform. There is one supreme source of all there is, God alone. He had made not only the universe and human beings, but heavenly beings as well. These are called "angels" or messengers of God. Their existence and personality, their moral character and intelligence, are consistently taught throughout Scripture. The holy angels will dwell with the redeemed in heaven, and in some respects we shall be like them (Matt. 22:30). There seems to be gradations in these beings: we read of Michael the archangel (Jude 9), together with other angels, seraphim and cherubim (Gen. 3:24, Ex. 25:20, Ps. 18:10, Isai. 6:2ff), principalities, powers, thrones and authorities

55

(Eph. 1:21, 3:10, Col. 1:16, 2:10, 1 Pet. 3:22). They surround the heavenly throne in worship and constitute the "ministering spirits" of the Almighty (Heb. 1:14). This ministry includes messages to men of promise or warning (Matt. 1:20, Lk. 1:26, Gen. 18:1–15, 19:1ff), sheer adoration of God (Lk. 2:13, Rev. 5:11), protection of men (Ps. 95:11, Matt. 18:10). We find angels at the birth of Jesus, at his resurrection, and they will accompany his return in judgement (Mk. 8:38, Matt. 25:31, 2 Thess. 1:7). Indeed, Rev. 21:12 speaks of twelve angels at the twelve gates of the celestial city. They occupy a significant place in Scripture. They figure in the giving of the Law (Acts 7:53, Gal. 3:19), in the teachings of Jesus (e.g. Lk. 16:22, Matt. 13:39), in the mission and sufferings of the church (1 Cor. 4:9, Rom. 8:38, Eph. 3:9f, 1 Pet. 1:12, Heb. 12:22) and they are even mentioned in an abbreviated early creed:

> Great, we confess, is the mystery of our religion
> He was manifested in the flesh
> Vindicated in the Spirit
> Seen by angels
> Preached among the nations
> Believed on in the world
> Taken up in glory
>
> (1 Tim. 3:16)

Such is some of the Bible's teaching about the angels of God. But Satan too, has his followers from the angelic realms. "God spared not the angels that sinned, but cast them down to hell, and delivered them into chains of darkness to be reserved for judgement" (2 Pet. 2:4). "The angels that did not keep their own position, but left their proper dwelling have been kept by him in eternal chains in the nether gloom until the judgement of the great day" (Jude 6). Clearly, the devil influenced some of the heavenly beings to join his revolt against God. And so they fell and came under the judgement of God. These forces are sufficiently numerous and powerful to constitute a kingdom of darkness. Their aim is to fight against the light and the good in every way possible. It is these malign forces which the

Scriptures maintain are behind the destructive powers in our world which we call demonic. We shall look more closely into this area in chapters four and five.

## Ourselves

Before we leave this chapter, one further ally of Satan deserves a mention: ourselves. Time and again we give in to the devil when we could quite well have held out. Our will is a casualty of the Fall. All too often we have ruefully to echo what G. K. Chesterton wrote to *The Times* on one famous occasion when there was a correspondence on what is wrong with the world.

"Sir," he wrote, "I am."

## CHAPTER 3

## Temptation

### The Targets of the Enemy

IN THE FOLLOWING chapters we shall look at four major ways in which the Enemy seeks the ruin of what God has created. It is a situation of total war, and it is important to be clear about the Tempter's targets in his war effort.

### God

His prime target is God Almighty. Such is his overweening arrogance and bitter hatred, that he dares to set himself against God. Never is this more clearly demonstrated than in the temptations of God incarnate, Jesus Christ. In those seductive temptations he aimed to separate Jesus from his Father by doubt, by disobedience, by distrust, by disloyalty, by compromise, by exhibitionism, by idolatry and by short-circuiting Calvary. He was launching through his assault on Jesus Christ, an all-out attack on God.

### The World

Second, he is determined to spoil the whole world, and his methods of doing so are legion. Some of them are highlighted in a fascinating passage in Revelation chapter 6. In the previous chapter John shows that only "the Lamb once slain who is in the midst of the throne of God" has the right to break the seals on the scroll of human destiny. Only in the light of his self-sacrificing and victorious love can history be rightly understood. And as Christ opens those seals, terrible things emerge in a world where Satan's trail is evident. We see, first, the white horse with its armed rider, "conquering and to conquer" (v.2). That speaks of ruthless, unrestrained militarism. The second is internecine strife, civil war, "the red horse that was permitted to take peace from the earth so that men should slay one another" (v.4). Third come ecological and social ravages. Famine conditions in which a quart of wheat costs a day's wage – whereas the oil and the wine, the luxuries, remain untouched. The disparity between the haves and the have-nots could scarcely be portrayed more graphically.

Fourth comes death by pestilence and malnutrition (v.8); fifth, the persecution of believers (v. 9–11); and sixth, disturbances in the sky and earthquakes terrible enough to induce men to hide in terror among the caves and rocks of the mountains. It would be a passable description of a nuclear holocaust.

These six seals, opening up and indicating something of the direction of history, are always contemporary. They show the way the Enemy operates in his attacks on God's world and all who live in it. The seventh seal leads us into two chapters concentrating on seven trumpets (for the warning of the nations). You might expect the last seal to bring us to the very edge of the Advent; instead, it ushers in seven fresh visions, similar to the preceding ones, but more awesome. The same process is adopted in chapter eleven as seven woes fall on an impenitent earth. This is more devastating still, as if God shouts to rouse those who will not listen. For 9:20 had told us that "the rest of mankind, who were not killed by these plagues, did not repent of the works of their hands nor give up worshipping demons and idols of gold and silver and bronze and stone and wood, which cannot either see or hear or walk; nor did they repent of their murders, of their sorceries (literally, drugs used for occult practices!) or their immorality or their thefts." It could have come from this week's *News of the World*. It is precisely true to life. And it shows the Enemy of mankind fostering every means to wreck God's world.

## Christians

His targets are God, the world, and then particularly Christians. He does not need to bother too much about those who are already safely in his control. But those who have defied him and committed themselves to his arch foe, these are major targets. That is why it often seems that temptation increases when we become Christians. Actually

59

it does increase: it is no illusion. We pass from security into the firing line.

This superb pictorial book of Revelation gives two graphic images of the way he attacks Christians. One is the image of the bloodthirsty dragon, waging war against "the seed of the woman, those who keeps the commandments of God and bear testimony to Jesus" (chapter 12). The other is the picture of the seductive prostitute (with overtones of Jezebel and Cleopatra, Babylon and Rome) in "the woman sitting on a scarlet beast which was full of blasphemous names, and it had seven heads and ten horns. The woman was arrayed in purple and scarlet, and bedecked with gold and jewels and pearls, holding in her hand a golden cup full of abominations and the impurities of her fornication; and on her forehead was written a mysterious name: 'Babylon the great, mother of harlots and of earth's abominations.' And I saw the woman, drunk with the blood of the saints, and the blood of the martyrs of Jesus" (17.3ff). A complicated picture, but the main theme is clear enough. Seduction this time, rather than outright opposition: but the overall aim is precisely the same in both cases – the liquidation of the people of God.

Leaving, then, to later chapters Satan's grip of nations and institutions through the principalities and powers, his encouragement of occult bondage, and his use of counterfeit religion, let us look in this chapter at the temptation of human beings which is Satan's stock in trade.

### The Nature of Temptation

In a world where good and devil are genuine options and where man has a measure of freedom to choose, temptation is inevitable. Interestingly enough, the biblical word for temptation can equally mean testing. It is morally neutral. When God allows pressures to come upon us, he wants us to overcome, and be all the stronger for it. God can neither be tempted by evil, nor does he tempt us. "Let no-one when he is tempted say, 'I am tempted by God'; for God cannot be tempted with evil, and he himself tempts no one" (Jas. 1:13). But it is quite otherwise when Satan brings those very same pressures to bear on us. He wants us to be overwhelmed by them, and to be all the weaker afterwards. Paul fears that the Tempter has tempted the Thessalonians to such an extent that his labour among them might be in jeopardy. Temptation is, therefore, something like the Basic Training in the Army. It is designed by the general to strengthen and discipline raw recruits. But it is not very pleasant, and those undergoing it may be pardoned for being oblivious of the general's designs and only too painfully aware of the sadism of the N.C.Os who, far from strengthening you, appear to be out to wreck your self-respect and break your spirit.

However, lest we should become conceited and see ourselves as a moral battleground between opposing cosmic forces, God and the devil, James has a practical and deflating thing to say. "Each person is tempted when he is lured and enticed by his own lust" (Jas. 1:14). He continues with a powerful analogy: "Then lust when it has conceived gives birth to sin, and sin when it is full grown brings forth death." We cannot escape responsibility by throwing all the blame on the devil. He is powerless until we say "Yes".

This is a point worth staying with for a moment. Many people feel that they must be particularly wicked because they get tempted so much. Not at all. Temptation is not sin: "Jesus was tempted in every respect as we are, yet without sinning" (Heb. 4:15). It is not the fact of temptation, but the giving in to it which is wrong.

What is undoubtedly true is that temptation becomes harder to combat the more we give in to it. As Peter observes, "whatever overcomes a man, to that he is enslaved" (2 Peter 2:19). The thought hardens into the word, and the word into the deed, and the deed into the habit, and the habit into the character – and the character into the destiny. No wonder the repeated call of the New Testament is, "Watch and pray that you may not enter into temptation." No wonder concern about this vital matter figures prominently in the Lord's Prayer. No wonder the writer to the Hebrews warns us against becoming "hardened by the deceitfulness of sin" (3:13).

It is true that temptation given in to is the harder to

combat next time, but temptation resisted does not necessarily mean that things become easier next time: it may simply mean that we become exposed to a stronger degree of temptation than before. That is how, I think, we should assess the true magnitude of Jesus' achievement. I used to think that because he never sinned, it must somehow have been easier for him. I now appreciate that whereas I never get the full blast of temptation – I fall before it gets that far – he did face just that without yielding: and he did so time after time. The rope that stands the test of repeated jolts is stronger than one which parts under the strain.

## The Tempter's Motivation and Strategy

### His global strategy

What is the motivation which goads the Tempter into continually seeking the downfall of man? The answer is his ambition. He was created, as we have seen, a creature of immense power, beauty and intelligence. When the recipient of qualities like that sees them as gifts of God, they induce awe, dependence and gratitude. Satan did not see them in that way. They were the basis of his power. All power tends to corrupt, and in Satan's case, it has corrupted absolutely. His god is no longer the Lord but himself. He must replace the Almighty. He must have pride of place. Therefore his aim is to get every man, woman and child in this world to owe him suzerainty.

His success is phenomenal. As we have seen, he is viewed in the Bible as the usurper prince of this world, and there is an important passage in 2 Corinthians 4 which sheds light on his ultimate strategy and present methods.

"If our gospel is veiled, it is veiled to those who are perishing. In their case the god of this world has blinded the minds of the unbelievers to keep them from seeing the light of the gospel of the glory of Christ, who is the likeness of God." (2 Cor. 4:3ff). Paul is speaking about the problems encountered in his ministry of preaching the gospel. It is hard work. It demands high motivation, holy living, courageous proclamation and dogged persistence. There is a great unseen adversary, Satan. He does not take kindly to seeing his kingdom assailed and his captives released. He is the god of this world. He has, for all practical purposes, taken the place of God in the lives of many people. He does not require that they should be very evil, very devilish. In fact he does not mind how kind they are, how devoted to philanthropic causes, how well educated or how generous. His great concern is to keep the light of the gospel of Jesus Christ who is the likeness of God, from breaking upon them. The weapon he uses for for this purpose, and with devastating effect, is blindness. He blinds the minds of unbelievers. They are blind to his machinations. They are blind to their danger. They are blind to the attractiveness of the divine likeness and glory in Jesus. They are not bad men; they simply don't see. And that is precisely the aim of the Tempter.

Imagine the situation behind the Iron Curtain, where the people are subjected all the time to official Soviet propaganda. They will not even see what things are like in a free country, let alone try to escape thither. But when some of them do see, when some of them attempt – and achieve – an escape, then the full wrath of the Soviet government is turned against them. It is a bit like that with Satan. So long as men stay within his realm and do not cross out of it into God's; so long as they believe his propaganda about the dullness of the Christian life and the injustice and meanness of God; so long he is content. But let them once doubt the propaganda, let them begin to be attracted by the glorious image of God in Jesus – then that spells danger. And the murderer of souls pursues them vigorously.

He does everything he can to prevent a man responding to the gospel of Christ. Jesus said as much in the parable of the sower. "The seed is the Word of God. The ones along the path are those who have heard; then the devil comes and takes away the Word from their hearts, that they may not believe and be saved" (Lk. 8:12). He seeks to lure men to destruction and does not mind what inducements he offers them en route. There is a delightful story told of the celebrated eighteenth-century preacher, Rowland Hill. He was walking down the street one day when he saw a drove of pigs following a man. "This", said Hill, "excited my curiosity so much that I determined to follow. I did so, and to my great surprise I saw them follow him to the slaughter-house. I said to the man, 'My friend, how did you induce the pigs to follow you here?' He replied, 'I had a basket of beans under my arm, and I dropped a few as I came along, and so they followed me.'"

That is precisely Satan's strategy. But when he is foiled and a man becomes a Christian, then he attacks that man mercilessly in order to spoil his Christian life. As Jesus taught in another of his parables, Satan is always out to quench the beginnings of spiritual life. "He who sows the good seed is the Son of man. The field is the world, and the good seed means the sons of the Kingdom. The weeds are the sons of the evil one. The enemy who sowed them is the devil" (Matt. 13:37ff). He can afford to allow men long rope while they are within his borders. When they cross over he sends his guerilla forces to harry them. These are obvious but good tactics.

In pursuit of his strategic aim to ruin men's lives and keep them from the Christ who alone can rescue and transform them, Satan has certain favourite stratagems which he repeats to excellent effect time and again.

### Scepticism

He discredits the message of the Bible. He can do this just as effectively by means of the charade of an Assembly and Religious Instruction period mandatory in English schools, as by the separation between religion and education in the U.S.A., or the inculcation of materialistic atheism which pours scorn on the Scriptures in the Soviet Union. He can do it as well by the old-fashioned fundamentalist who comes out with insensitive quotations in Shakespearean English on the street corner, as by the sceptical theologian who points out as many "errors" in Scripture as he can find. He can do it as well through the brass-bound King James Bible sitting unread in the front room, as through the publication and use of the Satanist Bible in many Western countries today. He achieves the same end by unlovely narrowness of mind among Christians who honour the Bible, as by excessive breadth of mind among those who do not, and who maintain that all religions lead to God and therefore it does not matter which, if any, you take up. In all these cases, men and women are effectively insulated from the life-giving message of the gospel.

## Silence

He keeps Christians silent. If, as the Book of Revelation maintains, "the word of their testimony" is one of the chief means whereby Satan's plans are thwarted, then the gagging of believers is obviously a prime necessity. Satan encourages this through a variety of means. Some are too fearful to open their mouths. Others maintain that life alone is what matters, and lips are at a discount. Others still are very dubious as to whether or not there is any good news to share. Others feel their lives are not good enough advertisement for them to come out of the closet. Others feel religion is too private a matter to speak of to others, or that it would be presumptuous to do so. Others have so small a grasp on the faith that they are easily persuaded that atheists who do not go to church but lead kind lives are just as good Christians as believers who worship God regularly. The means are legion: the result is the same. A silent church instead of a people who tell forth the praises of him who called them out of darkness into his marvellous light (1 Peter 2:9).

## Disunity

He loves to keep Christians divided. The Holy Spirit makes for unity. The Unholy Spirit makes for discord, hatred and division. How Satan must revel in the denominational structure of the churches. "By our denominations we show how much we hate one another," declared Bishop Festo Kivengere, and he is right. The scandal of a disunited church seeking to proclaim the gospel of reconciliation to a divided world would be ludicrous if it were not so sad. It is not only between denominations that cruel divisions exist, but between Christians in the same congregation. James in his Epistle draws attention to the disastrous effect of gossip and class consciousness in some churches, (3:5ff, 2:1ff), two weaknesses which are calculated to keep enquirers from coming to "the faith of our Lord Jesus Christ, the Lord of glory".

## Seduction

Another extremely common and effective tactic in pursuit of his overall strategy is to encourage Christians to fall in love with and marry a partner who has no interest in or only the most formal attachment to the Christian faith. For the sake of peace the enthusiastic partner cools down, in nine cases out of ten, and what could have been an effective Christian home is silenced. "Do not be mismated with unbelievers," urges St. Paul. "For what partnership has Christ with Beliar? Or what has a believer in common with an unbeliever? What agreement has the temple of God with idols? For we are the temple of the living God" (2 Cor. 6:14). But Satan learnt at the outset of his operations that if he can control one member of a marriage he can influence the pair. And by putting a hook in the nose of our sexuality he can draw us conveniently away from obedience to Christ and into a compromise which effectively quashes any witness to the gospel we might otherwise have made.

## Coercion

If seduction fails, coercion is another of his favourite expedients. In order to keep men from Christ, state persecution, torture, social pressures, economic disadvantage can all be employed. There are many countries in the world where to be a Christian leads to social discrimination, economic poverty, the closure of educational or medical facilities, the certainty not to get a good job, the loss of home, the loss of liberty or the loss of life – both for yourself and for your family. That is sober truth, and many millions of Christians throughout the world are undergoing some part of that list as I write. Satan rejoices. It all helps his war effort – except when he overreaches himself and the whole thing backfires, with the emergence of compassion, a change of government, pressure from world opinion, or the sheer counterproductive effect of martyrs going singing to their deaths as has happened in the Mau Mau risings in Kenya and often in Russia and Uganda.

These are among the most common expedients employed by the Destroyer to keep men in the dark. He is the utterly anti-God spirit. He is consumed with the corrupting lust for power which knows only one sovereign, himself. He will not rest satisfied until everyone recognises that power. Defeated by Jesus Christ, his great concern is to keep men from giving their allegiance to his conqueror. And if they do, he will attack them relentlessly. Let us see how.

## The Tempter's Methods

### Fiery arrows

In the celebrated passage about the Christian armour in Ephesians 6 Paul warns his readers that they have a resolute foe in the prince of darkness. Satan is like a wrestler full of tricks, like a soldier on the attack, or like an army assailing a castle with flaming arrows. What are some of these "flaming arrows of the evil one"?

There are many ways of looking at this question. If only Satan can prevent men from keeping the two great commandments to love God and our neighbour, he has totally achieved his purpose. If he can get us to break the Ten Commandments he is delighted. And which of us has put God first, and has not made our own conception of him, taken his name in vain and despised his day? Which of us has had a proper attitude to our parents? Which of us has not killed by deed, word or look, or committed adultery in fact or desire? Stealing, untruths about others and the cult of covetousness are characteristic of Western life. I cannot personally face any one of those ten commandments with equanimity. Can you? The flaming arrows of the Enemy have found their mark.

### Pride

Pride is one of the main ways in which Satan attacks mankind. This is not surprising, for he himself fell through pride. "Let anyone who thinks that he stands take heed lest he fall," said Paul (1 Cor. 10:12). It was pride that led King David to number his forces, and that pride was nurtured by Satan (1 Chron. 21:1). It was pride that kept the Pharisee, modern no less than ancient, from going home justified: "O God I thank thee that I am not like other men, extortioners, unjust, adulterers . . ." (Lk. 18:11). As John Wesley White says in his book *The Devil* (to which I have been indebted): "Pride is a strange illness – it makes everyone sick but the one who has it." "God resists the proud," says Peter, and it is in this context that he warns his readers to be watchful against their adversary the devil (1 Peter 5:5, 8).

## Lust

Lust is another most obvious flaming arrow which daily assails us from the hoardings, the movies, and the newsstands. The story of David and Bathsheba is a salutary reminder that position in society and experience of life are no safeguard against this temptation. A casual sight of a naked woman, that image dwelt on in the mind, adultery, and the whole network of intrigue and evil springing from it – treachery, complicity, disloyalty, murder, lying and disgrace. It is a story that has been repeated countless times. Indeed, lust has become one of the major weapons, perhaps the most important of all, in Satan's armoury. The permissive society has simply surrendered to lust. "I want it now, and I intend to have it" is the attitude, and its results are very serious. They include the massive escalation of divorce: "falling in love" with someone else dispenses us from any vows we may have made to our partner and any responsibilities to provide a stable home for our children. They include the sexual promiscuity which is now so prevalent that a virgin at marriage is the exception rather than the rule. They include a massive and lucrative industry in pornography – films, books, and an ever increasing rash of magazines. They include the upsurge of homosexuality, of wife-swapping, of orgies. They include the pill for the unmarried so that they can fornicate without producing children, and free abortion for them if they are careless.

Lust, sheer lust, lies behind all these things, not to mention the advertising which needs a pretty and practically naked girl if it is to sell any product effectively.

## False asceticism

At the other extreme the devil is skilful at inducing a false asceticism. Those who "forbid marriage and enjoin abstinence from foods which God created to be received with thanksgiving by those who believe and know the truth" are roundly said to be giving heed to demonic doctrines (1 Tim. 4:3). The devil can wear the hair shirt as well as anyone, and the mental torment of men of God like Origen (who castrated himself to avoid lust) or the anchorites (whose minds were often consumed with lustful thoughts as a result of their enforced abstinence from marriage) are good examples of the success of this particular flaming arrow.

## Doubts

Satan loves to tempt men by doubts. He did it in tempting Eve. "*Did* God say. . . ?" He did it in tempting Jesus – "*If* you are the Son of God . . ." It is clearly one of his most effective weapons. A great many Christians are racked by doubts about their own standing with God. Satan repeated this type of assault on Jesus through the agency of Simon Peter just after his great confession of faith at Caesarea Philippi. God had spoken through Peter, but then at once Satan spoke through him (Matt. 16:16f, Mk. 8:32f). This was a very subtle attack of doubt. But Jesus discerned it immediately, rebuked Peter and said, "Get behind me, Satan!" (Mk. 8:33). In so doing he left us an example of how to handle doubts.

## Disaster

Temptation can come on a man through disasters or physical misfortune. Satan well knows how to orchestrate that. Job is the classic case. His loss of animals and property, his bereavement, his physical illness were all satanically induced, though never out of God's control. This is not to say that every run of bad luck, every physical ailment is brought on by the devil; merely that it may be. It was so in the case of Paul, and his "thorn in the flesh". To be sure it was the occasion of his receiving special strength from God to deal with it; nevertheless he is quite clear that it was "the messenger of Satan" for whose removal he earnestly, though vainly prayed (2 Cor. 12:7ff).

## Depression
On the other hand, temptation can come with equal force through the mind, in the shape of depression and discouragement. 1 Samuel 18 relates how an "evil spirit from the Lord" (note the consistent monotheism which is boldly impatient of secondary causes) troubled Saul and turned him not merely into a depressive but a manic depressive (18:10). Elijah after his great victory over the prophets of Baal (and we are never more vulnerable than after a great spiritual triumph) retired into the wildnerness in deep depression and felt God's cause was lost and that only he was left (1 Kings 18). It is highly probable that some, not all, of the supposedly depressive illnesses are caused by demonic attacks. When rebuked in the name of Jesus a depression or migraine disapppears at once if it is demonic in origin; if not, it stays put. We shall be looking further at this type of release in chapter five.

## Fear
Fear is a very effective flaming arrow of which the Adversary makes much use. It was when Satan was sifting Peter like wheat on the night of Jesus' arrest that Peter had not the courage to tell even a maidservant of his allegiance to Jesus (Lk. 22:31ff). The link between Satan and fear is very strong. Like Peter, many are terrified to confess Christ in their homes, in the office, in the factory or at the football club. It would be asking too much! The fear syndrome is powerfully at work, and behind it is the Enemy.

## The suit of dirty clothes
There are many other fiery arrows in the Evil One's quiver. Sometimes the New Testament writers see these temptations not so much as arrows but as dirty clothes which

need to be stripped off. "Put off your old nature which belongs to your former manner of life and is corrupt through deceitful lusts," says Paul, and then enumerates some of the filthy old clothes that need to be removed: lies, anger and moodiness, stealing, laziness, filthy talk, malice, bitterness, bad temper, slander, fornication and idolatry are among the things he mentions (Eph. 4:22ff). The suit of dirty clothes which needs to be "put off" is described in Colossians (3:5ff) as fornication, impurity, covetousness, idolatry, malice, anger, slander, filthy talk. Equally Peter calls on his readers to "put off" malice and all guile and insincerity and envy and all slander (2:1ff). James says "put off all filthiness and rank growth of wickedness" (1:21) while Romans 13:12 says "put away the works of darkness" and indicates some of them in the list which follows –revelling and drunkenness, debauchery, licentiousness, quarrelling and jealousy. So there clearly was a common mind among the early Christians about the need to stand firm against temptation, and the very practical steps that must be taken, in the power of Christ, to get rid of embarrassingly particular failings. Just because Satan is so deceptively subtle (2 Cor. 11:3), just because sin is so enticing (James 1:14), just because sin's effect is so hardening (Heb. 3:13), Christians cannot afford to compromise. They must be willing to throw off the whole suit of dirty clothes. They must be willing to wear the whole armour of God and stand firm amid the rain of flaming arrows that Satan will assuredly shower on them.

### The Tempter at Work

It would be foolish to end this chapter without a careful look at the archetypal temptation in the Garden of Eden. This gives us profound insight into how the Tempter works.

### Satan in Eden

The idyllic third chapter of Genesis is much neglected. Everybody knows about it, but nobody profits by it. Why? Because some are so busy arguing that it is historical that they do not take to heart the lesson it is teaching; while others are so sure it is not historical that they feel at liberty to neglect what it is saying. And Satan laughs. He is anxious to divert attention away from Genesis 3. No undercover agent likes to have his disguise seen through and his methods exposed. So let us leave aside the secondary question of the literary category of this marvellous story, and see what it has to teach us about the Tempter's methods of approach.

Eden is God's plan for mankind. A superb garden, a place of delight, it came straight from the hands of him who gives us richly all things to enjoy. It was a place of happiness, of purity, of companionship, and of obedience. And this matchless story tells us how it call came to nothing, and still does. For whatever the historical status of Adam and Eve, this story is our story. It remains as true of mankind today as when it was first written.

The two opening characteristics of temptation as we find it here are these. First, it catches Eve by surprise, coming as it did from a quite unexpected quarter. Temptation often does that. And second, Satan does not appear in his true colours: that would act as a dissuasive. He comes in disguise, relying on the subtlety, the grace, the fatal fascination of the serpent to achieve his purposes. As ever he is the master of disguise.

Satan has a clear aim: to encourage disobedience against God, and thus get man and woman under his control. This would sever their relationship with God just as surely as his own had been ruptured by pride and self-will. So he sets about accomplishing man's downfall. He has to row his boat down God's waterways: he has none of his own. Devoid of creativity, he can only spoil what God creates. And he comes to Eve down the perfectly natural channels of the body, the mind and the ambition, all of which are God-given faculties.

**Attack on the body**

First, he appeals to the body. There is nothing wrong with feeling hungry, and hunger was the first target for his attack. It still is. The amount of evil that comes into the world through the misuse of perfectly natural bodily functions, the desire for food, drink, sex, sleep, and strength is simply enormous. Most of the time, it is unnecessary for Satan to be very sophisticated in his approach. He can reach us very effectively through basic physical functions. The overfed West pursues slimming, while half the Third World starves. Alcoholism has become one of the great killers of our day, and is a major social menace. Laziness is a national characteristic in many parts of the world, and there is a disturbing cult of violence in literature, on film, and in the streets. An article on "The battlefield of tolerance" in *The Times* (30.5.78) pointed out that those who foster the taste for mental rape and murder imply that "satiation seems the only reason for existence. Yet the drive for satiation is an abject basis for existence; its fuel can only be crude sex or greed for money. The sense of power derived from them has to be among the most primitive human feelings." The writer remarked sardonically that our intellectual London culture has now reached this point: evil is idolised, and a modish nihilism is marketed at large in the literature put out for our entertainment. And yet we fondly imagine that Genesis 3 is too naïve to have anything to teach us!

**Attack on the mind**
Second, Satan concentrates on the mind of Eve. He is out to confuse her. He sows several varieties of doubt.

He invites her to doubt God's goodness. "Did God say 'You shall not eat of any tree in the garden?'" he asks. This was not only a flagrant misrepresentation of the facts, but carried the innuendo that God is a mean fellow, who is out to restrict her legitimate pleasures. It is a piece of satanic propaganda which continues to have widespread success today.

He encourages her to doubt God's word. "Did God say. . . ?" The innuendo is that God cannot be relied on and probably has not disclosed his will anyway. Doubts of this nature continue to be a prime source of temptation to those who are trying to live for God. Whenever faced by a prohibition we tend to wonder whether it may not be patient of some other interpretation, whether it is not outdated in our modern situation, or whether we may not be the exception to the rule. Such doubt and casuistry have become second nature – since Eve's day.

Satan infuses a third type of doubt: it is clearly one of his favourite weapons. He expressed doubts about God's holiness. "You will not die," the devil maintains. God is not so unkind as to make good his threats. All will turn out fine in the end, however disobedient man is. And that is a lie which has destroyed millions who assumed God was no more holy than themselves.

Satan assailed Eve's mind with a variety of doubts about what is right and whether or not to act in obedience to conscience. It remains a primal mode of temptation.

**Attack on ambition**
Third, Satan appeals to the ambitions which Eve nourishes. Naturally she would be attracted by delectable fruit, but even more so by the prospect of further knowledge. But the Tempter's master stroke was to instil the itch to be like God. "When you eat of it your eyes will be opened, and you will be like God." And today's "men like gods" school of technocrats, today's ruthless social and political ambition, today's pursuit of knowledge for knowledge's sake even if it should destroy mankind – these present us with a dry commentary on this passage, written many centuries ago but still painfully relevant.

All these three methods were designed by the Tempter to breach the citadel of Eve's will. However subtle his innuendos, however sparkling the hopes he held out, Eve did not fall until she yielded her will to the thoughts that were beleaguering her. She yielded. In this apparently trifling but profoundly significant matter she disobeyed God, and Satan's objective was achieved. She had declared open rebellion on God and had sided with the Tempter. The key had turned in the lock of that inner room of her will. Only then did temptation become sin. The first battle of the long war was decisively lost.

## Seven consequences of sin

The consequences of this action of hers are sketched with candour and poignancy in the pages of Genesis. They, too, are always contemporary.

First, Eve embroiled somebody else. Sin is generally like that. It is rarely that we do not hurt another person even by our more private sins. In this case she gained the complicity of Adam, and the partnership which was intended to be so mutually supportive became mutually destructive.

Second, they felt dirty. They had been naked all the time, but now they felt embarrassed at this very natural state. They "sewed fig leaves together and made themselves aprons". Sexuality suddenly became something of which they felt unaccountably ashamed. And for all the overt sexuality of our own day, such remains the case. The "feeling dirty" is not just sexual, of course. It accompanies a mean business trick, taking advantage of a colleague, slapping down someone who cannot stand up for himself. The fruit of sin always turns to ashes in the mouth. Part of that ashes is the sense of feeling defiled.

Third, they hid from God. The point is made with delicate humour but infinite pathos. "They heard the sound of the Lord God walking in the garden in the cool of the day, and the man and his wife hid themselves from the presence of the Lord God among the trees of the garden." Trees are not very good at hiding a man from God: they were not intended for that. Ever since that day man has been hiding from God. It is not God who has made the break, but man. "If God seems far away, guess who has moved", says the wayside poster. Man had moved from the path of obedience, and God seemed far away. Moreover he now seemed less desirable than he had been. Companionship with God had lost its charm. Sin always has that effect.

Fear is very evident, too. "I was afraid," said man. A surprising result of enlightenment, you might be pardoned for thinking. Yet so it is. The fear that paralyses the body, the fear that grips and haunts the mind, is the product of sin. When a man walks in company with his God, he finds that perfect love casts out fear. When those communications are ruptured, man is cut off from the only

75

psychological force greater than fear, namely love: and *Angst* is the natural partner to alienation. Fear in all its varied forms is one of the most notable characteristics of our own "enlightened" day.

Moral cowardice is another unlovely fruit of sin. Man has not the courage to say "I was wrong". Instead he blames someone else: "she gave me of the tree and I did eat." And he also blames God: "the woman whom thou gavest me . . ." Both are typical characteristics of man since the Fall. He blames anybody but himself: the game of passing the buck is the oldest in the world (Eve did it as well as Adam, v. 13). Notice too how he hits out at God: the first of the "Why does God allow it?" brigade.

A sixth fruit of their sin was spiritual death. I used to feel that the serpent was right: that Adam and Eve did *not* die when they disobeyed God, as he had said they would. Instead they lived on for many a long day. But I have come to see my view was much too shallow. They did die, and at once. When they sinned, the link of fellowship with God was broken. He at once seemed estranged. Guilt replaced confidence. They were dead while they lived, spiritually cut off from him, although mentally and physically still alive. And that, too has been the human situation ever since. Man is cut off from life at the deepest level. That is why Paul can correctly ascribe our pre-conversion state as "dead in trespasses and sins" (Eph. 2:1). That is also why Jesus can describe relationship with God as eternal life – with life at the deepest level restored (John 17:3).

Lastly, their sin brought judgement. God did not act unfairly. They had the chance of explaining their actions. They were condemned not so much by God as by their own actions and words. He merely underlined the assessment they gave of themselves. The serpent, the man, and the woman are all judged. Man is sent out of the garden. He has chosen to be separate from God: separate he shall be. The punishment fits the crime, as it always does with God, who is perfectly just.

That, I suppose, one could have expected. But what one could not expect is the heart of the great Lover. He comes and makes skins for the rebel pair. He clothes them, little though they deserve it. That is the God we worship. So far from being mean, as the Tempter suggests, he is unbelievably generous. He is the one who would later justify the ungodly, clothing them not with skins but with the righteousness of Christ, even though mankind had rejected him and revelled in rebellion. If it takes temptation and sin to show God in his true colours and Satan in his, something has been saved from the wreck. And in a later chapter we shall see how, in the generosity of that same God, Paradise lost became Paradise regained.

# CHAPTER 4

## Principalities and Powers

THERE IS, IN the heart of Oslo, a park where a fascinating display of bronzes adorns a large bridge and monument beyond it. The artist, Gustav Vigeland, is expressing his philosophy of life, and nowhere is it more clearly portrayed than in the central figures on either side of the bridge. One is of a man, one of a couple; and they are both gripped, encased by a circle from which they cannot break free.

Modern man feels that bondage. So did ancient man. Perhaps nobody has better grasped the flavour of Graeco-Roman paganism than Edwyn Bevan. He wrote in *Hellenism and Christianity*:

> When men looked up at the stars, they shuddered to see there powers whose mysterious influence held them in a mechanism of iron necessity; they were the World-Rulers who fixed men's destiny without any regard to human will and human tears. Effort, shrewdness, long-laid design could bring no liberation from the predestined law . . . It became an obsession. This earth, the sphere of their tyranny, took on a sinister and dreadful aspect.

Judaism shared this sense of bondage to forces beyond themselves. They were not so materialistic as to locate them in the stars, but rather in the principalities and powers which were at work in the universe. The matter is sufficiently important for us to examine it in some detail.

### The Principalities and Powers in Jewish Belief

When seen against the background of the demon-ridden world of the Middle East, Judaism presents a very different emphasis, concentrating on the one God, Creator of heaven and earth. However, the Old Testament teaches that there are many subordinate spirits under God's overall sovereignty. We looked at this in chapter two.

Sometimes in the Old Testament we read of the *kedoshim*, or "holy ones", a heavenly court presided over by the Lord himself (Ps. 89:6, 8, Job. 15:15, Deut. 33:2, Zech. 14:5). Frequently God is called *Yahweh Sabaoth*, "Lord of the powers", and here the gods of polytheism are seen as captives under his suzerainty. And we read of the *bene elohim* or "sons of God" in Job, the Psalms, and Genesis 6:3. But perhaps the most important passage of all is Deut. 32:8 where the best texts read that the God "fixed the bounds of all the peoples according to the number of the *bene elohim*, the sons of God. For the Lord's portion is his people, Jacob his allotted heritage." The meaning is well brought out elsewhere: Deut. 4:19 speaks of the moon, stars and hosts of heaven which the Lord has allotted to all the peoples under heaven, with the exception of Israel whom he has appointed for himself. Thus "He appointed a ruler for every nation, but Israel is the Lord's own portion" (Ecclus. 17:7).

In this way the Jews resolved the problem of the one and the many. There was only one God, and he was their God for ever. All other spiritual forces, be they good or bad, were ultimately of his creation, under his control and assigned as tutelary deities to other nations. Thus in the apocalyptic book of Daniel we find Michael appearing as God's champion for suffering Israel against the angel-prince (*sar*) of Persia and of Greece (Dan. 10:13, 20f, 12:1f). The nations which ruled the ancient world were under the supervision of their angel-princes, who in their turn were under the ultimate control of Yahweh, the Lord of heaven and earth, who had entered into a covenant relationship with his people Israel.

*The Principalities and Powers in the Graeco-Roman World*

As in any polytheistic culture, spirit forces figured largely in the Graeco-Roman culture into which Christianity was born. The world was subject to the guardianship of spirits, *daimones*, and the whole point of magic was to use formulae or objects to influence these "world rulers" or "elemental spirits". The physical objects and the spiritual powers associated with them were often given no clear distinction. Thus the Greeks used "Hephaestos" to mean both fire and the deity which supervised fire. The world, as Thales had long before maintained, was itself an entity with life and full of *daimones*.

There were many aspects to this basic conviction that the spiritual world was closely bound up with our own. One was astrology, which helped men to believe there was some sort of order in the world and that they were not the hapless victims of *Tychē*, Chance. It was enormously influential in the Hellenistic age. Major rulers all had their star. Bar Cochba in the early second century called himself "Son of a star" in the pursuance of messianic pretensions. And Vespasian, Tacitus and Josephus all bear testimony to the first-century belief that the stars had decreed that the ruler of the world would come from Judaea (Suetonius, *Vesp*. 4, Tacitus, *Hist*. 5.13, Josephus, *B. J.* vi. 5, 4). On the one hand the stars offered the hope of purpose in a world that seemed chaotic; on the other hand they imposed the iron bondage of Fate, from which men sought to escape through *gnosis*, magic, or the mystery religions.

Another branch of this interpenetration of the human and the superhuman was given emphasis in the concept of *daimones*. These were spiritual deputies of the gods (or God) who ruled the world. They had many names, "principalities, powers, rulers, thrones, world rulers, elemental spirits" and the like. It was from their clutches that men sought salvation through means ranging from philosophy to the occult. In a long line of writers, embracing Porphyry, the Hermetica and Celsus, these *daimones* (which act as intermediaries in the divine government of the world and as forces behind the human rulers and their state) are seen to be both bad and good. The good ones do not harm man, but preside over the state, commerce, medicine and the rest. The bad ones are not officially appointed by the gods but make up for this by trying to usurp authority, attract worship to themselves and denigrate the great gods (*Corpus Hermeticum* 16:13f, Origen, *Contra Celsum* 5:25, 7:68). The Christian writer Origen is not keen to establish any common ground with his pagan opponent, so he calls the evil spirits *daimones* and the good ones angels; none the less, he is operating with precisely the same cosmology. It was very widely accepted in antiquity that behind the rulers of the state lay their *daimones* – or, as some preferred to call it, the *numen* or *genius* of the ruler. There is, in short, such a correspondence between the world of sense and time and the invisible world that the two were, to the ancients, almost a single entity. As Philo put it, the one God rules through his powers or angels (*Conf.* 171, 181 and *Leg. Alleg.* 3:177f).

Naturally the same concept governed the growth of the imperial cult, in which the supreme ruler of the one world pacified by Roman arms became the representative of the divine power working through him. Worship of *Augustus* or the *numen Augusti* was seen as both a religious and a political expression of loyalty: yet the Christians faced it head on. Their refusal to worship the *daimon* of the emperor exposed them to the charge both of sedition and of atheism. Christians might argue about whether the ruler was at his task because of divine appointment by an angel of God (so Origen, *Contra Celsum* 8:9) or because of domination by a malevolent *daimon* (so Justin, *1 Apol.* 5:1, *Dial.* 18:3), but all were agreed that behind the human ruler lay his celestial principality or power. This was common ground to Christian, pagan and Jew alike.

### The Principalities and Powers in the New Testament

**Their prevalence**

Oscar Cullmann has repeatedly drawn attention (in books such as *Christ and Time* and *The State in the New Testament*) to a neglected area of New Testament studies by pointing out that superhuman forces are mentioned in almost every place where Christ's complete lordship is being discussed. The spirit world is a major factor in the teaching of the whole New Testament.

Somewhat curiously Dennis Whiteley, who recognises

this, maintains that the demons with which Jesus dealt in the Gospels are nothing to do with the principalities and powers that we find in the Pauline writings. "The demons of the Synoptic Gospels are the putative cause of afflictions which come upon individuals and are now treated, with varying success, by physicians and psychiatrists. The 'principalities and powers' are the concern of politicians, sociologists and others" (Whiteley, *op. cit.* p. 19). But Heinrich Schlier in his book *Principalities and Powers* has shown, conclusively to my mind, that this distinction is not supported by the evidence of the New Testament. He instances the enormous number of names which the New Testament writers employ to describe this conglomeration of evil forces: they include principalities, powers, dominions (*kuriotētes*) thrones, names, princes (*archontes*) lords, gods, angels, spirits, unclean spirits, wicked spirits, elemental spirits (*stoicheia*). This is in addition to the many synonyms for Satan (the devil, the serpent, the lion, the strong one, the wicked one, the accuser, the tempter, the adversary, the enemy, the liar, the murderer, the god of this age, the prince of this world, the prince of the power of the air, Beelzebub and Beliar).

This astonishing collection of names indicates a number of things. First, concern with these spiritual forces was a very important matter to the New Testament writers, and continued to be in the subapostolic age.

Second, despite the variety in nomenclature, the overall picture is the same throughout the Bible; a variety of evil forces under a unified head. It would be foolish and misleading to try to separate the principalities and powers of the Pauline letters from the demons of the Gospels.

Third, the very number and variety of the names for these things shows us that the New Testament writers, unlike their Jewish and pagan predecessors, had no interest in building up demonologies; they enumerated at random, only in order to show that these enemy forces were one and all disarmed by Jesus Christ. You have only to compare the New Testament writings with the Book of Enoch to see the startling contrast. There is no need, as the Apocalypse put it, to search out "the deep things of Satan" (Rev. 2:24):

merely to know and count on the power of the ascended and reigning Christ.

Fourth, the prevalence of this belief in the demonic throughout the ancient world is significant. In Schlier's words, "In some way relevation absorbed these phenomena from the tradition of universal human experience" (*op. cit.* p. 13). Nowhere does Jesus have to explain himself when exorcising, either on Jewish or Gentile soil. The same applies to the apostles. And the same is true in the subapostolic age. Justin is typical. He castigates those who "yielding to unreasoning passion and the instigation of demons" persecute the Christians. He is at pains to point out that what the heathen call gods are demonic spirits, and shows how when Socrates tried to make this plain "the demons themselves, by means of men who rejoiced in wickedness, procured his death as an atheist and a profane person on the charge that he was introducing 'new divinities'; which is just what they do in our case" (*1 Apol.* 5, cf. 14:1, 44:12, *Dial.* 18:3).

## Their source and habitation

As we have seen in chapter two, these principalities and power are regularly portrayed as the subordinates of the quintessential spirit of evil, Satan himself. In Matthew 25:41 Jesus speaks of "the devil and all his angels", clearly indicating demonic powers. In Revelation 16:13, 14 it is plain that demons and unclean spirits are identical: they are lieutenants of Satan. The Beelzebub controversy puts the matter beyond doubt (Matt. 12:22–29). The Pharisees charged Jesus with casting out demons through Beelzebub, the prince of demons, and Jesus rebutted their charge. But both parties were agreed on the nature of these unclean spirits: they derive from the Unholy Spirit himself.

These mighty forces are not merely powerful; they are power. That is their name and definition: "dominion", "power", "might" and "authority". They are said to inhabit "the air" or "the heavenly places" (Eph. 2:2, 6:12). How much we should read into these rather vague cosmological statements it is hard to know. But Paul certainly does not simply mean by "the heavenlies" the home of

God, but the surroundings of the material world. They interpenetrate the climate of a country, the *Tendenz* of its politics and the *nuances* of its culture. I am not inclined to press the language unduly, despite the attention of various ingenious authors.* The "heavenly places" include the abode both of the principalities and powers (Eph. 6:12) and of the God who in Christ exercises his reign over them (Eph. 1:20). Indeed, the believer is in some sense already seated in the heavenlies (Eph. 2:6) and it is there that he is blessed with all spiritual blessings in Christ (Eph. 1:3). We are at the extremities of language, and perhaps all we should assume is that these forces of evil are so located that they can influence the world the people in it, although they are not autonomous, as they would wish, but are at the end of a long rope held by Almighty God.

## Their nature
In recent years a substantial debate has arisen about the nature of these principalities and powers. There has been a tendency to demythologise the concept, and regard them as not as fallen spiritual beings but rather as the structures of earthly existence – the state, class struggle, propaganda, international corporations and the like, when they become either tyrannical or objects of man's total allegiance. This has the double attraction of divesting ourselves of belief in so unfashionable a concept as a hierarchy of angels, good and evil, stretching between man and God; it also enables us to find a good deal more in the New Testament about our very modern preoccupation with social structures. Often this debate has been conducted more on the basis of presupposition than of exegesis.

The truth of the matter is that words like principalities, powers and thrones are used both of human rulers and of the spiritual forces which lie behind them. This is readily demonstrable. Lk. 12:11 clearly refers to men when it says, "When they bring you before the synagogues and the rulers

* See Schlier, *Christus und die Kirche im Epheserbrief*, p. 1–18 and Chrys Caragounis, *The Ephesian Mysterion*, Excursus A.

and authorities". Acts. 4:26 equally obviously indicates
men, "The kings of the earth set themselves in array and
the rulers were gathered together, against the Lord and
against his Anointed." On the other hand, it is perfectly
manifest that the powers and thrones and authorities in
Col. 1:16, 2:15, Rom. 8:38, Eph. 6:12 are superhuman
powers. There are some passages which could be taken
either way, notably 1 Cor. 2:8, Titus 3:1, Romans 13:1.
Probably the ambiguity is deliberate.

The main thrust of New Testament teaching is to see
these powers as spiritual entities in "the heavenlies" i.e. the
spiritual world. In Ephesians, for example, they figure
three times, and in each case they are described as being "in
the heavenlies" which, as John Stott points out in his *God's
New Society*, makes it almost impossible to believe that
earthly forces are in view. This does not for one moment
mean that the principalities and powers may not infest
government, public opinion and the like. It simply avoids
the confusion of identifying them. As Stott goes on to infer,
if these principalities and powers are identified with
structures and institutions, serious consequences follow.


First, we lack an adequate explanation why structures so regularly, but not always, become tyrannical.
Secondly, we unjustifiably restrict our understanding
of the malevolent activity of the devil, whereas he is
too versatile to be limited to the structural. Thirdly, we
become too negative towards society and its structures. For the Powers are evil, dethroned and to be
fought. So if the Powers are structures, this becomes
our attitude to structures. We find it hard to believe or
say anything good about them, so corrupt do they
appear. Advocates of the new theory warn us against
deifying structures; I want to warn them against
demonising them. Both are extremes to avoid. By all
means let the church as God's new society question the
standards and values of contemporary society,
challenge them, and demonstrate a viable alternative.
But if God blesses her witness, some structures may

become changed for the good; then what will happen to the new theology of the Powers?

(J. R. W. Stott, *op. cit.* p. 274f)

It is important, then, to realise the flexibility of such terms as principalities and powers in the usage of the New Testament. They do, on occasion, refer to human authorities. They do, for the main part, refer to super-human agencies in the spiritual world. And even here there is ambiguity. The most probable interpretation of these powers in Ephesians 1:21f, 3:10 is that they refer to angelic spirits in the court of heaven. The certain interpretation of these powers in Eph. 2:1f, 6:12ff is that they are demonic spirits under Satan's control. And yet the same words are used! It is perhaps an implicit reminder that all power is ultimately God's, and that the fallen spirits were angels before they fell, which is, of course, the consistent teaching of the Bible.

**Their influence**
The New Testament attributes a widespread influence to these principalities and powers.

i) We see it in the realm of illness. The woman with "a spirit of infirmity eighteen years who was bowed together and could not look up" was described by Jesus as "this daughter of Abraham whom Satan has bound" (Lk. 13:16). The dumb man of Matthew 9:32 was suffering from a demon, and when Jesus had cast it out he was free to speak. In Lk. 9:42 epilepsy is attributed to demonic interference, and in Matthew 12:22 blindness.

It is commonly said that the benighted New Testament writers put all illness down to demonic activity because they knew nothing of medicine. However, granted their medical ignorance, it is all the more significant that generally they make rather a careful distinction between the two. They believe (and why not?) that all illness comes from the fact that the world is out of joint and lacks the wholeness that God intended: in short, it is an aspect of the Fall. They see suffering as one of the ways in which Satan binds mankind. They maintain that God allows it in his inscrutable wisdom, that he longs to give wholeness, that he shared human suffering to the uttermost, and rose triumphant over it. That is why they can look forward in confidence to the Age to Come where there will be no more sorrow, or crying, or pain or death (Rev. 21:4).

But although Satan is the great wrecker of human wholeness and delights to inflict illness (as with Job), the Bible writers decline to attribute all illness to direct satanic activity. They distinguish between "healing" and "casting out demons" (Lk. 13:32, 4:40f, 9:1f). Demons are expelled; diseases are healed. The two are not the same, though the symptoms may be identical. Some cases of epilepsy, for example, may be demonic: but that does not mean all are. I personally recall a student whose epilepsy seems to have been of the type brought about by the Enemy. He read one day of Jesus' deliverance of the epileptic boy, told the Lord in prayer that he believed the same could happen to him – and never had another attack. That man is in the ordained ministry today.

ii) We see it in some historical situations. "Behold, the devil will cast some of you into prison" warns the Book of Revelation, and refers to the place "where Satan's seat is" (Rev. 2:10, 13). Since this was written to Pergamum, the seat of political power in Roman Asia, we are surely right in seeing that Satan had a particular grip of that historical situation. It was the place where "My faithful witness, Antipas" was matryred for his loyalty to Christ in the midst of political pressures to secede. And who can doubt that such massive extirpations of millions of mankind such as our generation has seen in many parts of the world is demonic? In historical manifestations like this we come close to the meaning of the "beast" in Daniel and Revelation. In Dan. 2:27, for instance, we have three closely related concepts in a concrete historical situation. First the human ruler; then the invisible "power"; and the two taken in collusion are described as the wild beast. "When this complex mechanism is in operation the wild beast is active: when it breaks down the wild beast is slain. That is to say, the *archon* has been robbed of his power, his underling the king has become powerless, and the system has collapsed.

The apocalytic Daniel views the changes in world affairs on a plane far above the earthly, in the region where the fight is going on between the *genii*, the guardian spirits of nations" (Caragounis, *op. cit.* p. 160).

iii) We see the influence of the principalities and powers in nature. The whole mythological figure of chaos and leviathan in the Old Testament is an expression of the demonic. So apparently, is the incident of Jesus' walking on the water and stilling the storm. He says, "Peace, be still," (literally, "Be muzzled") as if to a living entity, the spiritual force which was whipping up that storm into a welter of destruction. Again, the "weak and beggarly elements" to which the Galatians had become enslaved were almost certainly the stars, seen not only as luminaries but as astrological powers which directed the affairs of men. The principalities which governed the stars made them "who by nature are not gods" (Gal. 4:8) appear as gods. And resembling the elements which they infest so closely, it is by the name of these same elements that they are known.

iv) We see the principalities and powers in even the Jewish law, as G. B. Caird shows in *Principalities and Powers*, chapter two. So much so that the law which was intended by God for the life of the hearers became their death warrant (Rom. 7:10–14). It had ceased to be understood as the expression of God's love and faithfulness to his people and had become their justification for nomism. To this extent the law given by angels had fallen under the hand of the Enemy who encourages self-righteousness and self-seeking. The same had happened to the chosen people themselves. "You belong to your father the devil," says Jesus (John 8:44) to Jews who in the name of the law were seeking to destroy him to whom the whole law pointed forward. And in Rev. 2:9 the Jewish synagogue is described as the "synagogue of Satan". The Enemy of souls had gripped both the law and the people of the covenant.

v) Christians are certainly not exempt from the principalities and powers. Paul speaks of "false apostles" who have entered into his churches, disguising themselves as apostles of Christ. "And no wonder, for even Satan disguises himself as an angel of light. So it is not strange if his servants also disguise themselves as servants of righteousness" (2 Cor. 11:13–15). And heresy, which is incipient throughout the New Testament period, is assigned unambiguously to their agency. "Do not believe every spirit," urges John in 1 John 4:1. "The Spirit expressly says that in the last times some will depart from the faith by giving heed to seducing spirits and doctrines of demons" (1 Tim. 4:1). Christian teaching and Christian teachers alike are subject to attack and distortion by the principalities and powers.

vi) Behind human sin there is the activity of these evil forces. "I can't think what made me do it," we exclaim, surprised at the reservoirs of evil within us. "It is not I who do it, but sin which dwells in me," claimed Paul, reflecting on the force beyond himself which held him in captivity even when he wanted to do the right thing. Such is the human tragedy of Romans 7. Give too much emphasis to this force outside of us, and you rob human beings of responsibility, and make them mere pawns in a celestial tug of war between God and the devil. Give too little weight to it, and you fail to explain the persistent and overwhelming wickedness of mankind, individually and collectively.

vii) The state is obviously susceptible to the influence of the principalities and powers. How could it be otherwise when the state is in control of all the other power structures under it? We shall be looking at this later on, but the point is obvious enough whether you think of the Mafia or the Central Intelligence Agency; of the multinationals or the corruption of the police; of the fruitless deadlock between management and labour in England or the endless succession of administrations in Italy. Inflation and unemployment, the arms race and the corruption of morals, these are all manifestations in the modern state of the principalities and powers. The state does not want these things, for the most part. It struggles hard to get rid of them. But it fails. It is in the grip of a power beyond its own.

viii) The last and greatest of the powers to which we are exposed by Satan and his emissaries is death. To say that death was in the world before man is beside the point. For all we know, man, had he remained unfallen, might have had a natural transition through death without pain or *Angst*. As it is, men "through fear of death are in lifetime bondage to him who has the power over death, that is the devil" (Heb. 2:14). Death is, accordingly, the supreme locus of these enemy forces. They smell of death. They revel in it. They spread it. This is superbly portrayed in the story of the Gerasene demoniac. The man is possessed by unclean spirits. He has a strange fascination for death. He lives in the place of death, the tombs. He is tormented by the prospect of release from this living death through Jesus, because he is content with his ruined world and life. He has the inner urge towards the destruction both of his environment and of himself – hence the superhuman strength and masochism. And the climax of this compulsion comes when, with the release of the unclean spirits, death claims the pigs, thus setting him free from his longstanding bondage to death and destruction.

## An apocalyptic insight on the powers

Perhaps the most telling picture of the powers in all their naked might comes in the Book of Revelation, beginning with chapter 12. Here we see the Satanic trinity at work, destroying and seducing mankind. Unable to hurt God on whom he has declared war, foiled in his attack on Christ who is caught up on God's throne, the great Dragon is reduced to trying to spoil the lives of men who have done him no harm. He does so by means of two infernal allies.

The first is the Beast from the Sea, which, in context, clearly indicates the persecuting world power of Domitian's Rome, uniting in itself and indeed surpassing all the horrors of Daniel's royal beasts. Equipped with the crowned horns of world dominion, its political heads (the successive emperors) blasphemously claim the name of God (13:1). True, one of the Beast's heads had received a mortal wound, but it had recovered (3 – perhaps indicating that the anti-Christian policies of Nero had been revived by that *Nero redivivus*, Domitian) and the whole world goes after him. Resistance is impossible: "who is like the Beast and who can fight against it?" (4). The whole picture presents us with a counterfeit Messiah, with world dominion, blasphemous claims, a wound that has been healed, and universal worship. And this picture is not merely confined to the first century. It is always contemporary. The course of history is to a large extent dominated by the anti-God spirit, which seems to be *and is* victorious within the course of history (v.7) but ultimately will be defeated and annihilated by Christ the holder of all dominion. In the inscrutable permissive will of God "The Beast *was given* a mouth uttering blasphemies and *was allowed* to exercise authority for forty-two months (the symbolical time of three and a half years between the Advents, half of the perfect number seven for the years of human history) . . . Also it *was allowed* to make war on the saints and to overcome them." It ends aptly, "here is a call for the endurance and faith of the saints" (v. 10).

The Beast from the Earth completes the Satanic trinity. In Rev. 16:13, 19:20 it is identified with "the false prophet" and is manifestly a caricature of true religion, with particular reference to first-century Asia. For in the Beast from the Earth which cooperates with the first Beast, makes an image of it and causes people to worship it, we see the chief priest of the imperial cult on the mainland of Asia, the Ephesian Asiarch. He wore the garments of religion, but his whole function was political, to unite all Asia in loyal obedience to the emperor (v. 12). His first method was propaganda (v. 13–15) with trick miracles and a pseudo-messianic celebration. Failing that, he resorted to terror tactics, including both economic boycott (v. 16) and physical persecution (15). For the Asiarch wore upon his brow an image of the emperor with its blasphemous claims to deity: exactly the same claims were embossed on the coinage, so that unless you had the mark of the Beast in your hand you could neither buy nor sell.

In these two chapters we have the history of the church in apocalyptic language: the birth, death, ascension and rule of the Christ; the opposition of Satan showing itself in a combination of political and ideological onslaught on the followers of Christ. It would take us too far away to examine the counterpart in the heavenly places to this opposition – the Lamb and his redeemed ones (ch. 14) who celebrate his victory, and that victory dominates the rest of the Apocalypse. Suffice it to point out that the seer has acutely caught the flavour of the age-old conflict with the principalities and powers of evil, and the final outcome.

And why, we may ask, is the New Testament so confident that the outcome is assured? Because of Jesus Christ.

## The Defeat of the Principalities and Powers

1 John 3:8 has a very succinct summary of the reason for the coming of Jesus Christ. "The reason the Son of God appeared was to destroy the works of the devil." That takes us to the heart of the matter. It helps to account for the tremendous burst of satanic activity that faces us in the Gospels, and supremely on the cross. During those thirty odd years the key battle of the history of the universe was being conducted, and both sides knew it.

The triumph of Jesus Christ at every juncture over the powers and principalities of evil is a major theme of the New Testament. He was tested by persecution at his birth and throughout his life. He was tested by false friends, by hostile religious leaders, by Jewish and Gentile civil authorities. He was tested in the healings, the exorcisms, the temptations in the wilderness. The principalities and powers attacked him through opposition from within his own circle. His own family assigned his notoriety to the devil (Mk. 3:20–35) and one of his intimate friends sold him for thirty pieces of silver. No man was ever tested like Jesus Christ. He faced it all, and overcame it all, as no man before or since has done. The secret of his life was his determination to please his heavenly Father at all points (John 8:29). The spirits of disobedience had never before in the history of mankind discovered a person who was both totally obedient and totally fulfilled in that obedience. No wonder they could get no grip on him. No wonder the demons felt threatened at the very presence of Jesus: "Have you come here to torment us before the time?" (Matt. 8:29). The evil spirits perceived the ultimate judgement, and they realised that in Jesus Christ the end-time had broken in – and that his appearance in the world spelt their doom.

## Three aspects of the cross of Christ

But it was at the cross that Jesus Christ won the greatest and most conclusive victory over the powers of evil. He destroyed their sovereignty over man by utterly submitting to it all the way to the scaffold. In submitting he conquered; just as, conversely, in rebelling they had fallen. Unlike Satan, unlike the powers, unlike Adam, Jesus had not considered being equal with God as a thing to be seized.

> His very obedience unto death is in itself not only the sign but also the firstfruits of an authentic, restored humanity. Here we have for the first time to do with a man who is not the slave of any power, of any law or custom, community or institution, value or theory. Not even to save his own life will he let himself be made a slave of these Powers. This authentic humanity included his free acceptance of death at their hands. Therefore it is his death that provided his victory
>
> (J. H. Yoder, *The Politics of Jesus*, p. 148)

Back in 1951 Professor James Stewart made a plea in the *Scottish Journal of Theology* for a recovery of the dimension of the cosmic battle in our theology. Nowhere, he maintained, is it more important than in understanding the meaning of the cross of Christ. He showed how each of the three major factors which led Christ to Golgotha is illuminated by giving full weight to the influence of the invisible cosmic powers.

Behind the cross there lay, first and foremost, the design of man. Basic human failings like pride, jealousy, and greed combined with the self-righteousness and traditionalism of Jewish religion, the injustice of Roman politics, and the apathy of the crowd to take Christ to that gibbet. But behind these religious, political and social pressures stood the principalities and powers of evil. Thus organised religion was there at the cross: all the more dangerous because masquerading as true religion. Politics were there at the cross: but behind Herod and Pilate, the earthly rulers (*archontes*) lay the invisible powers (*archontes*) and it was they who crucified the Lord of glory

(1 Cor. 2:8). The average man was there at the cross: but the New Testament takes us to a more profound level here too. When the crowd cried, "His blood be upon us and upon our children," we see them driven by forces beyond themselves to a conclusion they could never have envisaged.

Second, behind the cross there lay the will of Jesus himself. He chose with his eyes open. He came to give his life a ransom for many. But here again we are driven to look deeper. Why was it necessary? Because of the grip the strong man had upon the house: the stronger than the strong was needed to set the place free. It was only by facing these forces in the place where they exercised their power that he could break that power. The cross was that place of victory over all the forces of the Enemy. By submitting in perfect obedience right up to death, he broke the power of him who held men in thraldom through its dread. In that cross he conquered. "There is no tribunal so magnificent," wrote Calvin, "no throne so stately, no show of triumph so distinguished, no chariot so elevated as is the gibbet on which Christ has subdued death and the devil and trodden them under his feet."

Third, behind the cross there lay the predestination of God. If God ever acted in history he acted then. But look deeper. In that will of God we see not only his reconciliation of sinners but the complete rebuttal of dualism. These principalities and powers which thwart his will are not independent military units opposing his own army. They are rebel forces of his own. In Christ they were created (Col. 1:16) and in Christ they were defeated (Col. 2:15). Phil. 2:10 makes it quite plain that they must own his sway whether they like it or not. His lordship, since the resurrection, has been beyond cavil among beings celestial, terrestrial and subterranean. "In the end," writes Stewart, "the same invisible powers are the tribute which the Son hands over to the Father, that 'God may be all in all'." He concludes this short but important article by pointing out that our real battle is not "with Communism or Caesarism but with the invisible realm where sinister forces stand flaming and fanatic against the rule of Christ. And the only way to meet that demonic mystic passion is with the passion of the Lord."

There is little doubt that Stewart has stressed a critical aspect in the cross of Christ, one to which Gustav Aulen has drawn attention in his *Christus Victor*. The power of Satan was shattered on that cross, shattered by the invincible power of love. "Now is the judgement of this world, when the prince of this world will be cast out," said Jesus as he faced the cross (John 12:30, cf. 16:11, 14:30). And I think Stewart is right in seeing a studied ambivalence in the "rulers" of 1 Cor. 2:8. It refers both to Herod and Pilate on the one hand and to the invisible powers on the other. They worked hard to get the Lord of glory on the cross. But in so doing they overreached themselves, and lost the battle. Had they known the outcome they would never have conspired to bring Calvary about. Not only was obedient love stronger than death, but in dying it destroyed all life apart from God, as Paul explains in Col. 2:15. Jesus despoiled the principalities and powers, and made an open show of them, triumphing over them in it (i.e. the cross).

Those three verbs are worth considering. Jesus *made a public example* of these hidden principalities and powers. The cross was their unmasking. Hitherto in both Jewish and Gentile circles they had been accepted as the most basic realities, the gods of this age. And then the true God appeared in Christ Jesus. The powers were seen to be deceivers. They were shown up in their real light as enemies of God. The cross was the public example when much-vaunted Roman justice and Jewish religion were seen in their own pathetic rags, and it became clear that Pilate and the Pharisees were the puppets of powers far more mighty than themselves, and utterly malign.

Moreover, Jesus *triumphed over* them in the cross. He showed by that cross and subsequent resurrection that he had penetrated into their territory and captured their stronghold. Christ was indeed reigning from that tree, as the Fathers loved to insist.

And that cross of Christ *despoiled* the principalities and powers. The imagery in the word is of a person stripping off a suit of dirty clothes. He showed his sovereignty and his holiness in this graphic gesture of triumphant rejection.

On the cross the principalities and powers incurred the defeat that indicates the outcome of the whole war. But what is their present condition?

## The Present Status of the Principalities and Powers

Since Scripture is not very explicit on this matter, it may be safest to proceed by way of some negatives.

It is not the case that their defeat is only provisional until the last day, as if some theoretical transfer of power has taken place which does not affect anybody or anything. In the coming, the cross and the resurrection of Christ even the greatest of the powers, death, has been affected. And to concentrate on that particular power may help us see what Christ's victory has done to the others. Men still die. Of course they do, and to that extent the power of death is still operative. But the New Testament maintains that death is a defeated foe. It has been robbed of its fangs. Sin, its major adjunct, has been forgiven for the believer, and therefore death no longer has the dread of final separation from the God who is light and love. Moreover in the resurrection of Jesus we see foreshadowed the destiny of every believer: we shall be with him, and we shall be like him (1 Cor. 15:20, 1 John 3:2). In these two respects death has been shorn of its terrors, though we still have to go through it. We know that, evil power and enemy though it is, our Lord holds the key to its defeat and ultimate annihilation.

It is not the case that the principalities and powers have lost their grip on the cosmos at large. True, they have received their death blow, but like a thirty-foot conger with its throat cut which continues for hours thrashing about in a fishing boat, the principalities and powers refuse to lie down and die. They are willing to admit defeat only when faced with the name of Jesus Christ. He is the conqueror and they are vulnerable only when approached on the ground of his victory.

Yet it is not the case that the principalities and powers continue just as they were before the cross of Christ. Their defeat is indeed hidden at present, but they are nevertheless passing away, *katargoumenoi*, as Paul puts it in 1 Cor. 2:6. They have no other expectation than final ruin. And this produces an increasing tempo of chaos; could that be why Jesus forecast wars, rumours of wars and men's heart failing them for fear as the end approached? As time runs out, the atmosphere of history is increasingly filled with the fear of time. Man forgets his transience and dreams of eternity, while the devil knows he has lost eternity and rages at the ever shortening span of time open to him. "Rejoice O Heaven, and you that dwell therein. But woe to you, O earth and sea, for the devil has come down to you in great rage because he knows that his time is short" (Rev. 12:12).

Therefore it is not the case that things will get better and better and a millennium be created by man on earth. Such facile optimism whether based on Communist, evolutionary or humanistic presuppositions is totally at odds not only with the news but with the teaching of the Bible, which indicates that things will get worse and worse, and men's hearts will cry out for fear. The events prophesied by Jesus in Mark 13, the preoccupation with the loss of time, the tensions between men and nations, the willingness to believe propaganda, the very tremors of the world itself are all manifestations of the frenzied kickings of the satanic bull in God's net as the rope gets drawn tighter. Nor is it surprising that the attacks of the Enemy are primarily directed against the church, whether through heresy from within or seduction or persecution from without. For in the church, however heavily veiled, the principalities and powers discern the person of their conqueror, the Lord Christ. The powers of the age to come are already at work in her, frail and fallible though she is. And as such she reminds the principalities and powers of their doom.

For doom is what awaits them. There is no hint in Scripture that all will come right in the end for the principalities and powers of evil, and for their satanic master. All that offends will be wiped out and will not come into the eternal city (Rev. 21:27). It is not the principalities and powers that have been reconciled by the death of Christ. They have been despoiled, and the church has been reconciled. They have been defeated and the church has been brought out of the power of Satan unto God. The focus of Christ's victory is not to be sought in the principalities and powers but in the church, in those who believe. The genial generosity of those who, like Alan Richardson, maintain that the rebellious powers of evil are in the end to be saved has neither logic nor Scripture to commend it.

The rebellious spirits have locked themselves in a hell which is chained both by their own choice on the inside, and by God on the outside. As Milton, with prophetic insight and poetic brilliance shows in *Paradise Lost*, the great debate between Satan's followers is how to find a way out of that situation other than the one way which exists, the way of repentance and restitution, against which they have resolutely set their faces. But there is no other way. Moloch uses the weapon of blind rage: anything is better than the frustration and agony of fallenness. Belial uses the weapon of caution: gradual acclimatisation to alienation is better than a traumatic reliving of the great rebellion. And Mammon seeks a solution by trying to make hell a substitute for heaven. Indeed, one wonders whether he had really seen the difference between the two! The way of rage, of getting used to one's lot, of blind substitution sometimes works on this earth. But in the ultimacy of the Beyond, Milton knows it cannot be so. Hell is their dungeon, not their safe retreat (2.317).

If logic points this way, so too does Scripture. It does not see the conquered powers as some scholars have seen them: now tamed and domesticated to do the will of Jesus Christ. They have indeed to confess his sway (Phil. 2:10). The archetypal sinners of Gen. 6:3 have heard the proclamation of his achievement (1 Pet. 3:18ff). But rebels they remain, like many of mankind whom they control (Rev. 9:20, 21). A great bottomless pit is reserved for the devil and his angels: so is the lake of fire. And at the end the satanic trinity are found in this place of final ruin while the heavenly Trinity rejoice with the Bride, the church, for ever (Rev. 20:2f, 14, and compare 21:1ff). The destiny of the forces of evil is destruction. They are given over to the ruin which they have chosen and which they propagate. The end is inescapable: any other would be unjust. It is the logical and necessary outcome of the victory already gained through the cross and resurrection. That is why Christians can lift up their heads, however black the clouds. Their hope does not rest upon fairy tales and the hope of pie in the sky, but rather on the solid achievements of Bethlehem, Golgotha and the first Easter Day.

## Can We Believe This Account of the World?

This is our problem today. It is all very well to see the great significance attached by the New Testament to the principalities and powers of evil, under the control of the prince of darkness, Satan. But is this sort of thing credible in the modern world? As we saw in chapter one, Rudolf Bultmann met this problem head on, and replied in the negative. In his famous article "*Die Entmythologisierung des Neuen Testament*" he poured scorn on the possibility of believing in demons and spirits in an age of radio sets and modern medicine. Alexander Solzhenitsyn on the other hand is in no doubt whatever about the element of the demonic which is gripping the world and inexorably drawing Western civilisation towards final catastrophe. Which shall we believe?

### Factors in society

It is a commonplace among sociologists that the whole is much more than the sum of its parts, that our world is in the grip of institutions and ideologies which transcend the individual and condition his lifestyle. Let us glance at a number, first in the world at large and then in the church: it may help us in deciding whether or not we are in a position to dispense with the idea of principalities and powers.

Ours is an age of the consumer society in which technology is applied to an ever increasing production. Standards of living are seen in terms of money and what commodities money can buy. Our conviction that a man's life consists in the multitude of things which he possesses is not only in direct opposition to the teaching of Jesus: it is, as he maintained, blind folly. For the present industrial system turns man into a small cog in a vast machine, robbing him, in most cases, of pride in his work and job satisfaction. It sharpens the divides between the "haves" and the "have-nots" in society and between nations. It blinds the wealthy countries to the collision course on which the world is set between rich and poor nations. In a world where the U.S.A. with six per cent of the world's population consumes a third of its energy and raw materials, is there not some massive blindness, a blindness that must inevitably lead to confrontation?

Ours is an age of the hidden persuaders. We tend to believe whatever propaganda the television or newspapers put out. It has only to be in print to be given at least some credit. We have simply sold out to propaganda. It is evident in the selection of news. It is evident in the massive influence advertising has on the population. Property is not seen as a service to the community but as personal enrichment, and advertising falsely persuades us that we need more and more of it. The consumer mentality conditions men to work so as to make money so as to buy things . . . and from these things purchase some value for themselves, having long ago forgotten their true value – so valuable that for us men and our salvation our Lord was content to die.

Ours is an age of multi-national companies which exercise an iron grip on the poor among primary producers. Despite the coming of political independence to Latin America in the nineteenth century, First World countries continue to colonise their economy, control the international money system, dominate international trade, and use their political and military power to preserve the *status quo*. Let us take three examples of "the system".

First, coffee. While the West complains of the high price, labourers in El Salvador earn between one and three dollars a day in the season for a long day's picking in the coffee fields – about half of what they need to stay alive. Coffee makes up only one per cent of world trade, and it is not crucial to an industrialised economy. But for the 350,000 coffee workers in El Salvador the price of coffee on the world market makes the difference between a hazardous livelihood and death. Moreover, the terms of trade are very much against primary producers like El Salvador. Eighty per cent of what they purchase from abroad is manufactured goods, whose price is always inflating, while coffee sometimes goes down. A tractor which cost 165 bags of coffee in 1960 cost 316 ten years later. The international monetary system, which governs capital investment and control of goods and services in underdeveloped countries, is in the hands of the "Group of Ten" – rich nations of the non-Communist bloc who do not even number one Third World member among them. The system is so weighted against the poor nations that it seems beyond the power of any man, organisation or state to rectify – even if they wanted to. But do not rich lands like the U.S.A. give much financial aid to countries like El Salvador? The answer is "No". Most of such aid consists in loans, not grants, and they are repayable with interest. The main beneficiary is the donor nation, as Eugene Black, then president of the World Bank, pointed out in 1965: "Foreign aid provides a substantial and immediate market for U.S. goods and services. Foreign aid stimulates the development of new overseas markets for U.S. companies. Foreign aid orients national economies towards a free enterprise system in which U.S. private firms can prosper." In a word, the rich countries get richer and the poor poorer. Latin America's trade balance was two and a half times worse in 1970 than in 1960, because of the operation of these impersonal factors mentioned above, which I believe to be one expression of the principalities and powers of evil.

A second example is powdered milk. Third World babies are dying in their thousands because mothers, living in absolute squalor, are succumbing to advertising pressure to feed their babies with Western style infant milk. Nestle's and Cow and Gate have made a vast sales drive in the Third World countries, carried out by sales girls in nurses' uniforms, with the result that in lands like Nigeria, Jamaica and Chile there has been widespread abandonment of breast feeding; and this is contributing enormously to malnutrition and liability to disease among the children. Human milk, of course, provides the best protection

101

against infection as well as the best nutrition for infants. Despite the fact that both Cow and Gate and Nestle's admit in their advertising that breast feeding is best, that is not the message that is heard, nor is it intended to be. The lure of urbanisation, of modernity, the sheer power of television and radio advertisement have had their effect, and the graveyards of the Third World bear silent testimony to the grip the principalities and powers exercise upon something as basic as baby foods.*

Bananas may serve as a third example. The marketing of bananas is a highly integrated operation, because the fruit is easily spoiled and the maximum period between picking and selling must be no more than three weeks. The only flexibility comes from refrigerated shipping and ripening rooms in the developed importing country. Thus banana producing countries are at the mercy of large well-equipped companies like Fyffes and Geest. Whilst Geest has put a great deal of money and imagination into developing both the crops and the standard of living in the Windward Islands, Fyffes, which controls nearly eighty per cent of Jamaica's crop, has a policy of maximising profits for shareholders. The result? A few pence per pound for the growers, and virtually no contribution towards the good of the country by Fyffes. It is hardly surprising that the Jamaican banana crop is in decline. Here is a classic example of the destructive power of a monopoly. It is one small facet of the principalities and powers which are so deeply entrenched in the economies of the world.

Archbishop Helder Camara of Brazil states the issue forcefully. "What is to stop the developed world from moving further apart from the underdeveloped world? Today eighty-five per cent of the world's population lives in poverty to make possible the luxury of the comfortable fifteen per cent. Tomorrow it will be the ninety per cent catering for the luxury of the ten per cent." We know this is going on. We know that this way lies Armageddon. Yet successive world trade conferences have failed to change

* Those interested in pursuing this further should read *The Baby Killer*, by Mike Muller, published by War on Want, March 1974.

anything of substance. Are we not in the grip of forces beyond ourselves?

Ours is an age of warped priorities. I think of the appalling conditions I have seen in Quito, Ecuador, where work was continuing on a totally unneccessary and non-functional prestige building for the government while the housing conditions around it were among the worst in the world. It is a curious irony that the generation which sent men to the moon should be the generation which has faced, and notably failed to meet unprecedented hunger among the citizens of this planet, sixty-five per cent of whose population suffers from hunger.

Ours is an age of horrendous cruelty and war. More people have met a violent end in our generation than at any time in the history of the world – indeed, in all generations of mankind put together. Torture is practised by almost every country in the world. Oppressive regimes, supported by naked force, direct the affairs of by far the major part of the world's population. In the past thirty years the human race has spent nearly a thousand pounds per head on armaments. There have been a hundred and thirty wars which, between them, have accounted for more dead than World War Two. And the armaments race is accelerating.

Ours is an age dominated by the nuclear factor. The clock can never be put back. Instead, we simply try to forget. By 1975 the American armed forces held a nuclear megatonnage with an explosive force equivalent to 615,000 Hiroshimas, and the Russians had more still – not to mention the Chinese, the French and the rest of the nuclear club. One day some fool is going to press the trigger . . .

Ours is an age where absolutes are gone. Words like "good" and "bad" are totally devalued: they mean "good for me", "bad for me". I do my own thing: you do yours. The relative is paramount. There are no absolutes. God, the Universal or Absolute, has for all practical purposes been dethroned: everyone does what he feels like or can get away with. Ethics and religion alike are reduced from a quest for truth to the counting of heads.

Ours is an age where greed has both fouled the nest and grabbed non-renewable resources to a point unequalled in

103

history. The atmosphere, the land and the oceans are polluted and poisoned. Fossil fuels will run out before long, and the present-day impact of control of oil by OPEC countries shows both the lengths to which countries will go to get this scarce resource and the vast potential for blackmail and violence which its possession makes possible. How can we go on allowing ourselves ever larger slices of a strictly limited cake? Yet every politician cries out for more for his own supporters and advocates the utterly self-destructive pursuit of economic growth. Would the visitor from Mars not conclude that we were mad – or had a demon?

Ours is an age when ideology has a terrifying grip on its adherents. It may be the ideology of nationalism, ludicrously growing in a world which is contracting into a village. It may be the ideology of resurgent religion, militant and ruthless like Islam in the Middle East and Pakistan. It may be the ideology of liberation so popular in Africa and Latin America: utterly justified on the one hand because of past exploitation, but on the other utterly blinded in the exchange of one domination for another. It may be the ideology of Communism, a false religion based on hate not love, on blind economic forces not God or humanity, and on propaganda not truth. It may be the ideology of liberal Westerners who refuse to watch rugby matches involving the "racist" South Africans but cheerfully support the Olympic Games in Moscow. Or it may be the consumer ideology of Western capitalists, as selfish and as degrading as it will soon prove self-destructive.

Ours is an age when sexuality has become devalued. The distinctions between men and women vanish into "Unisex". Homosexuality and heterosexuality are equal and alternative options. Women for all their bravado are sex objects, and *Playboy* magazine has the highest circulation of all periodicals in the West after *Reader's Digest*. Never has the quest for sexual satisfaction been more widespread and been deemed more enthusiastically the *summum bonum*: never has the amount of sexual misery and divorce been greater. Is there not some demonic force which turns our very pleasures into bondage and makes the grapes turn to ashes in our mouths?

104

Ours is an age of the revival of superstition. God has been shown the front door, by and large, and the demons he once dethroned have returned via the back door. Horoscopes sell by the million. Interest in the occult, in magic and transcendental meditation, in every aspect of the spiritual and paranormal is vast and growing in a generation which though still utterly materialistic for the most part, has discovered that materialism does not satisfy.

Ours is an age of confusion. As nations and as individuals we have no satisfying *raison d'être*. Our culture has subordinated every consideration to the scientific and then wondered why ultimate questions of our origin and destiny seem so improper that we dare not discuss them in polite society. But such questions refuse to be utterly shut out. They prey on people's minds. They necessitate enormous dependence on tranquillisers, the phenomenal upsurge of social workers and psychiatrists, and a massive bondage to drink, smoking and drugs – or the addictions of continuous background music, football, pornography, science fiction – or anything else that takes the mind away from the awfulness of reality.

Is it so incredible that forces of evil far greater than ourselves are somehow involved in the chaos of our world? Is it so incredible that we have not after all escaped their clutches, for all our sophistication? Was Shakespeare not near the mark when he interwove the tragic events of *Macbeth* with an atmosphere of the supernatural induced by the witches? The result is that Macbeth and his wife are seen in their true colours as wicked people, but we also recognise that they are caught up in a network of evil forces beyond their control. Could not the same be said about Hitler in his monomania and genocide?* And is it surprising that after the War there was a tremendous resurgence of

---

* As a matter of fact it was said, and by Hitler's biographer, Walter Langer, in *The Mind of Adolf Hitler*. "Hitler is not a single personality but two that inhabit the same body. The one is very soft and sentimental and indecisive. The other is hard, cruel and decisive. The first weeps at the death of a canary. The second cries that 'there will be no peace in the land until a body hangs from every lamppost . . . nothing but death, annihilation and hatred'."

interest in the demonic in German theological circles? To be sure there was an element of self-exculpation in this, but was there not an instinctive rightness in their hunch?

In his little book *Principalities and Powers* Gordon Rupp brings out this forgotten strand in world affairs with charm and historical perspective. Here is one example:

> Anybody who will stand in the ruins of Heidelberg Castle in Germany, or in the streets of Strasbourg down the Rhine, and will count up the number of times in which invading armies have harried first one and then the other side of that great valley, will understand why European cooperation is not the simple thing it seems in the blueprints of doctrinaire idealists. There is a bondage of the will of peoples as well as of individuals, and it may be as terrible and inexorable as the enslavement of any individual by the stain and chain of moral evil.

Here is another:

> Most startling of all has been the rise in the modern world of revolutionary movements, of ideologies which batten parasitically on public opinion, and which inspire millions of men and women with the fervour, sanctions, and inhibitions of a religion, able to swell into terrible systems of tyranny and power.

He turns to the Kittel article on Principalities and Powers in the celebrated *Wörterbuch*, and is fascinated by the word *Schickalzusammenhang* "bound together in a common fate and destiny". Such is our situation.

> There are forces at work in human history which represent human solidarities perverted and twisted and full of danger. They are part of the pattern of evil. They are part of the conflict in our human existence. If the Christian gospel were only concerned with the moral problems of individual men and women, it would be defective indeed. But the first Christians

106

knew better when they affirmed, "Christ has conquered sin and death and the principalities and powers."

(op. cit. pp. 16–18)

It is not possible to prove that there are trans-human forces at work in the network of evil in society. But at least the evidence is as strong in the twentieth century as it was in the first, when Jesus believed it. We can scarcely be said to have advanced to such an extent that hypotheses of organised cosmic evil are no longer applicable or relevant. In a generation where Utopias have given place to Dystopias and the doomwatch writers have much grist to their mill, it might be worth giving ear afresh to the New Testament which asserts that the service of God and mammon are mutually exclusive and that the only way in which we can escape the grip of the principalities and powers of evil is to surrender ourselves without reserve to the Lord of spirits.

As A. M. Hunter expressed it, "There is no metaphysical reason why the cosmos should not contain spirits higher than man, who have made evil their good, who are ill disposed to the human race, and whose activities are co-ordinated by a master-strategist" (*Interpreting Paul's Gospel*, p. 75). To my mind, the evidence points strongly that way, and so it is interpreted by a steadily increasing number of modern thinkers of the stature of Helmut Thielicke, William Stringfellow, Jacques Ellul, Robert Heilbroner and Ronald Higgins, to whom we shall return in chapter eight.

### Factors in the church

But it is not only in society at large, but, even more dangerously, in the church itself that the principalities and powers of evil exercise their grip. At least, that is the New Testament account of the matter. Can we credit it?

Ours is a church dominated by officialdom, and not only the duly constituted ministry, but the church lawyers, the financiers, the Church Commissioners, the curia – the tradition. Within those structures it is all too easy for the way of the world not the way of the gospel to govern the activities of the people of God.

Ours is a church where ethical standards are largely dictated by the outlook of the contemporary secular scene. This applies not only to permissive ethics in the areas of divorce, abortion and the like, but to social ethics too. Thus Christians tend either to take little notice of their brethren suffering under corrupt regimes (out of sight, out of mind) or else, along with the World Council of Churches, tend to support national liberation movements, thus matching repressive violence with revolutionary violence, in total disregard for the teaching and example of their Lord. Ours is a church where false belief is not only tolerated but even welcomed as a contribution towards truth. To be sure, there is truth in every heresy, or it would never gain ground. But it is not that which is welcomed. The very concept of truth has become devalued. The idea of revelation, so central to Christianity, is now at a discount.

Ours is a church which has surrendered to the mores of the consumer society. She has failed to demonstrate a distinctive and sacrificial life style. She has failed to be what Harvey Cox has called "the cultural exorcist". Some years ago the Bishop of Lichfield observed that inflation cannot be solved by economic and political measures alone. "Greed", he said, "must be exorcised by the spirit of service, and selfishness driven out." The demonic forces have been at work in the very fabric of society. What was once a quest for economic justice all round has turned into a trail of greed. As John Richards has shrewdly pointed out in an unpublished paper delivered at the Fountain Trust Westminster Conference in 1979, "Yesterday's books of spiritual warfare were mostly about 'possession'. Some of tomorrow's books are already here. Are not Bishop John Taylor's *Enough is Enough* and, more recently, Ronald Sider's *Rich Christians in an Age of Hunger* the successors to Michael Harper's *Spiritual Warfare*? Are not these writers with their call for a simpler lifestyle, and the transformation of economic relationships and social structures, are not these fighting against the powers in rebellion?"

Ours is a church which has surrendered to secularism at

many points, and notably in the area of the Christian mind. The surrender is so complete that for many Christians it is astonishing to hear it suggested that there is or ought to be a Christian mind at all. This is what makes Harry Blamires' book *The Christian Mind* both so necessary and so unusual. He shows how the modern church has swallowed almost completely the secular presuppositions of atheistic humanism, illustrates his theme powerfully, and then gives six distinctive marks of the authentically Christian outlook. His book should be required reading for Christian leaders. Fortunately it is not unique: the writings of a man like Dr. Francis Schaeffer constitute a challenging recall to the Christian mind, but such writers are rare in our culture.

Ours is a church where all too often charisma is stamped out by office – in striking contrast to the New Testament where the two respect and cooperate with each other. But you have only to see how suspicious central church circles are of spiritual renewal, or how prone the "renewed" are to secede or to make judgemental assessments, to see what a long way we have come from that.

Ours is a church where the members hate one another. Not, of course, with great personal vendettas; they do not normally get close enough to one another for that. But our denominationalism shows it very clearly. It is the non-theological factors of conservatism, class consciousness, lack of adaptability, ignorance of how other Christians think and feel, which keeps churches apart, far more than major dogmatic issues like the ministry and the eucharist. Persecution (and it still goes on between Protestants and Catholics in parts of South America) shows how much we hate one another. The correspondence columns of the church press indicate precisely the same. And worst of all is the disparaging way we gossip about one another, run one another down and damn each other with faint praise. "The tongue is a little member and boasts of great things. How great a forest is set ablaze by a small fire! And the tongue is a fire. . . , setting on fire the cycle of nature and itself set on fire by hell" (James 3:5ff). That is precisely how the principalities and powers love to grip the church of God: by setting tongues of members on fire from hell. It is illuminating to notice how both the Father of lies and the Spirit of truth concentrate on the tongue. Five of the nine gifts of the Spirit mentioned in 1 Cor. 12:8ff are concerned with the tongue. It is a crucial area.

Ours is a church which pitifully apes the secular setting in which it happens to be placed. One thinks of the surrender of official Russian and Chinese church leaders to the dictates of atheist governments placed there, in striking contrast to many of their congregations who declined to render to Caesar the things that are God's. In England, the church may not be the Tory Party at prayer any longer, but it bears undeniable similarities. It is fascinating to see how in almost all churches in recent years, even the Roman Catholic, there has been an ever increasing imitation of secular democratic systems. But whoever gave democracy this *fiat* of divine approval? How prominently does democracy figure in the many and varied patterns of ecclesial government in the New Testament? And does it work any better if you are responsible to a committee or to a synod than if you are responsible to a bishop? I know which I would prefer. But that is not the point. The point is the extent to which structures from outside the church have come to dominate it.

Ours is a church which has lost its vision. No longer does it seem to exist in order to "declare the wonderful deeds of him you called you out of darkness into his marvellous light" (1 Peter 2:9); it rather perpetuates itself for the benefit of those, its members, who like that sort of thing. Recently a book has emerged, entitled *Evangelism in Eclipse*. Written by Dr. Harvey Hoekstra, it shows gently and sympathetically but with immense power and documentation the way in which the World Council of Churches, which was founded to bind churches together in the evangelisation of the world, has now so retreated from its charter that evangelism figures as nothing more than one office with a single occupant in a substructure which is itself merely part of one unit in the headquarters of the World Council at Geneva! Has fifty years of wheeling and dealing and of committees reduced the World Council to this? Or is it reasonable to think that some force

110

beyond itself is gripping its priorities and blinding its vision?

René Padilla, writing from a highly perceptive and articulate Third World perspective, has no doubt of the way in which the principalities and powers have dominated the world structures with their worship of materialism and consumerism, and have dominated the church with its twin evils of secularised Christianity and culture-bound Christianity. He notes with approval E. Stauffer's laconic judgement, "In primitive Christianity there is no theology without demonology", and shows what a necessary concept it is for modern Christians.

> Those who limit the workings of the evil powers to the occult, demon possession and astrology, as well as those who consider the New Testament references to those powers as a sort of mythological shell from which the biblical message must be extracted, reduce the spirit of evil in the world to a personal problem, and Christian redemption to a merely personal experience. A better alternative is to accept the realism of the biblical description and to understand man's situation in the world in terms of enslavement to a spiritual realm from which he must be liberated.
>
> (René Padilla, *The New Face of Evangelicalism*, p. 212)

The New Testament writers talk a great deal more about sin as an active force in human affairs than the particular sins of which human beings are guilty. And it was very clear to them that behind sin and human bondage to it lies the Evil One and his hordes. As a society and as a church we have declined to recognise this. As a result we have blindly absolutised this present age with its materialism, collective egoism, racialism, scientific materialism, and the rest. We have believed the great lie that the good life lies in independence of the God who gave us life. This is precisely the path trod by the principalities and powers. And it is a path which God has judged in the cross of Christ and will continue to judge in individuals and in nations. For that way leads to ruin.

# CHAPTER 5

## The Fascination of the Occult

### Rise of Occultism

When I was ordained in the late 1950s, the whole question of demons and the occult was, for all practical purposes in Britain, a dead letter. Or so I would have thought – had I paused to consider the matter. It would not have been entirely true, for even then the occult explosion was beginning, but now it is in full spate.

You have only to look at the plethora of literature on this subject which floods the bookstalls. I took a note today of some of the titles in the bestseller range in Selfridges in Oxford. They included *The Wolfen* by Whitley Strieber, *The Case Against Satan* by Ray Russell, *The Devil's Maze* by Gerald Sanders, *Magic* by William Goldman, *The Devil Finds Work* by James Baldwin, *The Mysterious Unknown* by Robert Chevaux, *The Ancient Magic of the Pyramids* by Ken Johnson, a variety of books by Erich Von Daniken, *Messengers from the Stars* by W. R. Drake, *The Book of the Damned* by Charles Ford, *Psychic Archaeology* by Jeffrey Goodman – to name but a few. And that is merely the books: it takes no account of the horoscopes in most of the newspapers and magazines, the tarot cards and the manuals on black and white magic.

You have only to notice what films draw the largest numbers. The *Exorcist* had the biggest box office returns in history. *The Omen, The Anti-Christ* – these are the films people are watching, along with *The Exorcist's Daughter, The Demons, The Legions of Lucifer, The Devil's Wedding Night* and the like. The night I wrote these words the Queen of the Witches was appearing nationwide on a television programme.

You have only to notice the serious writers like Colin Wilson, following his magisterial book *The Occult* by an equally fascinating and comprehensive volume *Mysteries*, or Brian Inglis' *Natural and Supernatural, A History of the Paranormal*. Both of these are massive and scrupulously documented tomes: both are written by eminently sane, indeed by mature (and sceptical) authors. But like Sir Alister Hardy, the internationally celebrated biologist who has been exploring the religious nature of man from a scientific viewpoint, and has written books like *The Biology of God* and most recently *The Spiritual Nature of Man*, these men of letters have been driven to an account of the universe that treats materialism as out of date. Colin Wilson's comment in *The Occult* is representative:

> In science a new cycle has begun, a revolt against the old rigid reductionism, a recognition that "materialism" leaves half the universe unexplained. Biologists, psychologists and even physicists are cautiously trying to feel their way into new worlds. They are acknowledging at last that they are dealing with a *living* universe, a universe full of strange forces. The magic of the past was an intuitive attempt to understand and control these forces: the science of the future will be a fully conscious attempt.

It is much the same among psychologists. Although many of them have been trained in presuppositions which make the demonic unthinkable, there is evidence that this view is changing. I personally know a number of psychiatrists who use exorcism as well as normal psychiatric medicine, when need arises. In his book *Occult Bondage and Deliverance* Dr. Kurt Koch, probably the most experienced living practitioner in the ministry of deliverance, wrote as follows:

> The well-known doctor and preacher Dr. Martyn Lloyd-Jones had invited me to speak before a group of psychiatrists on the subject of occultism and occult oppression. Afterwards I was attacked by two psychiatrists who claimed that the biblical accounts of possession were merely cases of mental illness.
> Another man stood up and came to my defence. He

said from his own practice alone he could quote up to eleven different cases of possession. Another psychiatrist then endorsed what his colleague had just said, adding that he had come across three or four cases of possession himself. I found it unnecessary to defend myself any more.

The public is well aware of the rise of occultism. It has become a major industry in the past decade, involving many millions of pounds. Interest in magic, fortune telling, astrology and spiritism together with yoga and Eastern religions followed hard in the wake of the drug culture, and yet it is the middle-aged and middle-class who are the most avid investigators into the occult. In Britain, America, Germany and Scandinavia there has been in the last decade a monumental increase in preoccupation with astral powers, spiritism and Satanism. It is a remarkable turn in events away from the materialism of the previous decades. And it is ironical that the legislation against witchcraft in Britain, dating from the Middle Ages, should only have been repealed in the 1950s just when the resurgence was getting under way.

The church has been fully aware of all this, where clergy have been in touch with the people. In the Nottingham area at a meeting of the local clergy, I did not find one who had not had some recent experience of the occult in his pastoral work. During the past five years in supposedly sophisticated Oxford, I have seen more of it than in the previous eighteen years of my ministry. The Church of England has recently published a significant report, *Exorcism*, and recommended that every diocese appoint a Diocesan Exorcist. This Report was the fruit of a thorough Working Party which met over a number of years, and the Secretary of this Group, the Rev. John Richards, has written one of the most important books on the subject for many years, *But Deliver Us from Evil*, to which I am much indebted. The Pentecostal and neo-Pentecostal Churches have specialised in the ministry of deliverance, though not always with balance and discernment. The Church of Rome has followed suit, not only with its revision of the *Manuale*

114

*Theologiae Moralis* with ample provision – and advice –
on exorcism, nor only in the emphases of the Catholic
Charismatic Movement in the Roman Church, but also in
the direct warnings of Pope Paul VI on the matter.

## Reasons for the escalation

A variety of causes have combined to bring about this
remarkable *volte-face* in contemporary attitudes; so much
so that there appear to be as many witches as clergy in
Britain at present, and circles for black and white magic
exist in all universities and towns.

One reason is the barrenness of materialism. It simply
does not match up with life to believe that only what you
can touch and measure is real. Revulsion against sheer
materialism in goals and explanations set in during the
fifties in many cultural centres in the Western world, and .
prepared the way for the counter-culture with its acute
awareness of spiritual realities.

Another is the incurably religious instinct of mankind.
Man needs something greater than himself to revere and
relate to. With the decline of Christianity in the West (at
the same time as it was advancing all over the rest of the
world) the way was open for other forces to enter the
vacuum. At the very time when Western theologians were
proclaiming God to be dead, the star of his satanic
adversary was everywhere in the ascendant.

This leads to a closely connected factor in the situation,
the deadness of the Christian church in the West. Under
the influence of a Liberal theology (itself the fruit of
sceptical and rationalist presuppositions), first the virgin
birth, the demonic, then the miracles of Jesus, followed by
his resurrection, and his deity were all progressively denied
by *avant-garde* theologians, during the past fifty years. The
ordinands and priests did not know what to believe, and
churchmen on the whole seem to have given less and less
credit to the trans-historical aspects of the Christian
religion. It is fascinating to read in a Marplan survey of
British religious attitudes published in *Now!* for December
1979, that whereas seventy-six per cent of Britons claim to
be Christians, only seventy-three per cent even believe in

God let alone the deity of Christ. No less than twenty-eight per cent of those who claim to be Anglicans do not believe in something so central as an after-life, whilst another twenty-two per cent described their attitude as "Don't Know". Of the fifty per cent who do believe in an after-life, only one sixth accept the Bible's alternatives of heaven and hell, and the same proportion think they will be re-incarnated. When the church has grown so uncertain of its own beliefs, when it has become so preoccupied with its own structures, when it has degenerated very largely into a spectator sport for those who like that kind of thing, is it surprising that people have turned from it towards something that actually works? Ironically, the church may well prove to be the last sector in the community which comes to believe in the supernatural.

Hunger for thrills is another reason which has driven men towards the occult. Life is pretty dull for many people who have boring jobs and indifferent or unhappy homes. The horoscope offers them some purpose, expectancy and promise. Spiritism offers the consolation of some sort of communication with dead friends, and the vast increase of this cult after two world wars is not surprising. Eastern religions offer tranquillity in the midst of our pressurised existence, and demand little in the way of either morality or belief. Witchcraft and other forms of the occult were the natural next step for a generation that had reacted against the alcoholism of their parents and had realised the dangers of the drug cult which followed it. Where else was there to look for kicks?

Power over others is indubitably another attraction, especially for people whose employment and home life give them no power at all. There is a great excitement in making use of a power denied to the majority of men. It enhances the ego.

Nor should we underestimate the group instinct in a society which is increasingly disintegrating. The thrill of belonging to a group bound together by the closest of ties, a group in which the exciting and the forbidden are stock in trade and where secrecy is the essential – this has a great attraction. The séance, the coven, even the group of teenagers round an ouija board all meet the pyschological hunger of man for a group to which one can be committed. It may well go deeper still into the national background. In Iceland particularly, in Norway and Sweden to a considerable extent, the resurgence of the occult is merely a turning back to the old pagan deities. They had been dethroned by the coming of Christianity but they survived in the folk culture and had never died out. And once men pay attention to them again, they come under the grip of the demonic. Paul makes this clear in 1 Corinthians 10:19ff: "What do I imply? That an idol is anything? No. I imply that what pagans sacrifice they offer to demons and not to God. I do not want you to be partners with demons." In other words, it does not matter one iota that there is no substance in the deity being worshipped by a pagan: the mere fact that he is bowing down to a creature not the Creator opens him up to the grip of the principalities and powers.

And just possibly, in this apocalyptic age when the world could be destroyed in an instant, there is another reason for the growth in occultism and Satan worship. "Now the Spirit expressly says that in the last times some will depart from the faith by giving heed to deceitful spirits and doctrines of demons . . ." (1 Tim. 4:1). So far from becoming better and better, the Bible envisages the world as growing worse and worse. Jesus foretold widespread apostasy, the multiplication of wickedness, false religions boasting powers and wonders, utter godlessness and the shaking of all the foundations of the world before the end comes (Matthew 24 *passim*). Paul envisaged a time of great rebellion against God and the emergence of a man of sin, full of satanic power (2 Thess. 2:1, 3, 9). John in his vision saw a third of mankind annihilated and the rest refusing to repent or to give up their worship of demons, their sorceries and their murders (Rev. 9:18ff). Towards the end of the Apocalypse, he puts it another way. Satan will be loosed from the control which inhibits him and will come out to deceive the nations as never before. Such will be the prelude to the final Advent. We are bidden not to speculate on dates (history is white with the bones of those who have done so – and have got it wrong) but we are equally bidden not to be blind to the signs of the times.

## Varieties in the Occult

The "occult" means "the hidden things", and they are not easy to seek out or to describe. Scripture gives us no mandate for curiosity, and mercifully it is not necessary to know a great deal about the occult to be able to overcome it. For Jesus Christ is Lord, even of the demons who are encountered in this dark area. I did not imagine that I would live to see the day when the horrors of spirit worship from animistic countries would be widespread in Western Europe, but so it is. Satan is so sure of his hold on man's heart that he does not need any longer to fear the Christian influence and cover his tracks more in so-called Christian countries. His agents no longer need to work undercover. Even the black masses are often now not anti-Christian in their emphasis: they do not need to be, for Christians are not in large supply, and most of them are blind to the power of evil. So what need for concealment? Accordingly, the occult is now enormously prevalent, and information about it is available on every bookstall.

The main areas of occultism are magic, fortune-telling and spiritism. Let us glance at them in turn.

### Magic

Magic is the attempt to bring the spirit world under one's own knowledge and control. It is the precise opposite of religion, which seeks surrender to the divine, not control over it, and operates by faith not knowledge. Magic normally falls into the categories of black or white, depending on whether the envisaged purposes and the spirits invoked are evil or good. The black magician seeks to subjugate his enemy. The white magician seeks to help his friend. But in the last analysis both types of magic stem from the same stock: both are the attempts by means of hidden lore and secret ceremony to control. Both are an exercise in seeking power. And both conjure up spirits of the universe which are alien to Almighty God. Telepathy,

118

clairvoyance, clairaudience, ESP, automatic writing, charms, magic healing are at root no different from spiritism, fortune-telling, black magic, Satan worship and death magic. Kurt Koch distinguishes and illustrates with copious examples four different ways in which a person may fall into the practice of magic. It may come through hereditary involvement, and often does. It may come through occult experiments. It may come through occult transference from one person to another. And it may come from overt commitment to Satan. John Richards quotes a letter which came into his possession from one who had entered such a contract with Satan, and I have met others who have done just this. The letter reads:

> My Lord and Master Satan, I acknowledge you as my God and Prince, and promise to serve and obey you while I live. And I renounce the other god and Jesus Christ, the saints and the church and its sacraments and I promise to do whatever evil I can. And I renounce all the merits of Jesus Christ, and if I fail to serve and adore you, paying homage to you daily, I give you my life as your own. This pact was made the -th day of ---, 19--, signed ------.

*(op. cit. p. 82)*

**Fortune-telling**
Fortune-telling is, in effect, another branch of magic, though it is convenient to distinguish them since magic is primarily concerned with power and fortune-telling with knowledge. The most common forms are palmistry or acquiring knowledge through studying the lines of the hand; tarot cards, which are thrown to reveal a characteristic of the person involved; crystal gazing, a putative way of peering into the future; psychometry, whereby an object belonging to a person is held by the practitioner who then proceeds to make statements about the owner; and, most common of all, astrology. This assumes that the lives of men are controlled by the stars, and is a conviction almost as old as time which has occurred in most civilisations, not least, as we have seen, the world of the first century. There

119

is the astrology of the horoscope in the paper, with which millions of people in this country flirt daily. There is the astrology of prediction for business and politics. Both Germany and Britain made use of this in World War Two (see Richards, *op. cit.* p. 26 for details and primary sources). And then there is the astrology of personality traits and characteristics with which Jung concerned himself to a considerable extent. Some astrologers seek merely to determine astral events from the past; some seek from the stars predictions for the future. Both assume that life is largely determined by forces quite outside the control of man and therefore diminish human beings in the areas of their freedom and personal responsibility.

## Spiritism

The third main area of occultism is spiritism or spiritualism – the meanings are synonymous, although spiritualism is generally used by those who wish to add a semi-Christian façade to their sorceries, such as the Spiritualist Churches. The essence of spiritism is the attempt to communicate with the spirits of the dead. Whether this is in fact achieved, or whether people are put in touch with demonic forces masquerading as the spirits of the dead, is, for the moment, irrelevant. The point is that whereas much is chicanery and trickery in this area of the occult as in others, much is not. Through trances, through séances, through mediums and ouija boards, table-turning and the like, messages from "the other side" are often received. To be sure, they are usually trivial or banal. But it cannot be denied that time and again they do put men and women in touch with the spirit world. Nor can it be denied that this hunger to be in touch with the departed through necromancy often becomes an addiction and not infrequently leads to mental breakdown and suicide. We can assert beyond the possibility of cavil, that there is power in this whole area, and a most sinister power it is. Dennis Wheatley, himself infatuated with the occult and responsible for bringing it to every station bookstall, gives a solemn warning in an interview with the occult magazine, *Man, Myth and Magic*:

I do not approve of mediums attempting to contact the
dead. Mediums who get in touch with occult forces are
laying themselves open to serious danger. The powers
that mediums contact are not the dead, but evil
entities, and they are very dangerous indeed.


### The Biblical Attitude to the Occult

The teaching of the Bible is extraordinarily clear on this
matter, and extraordinarily explicit. All down the centuries
over which the Bible was being written the attitude is
precisely the same. We are warned to have nothing to do
with the occult.

We have already in chapter four examined both the
Jewish and the Graeco-Roman attitude to demons. It
remains here merely to note the explicit teaching of the
Bible on occult practices.


**Forbidden in the Old Testament**
The Old Testament had a lot to say on the subject, by
warning, precept and direct teaching. Deuteronomy 18:9ff,
is perhaps the *locus classicus*, for it explicitly forbids all
three main divisions of occultism: magic, fortune-telling
and spiritism.

> When you come into the land which the Lord your
> God gives you, you shall not learn to follow the
> abominable practices of those nations. There shall not
> be found among you anyone who burns his son or his
> daughter as an offering, anyone who practises divin-
> ation, a soothsayer, or an augur, or a sorcerer or a
> charmer, or a medium or a wizard or a necromancer.
> For whoever does these things is an abomination to the
> Lord, and because of these abominable practices the
> Lord is driving them out before you.

Spiritism became a capital offence in Israel: "you shall not
allow a sorceress to live" (Ex. 22:18). This applied to the
mighty as well as the lowly in the land. Saul, the first king of
Israel, is held up as a warning to posterity. "So Saul died for

121

his unfaithfulness . . . he did not keep the command of the Lord, and he also consulted a medium, seeking guidance, and did not ask guidance of the Lord. Therefore the Lord slew him" (1 Chron. 10:13f). The incident of the witch of Endor was not only the cause of Saul's personal downfall and death. It was the hinge on which the kingdom swung over to David. Had not Leviticus 19:31 said clearly, "Do not turn to mediums or wizards. Do not seek them out, to be defiled by them"?

Of course, human nature being what it is, Israel did not always obey, and the historical and prophetical books have a lot to relate of those who disobeyed this plain command and went after "the host of heaven", the *baalim*, necromancy and the like. Ahab was one of the most celebrated offenders, and Manasseh was arguably the most heavily involved and the most depraved. His story is told in 2 Kings 21. The Old Testament is clear that heathen idols were not, as Colin Wilson claims in his book *Mysteries*, merely defeated deities: the heathen gods are seen as demons in Scripture, part of the allied hosts of Satan. Thus Deuteronomy records Moses' complaint, "they sacrificed to demons which were no gods" (32:17) and Ps. 106, in recounting Israel's chequered history, is explicit: "they did not destroy the peoples as the Lord commanded them, but they mingled with the nations and learned to do as they did. They served their idols, which became a snare to them. They sacrificed their sons and daughters to the demons" (Ps. 106:34 cf. Deut. 12:31). From one point of view the gods of the heathen are non-entities, nothings; the word for "idol" in both Hebrew and Greek indicates "phantom, mere appearance". But behind these non-existent deities lurk the forces of the demonic. When men engage in idolatrous worship, the demons exercise power over them. That is why the prophets were so vehement against idolatry and spiritism. It was for this reason, among others, that God allowed the Exile (Is. 8:19, 29:4, 27:9, 19:3, 47:9–13, 1 Sam. 15:23, Jer. 27:10, 32:35, Ezek. 13:17–23, 21:21f, Micah 5:12). It is impossible to exaggerate the insistence of the Old Testament against idolatry in every form.

## Forbidden in the New Testament

In the New Testament it is just the same. Jesus Christ's own powerful opposition to the demonised is one of the most notable characteristics of the Gospels. We shall examine it below. Paul is emphatic that the Corinthians must not, for all their knowledge that "an idol has no real existence" (1 Cor. 8:4) "become partners with demons" by sharing in pagan sacrifices. "You cannot partake of the table of the Lord and the table of demons" (1 Cor. 10:20). But wherever you turn in the New Testament you find the same emphasis. Acts 16:16–18 tells of one of the slaves of a soothsayer who under the influence of a spirit of divination, or fortune-telling, pestered Paul and his company. Paul exorcised her, "I charge you in the name of Jesus Christ to come out of her." It did. Converted magicians at Ephesus burnt their books, aware that they could not serve both Christ and the demonic powers (Acts 19:19). In the Book of Revelation sorcery and those who practise it are condemned in the strongest terms. It is associated with murder, idolatry, fornication and theft in the passages where it is mentioned (Rev. 9:21, 18:23, 21:8, 22:15), and I have reason to believe that this is so today. The satanic origin of the whole thing is made abundantly plain from 16:12ff.

## Reasons for its banning

It is not difficult to see why the Bible should take so uncompromising an attitude towards all trafficking with the occult.

In the first place it is putting yourself under the control of a power that is not from God and is in fact rebellious against God. By worshipping idols in any shape or form we come under the control of demons (1 Cor. 10:19f).

Second, the lust for knowledge not normally available to man, which is the driving force in astrology and fortune-telling, is an attempt to bypass the boundaries God has set. It was by taking the fruit of the tree of knowledge in the Garden at the devil's suggestion that mankind fell under his power. He did gain this knowledge, but it brought sorrow and an evil dependence with it.

Third, the longing for power to dominate and control the

supernatural, which lies deep within magic, is the very antithesis of the proper attitude of creature to Creator. "What does the Lord require of you but to do justice and to love kindness and to walk humbly with your God?" (Micah 6:8). Ezekiel complains of those who put magic bands upon themselves (amulets?) in order to "hunt for souls" (13:18), and Isaiah mocks the Babylonians for their magic practices, the astrologers who seek the power to predict ("who at the new moons predict what shall befall you" 47:13), and the magicians who seek power to harm ("your many sorceries with which you have laboured from your youth; perhaps you may be able to succeed, perhaps you may inspire terror" 47:12). The attempt to gain illicit power over God or man is anathema.

Fourth, the demonic is dangerous and ultimately destructive to a man, and it is for that reason that God forbids it. Saul, Manasseh, Ahab and many other examples of this are brought before us in the Old Testament, and the same emphasis is implicit in stories such as the Gerasene demoniac or the woman "Satan has bound" in the New Testament. Being under control of a demonic spirit is like having your house captured by a foul and unwelcome invader, according to the teaching of Jesus (Mark 3:27). And God does not want that for his creatures.

Worst of all, surrender to the occult is hateful to God because it is straight disobedience. "Rebellion is as the sin of witchcraft" (1 Sam. 15:23). It is not by accident that witchcraft and immorality are so often mentioned in the same breath (Gal. 5:20, Rev. 9:21, Rev. 2:14, 1 Cor. 10:6–9, Acts. 15:29). The two are closely linked not only in Scripture, as with Manasseh and his like, but also in contemporary life. Power over women is one of the avowed aims of magic. Naked dances and multiple intercourse are regular features both of black and white magic. The altar is often the body of a girl. This is how one writer in *Esquire*, March 1970 described it:

> I was at this party, about eight months ago, where you were greeted at the door with a glass of special hallucinogenic formula; acids and a pinch of strychnine.

Rat poison. Makes the trip very physical. You went in and there were three altars. On two of them these boys were tied with leather thongs. They were sobbing. These two faggots dressed as nuns – one had a goatee – were beating them with big black rosaries. On the middle altar was a very young girl. This guy wearing a goat's head had crushed a live frog on her privates. When I came in he had just cut a little cross on her stomach; not deep, but the party had just started.

A Christian commitment would demand that a person turns round and repudiates this rebellion, whatever form it may take; and this many are not prepared to do. One of the charms of occult practice is that it gives rein to the religious instinct deep within a person but does not make upon him any claims for love, holiness, or service of others. In this sense it is a pseudo-religion, and justly deserves the name of "idolatry" which is so often attributed to it in the Bible. For idolatry is essentially the pursuit of the counterfeit. As we saw in the last chapter, Satan counterfeits the Messiah, and so do his lackeys. Their spiritual nature counterfeits the God who is spirit. Their predictions counterfeit prophecy. They can counterfeit the spiritual gifts of glossolalia and interpretation. They have a counterfeit healing, but generally it has very different end products from the wholeness that characterises God's healing and salvation. They have a counterfeit worship, but it brings bondage and fear not freedom and joy. The imitation is often uncannily like the real thing. But there is an unmistakable difference of tone. I have heard people speaking in tongues under the inspiration of the Holy Spirit and people opposing them in demonic tongues at the same time. Quite an experience! But the counterfeit stood out from the God-given. Nor is that in the last analysis surprising, when all allowance has been made for the Enemy's skill in deception, for whereas the Holy Spirit convicts men of sin, righteousness and judgement, the Unholy Spirit behind the occult excuses sin, denies the reality of judgement, and promotes either self-satisfied moral achievement or rank immorality. No wonder God forbids our involvement in anything of the sort.

## Demons in the Gospels

The whole Bible is emphatic that behind the occult lie those principalities and powers of evil often called *daimonia*, demons, in the New Testament. As we began to see in the last chapter, the Scriptures give a unified and coherent account of demons, even though much remains hidden from us.

It is noteworthy that they are not seen as influences but as something approaching personalities. They are credited with at least four of the criteria we should want to apply to personality. They have *knowledge*: the demon in the man at Capernaum says, "I know who you are, the holy one of God" (Mk. 1:24) and the demon in the man at Ephesus told the sons of Sceva, "Jesus I know and Paul I know, but who are you?" (Acts 19:5). Then they appear to have *emotion*. "What have you to do with us, Jesus of Nazareth? Have you come to destroy us?" (Mk. 1:24) is fraught with emotion, and James tells us that the devils believe in God – and tremble (Jas. 2:19). A third characteristic we associate with personality is *speech*. In the New Testament the demons are represented time and again as speaking. And fourthly, the demons have *willpower*. When despatched they have to leave: but in Matt. 12:44 the unclean spirit decides, "I will return to my house from which I came." On all four counts, therefore, it would seem proper to ascribe personality to the demons. Yet they are normally referred to by the neuter in Greek. Obviously these spirits are not personal in the same sense as man is personal, let alone the same sense as God is personal. But they share the characteristics of a living, purposeful, communicating being.

It is with these beings that Jesus is concerned in his ministry of delivering men and women. He came to destroy the works of the devil (1 John 3:8) and the Gospels show him at work. Demonic activity lies behind some diseases: blindness, dumbness (Matt. 12:22), deafness (Matt. 9:32), epilepsy (Matt. 17:14–18), mental illness (Lk. 8:27ff) and

126

perhaps we should include the woman with the crippled back (Lk. 13:11ff), and the high fever which Jesus "rebuked" in Simon's mother-in-law (Lk. 4:39).

As we have seen, the Bible writers do not believe that all illness is directly attributable to demonic possession. They make a careful distinction between healing and casting out demons. Jesus sent a message to Herod, "I cast out demons and perform cures" (Lk. 13:32). In Luke 4:40f we have a general picture of his liberating work, and find that whereas he laid hands on the sick and healed them, he did not lay hands on the demonised, but rebuked the demons and cast them out. In the Mission Charge he empowered the Twelve in two respects, not one: to have authority over demons and to heal diseases (Lk. 9:1f). Demons are expelled: diseases are healed. In other words, the Gospel writers seem to indicate that illness may be caused by direct demonic invasion though it certainly need not be. They are abundantly clear that there is a difference between healing and exorcism.

### The Ministry of Jesus to the Demonised

There are many general statements in the Gospels of the work of Jesus in setting free demonised people (see, e.g. Matt. 4:24, 8:16, Mk. 1:32–34, 39, 3:11, 6:13, Lk. 4:41, 6:18, 7:21). And there are seven accounts of his work on individuals. They are (i) the man with the unclean spirit in the synagogue (Mk. 1:21–28, Lk. 4:31–37), (ii) the blind and dumb demoniac (Matt. 12:22–29, Mk. 3:22–27, Lk. 11:14–22), (iii) the Gerasene demoniac (Matt. 8:28–34, Mk. 5:1–20, Lk. 8:26–39), (iv) the Syrophoenician woman's daughter (Matt. 15:21–28, Mk. 7:24–30), (v) the epileptic boy (Matt. 17:14–21, Mk. 9:14–29, Lk. 9:37–43), (vi) the woman with a spirit of infirmity (Lk. 13:10–17), (vii) the dumb demoniac (Matt. 9:32). In addition we may with probability include the healing of Simon's mother-in-law, whose fever he "rebuked" (Lk. 4:39).

I do not propose to go through these one by one, but it would be worth while to look at the three incidents which were deemed important enough to appear in all three

Synoptics, and then to draw from the remainder such lessons as might prove applicable today.

## The Beelzebub controversy

The first of the three major incidents is the Beelzebub controversy to which we have already given some attention. It is given prominence in all three Gospels because it shows that the Kingdom has broken in with power, a power which nobody can deny and about which nobody can be neutral. If it does not come from Satan then it must come from God. Like his healings, Jesus' exorcisms were an acted Christology. They challenged men as to who he was and what their response to him would be. Wilfully to call light darkness was to commit that sin against the Holy Spirit which cannot be forgiven for the simple reason that forgiveness needs to be received as well as offered. And it cannot be received by one who is impenitent and still calling Jesus Beelzebub.

## The Gerasene demoniac

If the first of these three major incidents with demons challenges the reader's attitude to the person and claims of Jesus and the provenance of his power, the second is descriptive of Jesus' handling of a particularly serious case of demonic possession. The Gerasene demoniac showed lack of control: nobody had the strength to subdue him. He showed lack of shame: Luke remarks that he lived naked among the tombs. He showed lack of peace: tortured by the demons, he was always crying and bruising himself with stones. And he showed profound lack of identity: he saw himself not as a unified personality but as a legion of conflicting impulses. A Roman legion, which the man may well have seen in Palestine or Syria, when up to full strength (as it usually was not) mustered five thousand men. This poor man felt himself not a person but an army.

The man's encounter with Jesus was no less instructive than his condition. His loud cry is typical of the demonised person when the demon is beginning to manifest itself. So is his insight into who Jesus was. Characteristically, the approach of Jesus both attracted and repelled him: the demons within are tortured by the person of Jesus and sense in him their conqueror. In this instance (the only one in the Gospels) Jesus asked the name of the man (*soi* Mk. 5:9): and the demons spoke through the man's mouth and said, "*We* are many." It sounds mad for a demon (or many demons) to talk through human lips, but I have heard it time and again. The pleading nature of the demons is emphasised, "they pleaded with him not to be sent out of the country." And so is their fear of being driven out. Jesus acceded to their request, possibly in order to give demonstrable evidence to the man that they were gone. He also, we learn, had to command them more than once to come out (Mk. 5:8, 13), and that is another common feature in deliverance ministry. The immediacy of the change, once the demons had gone, is a regular characteristic in deliverance as opposed to healing where nowadays the relief is often slower and more gradual in coming. When a demon is expelled the change is immediate. Luke tells of him "sitting and clothed and in his right mind", a source of amazement to all. But not all wanted to know anything about it – and the same remains true today. Relatives and friends of one who has been released from a demon and exhibits an amazing change in lifestyle still, like the Gadarenes, often indicate that Jesus is not wanted round these parts.

### The epileptic boy
The third passage on exorcism that is related in all three Gospels concerns the epileptic boy who was deaf and dumb. It is probably selected for several reasons. For one thing it shows how the contest with the demonic follows immediately after a time of special blessing on the Mount of Transfiguration, and, Luke adds, of prayer. Second, it demonstrates that Jesus took time in securing an analysis and diagnosis, and himself saw the spirits manifesting themselves. But the main reason is clearly the conclusion of the story. The crestfallen disciples ask why they failed to cast the demon out. And the answer shows more clearly than anywhere else in the Gospels that for this ministry there needs to be the most intimate relationship with God.

129

Their lack of faith (Matthew), their lack of prayer (Mark), meant that God could not work through them. Unquestionably that was a message intended for would-be Christian exorcists reading the Gospels. If ever exorcism is regarded as a technique possessed by man rather than an utter dependence on God for him to work, it is bound to fail. That is the main thrust of the story.

## Jesus exorcising

Other emphases which come out of the accounts of Jesus exorcising in the Gospels are as follows.

i) Jesus did not go seeking demonics. On almost every recorded occasion we read that they were brought to him by others.

ii) Jesus cast them out by a word (Matt. 8:16). He rebuked them (Mk. 9:25) and normally did not engage in argument with them. Indeed he forbade them to speak (Mk. 1:34), the only recorded exception being the case of the Gadarene demoniac.

iii) Jesus acted through the power of the Spirit of God (Matt. 12:28 – his "finger" as Luke calls it, with Old Testament overtones), and with faith, prayer and fasting (Mk. 9:29, Matt. 17:20).

iv) On some occasions Jesus had to repeat his commands to the demon to depart: they did not always obey immediately. We have noted Mk. 5:8 "For he *had* said 'Come out' ..." It is also implied in the (conative) imperfect tense used in Lk. 11:14. "And he was in process of casting out a demon" or "And he was seeking to cast out a demon".

v) On occasion he "muzzled" a demon before commanding it to come out (Lk. 4:35). Presumably this corresponds to the "binding of the strong man" before "ravaging his house", in the words of his own parable.

vi) He made a point sometimes of commanding the evil spirit never to return (Mk. 9:25). Once again, his own parable of the return of the evil spirit with others elucidates and emphasises the point.

vii) He always directed his commands to the demon, not to the man possessed by it.

viii) He made no distinction, as is sometimes fashionable

today, between those oppressed or possessed by a demon. The Greek word is *daimonizomai* "to be demonised" or sometimes *echein daimonion*, "to have a demon". The modern distinction between oppression and possession has no basis in the Greek New Testament.

ix) He did not heal those with demons. He *cast out* the demons, while he healed those who were sick. The distinction is important. Often, as in Lk. 9:1, 2, 13:32, the distinction is maintained whilst the link is strongly emphasised between the two. Frequently in modern exorcism the demon is not the only factor that has to be dealt with: in addition, healing of one sort or another is often requisite.

x) On one occasion Jesus is recorded as exorcising at a distance (Matt. 15:28). The context is one of exceptional faith and persistent, single-minded request.

xi) The authority of Jesus was noteworthy in this ministry of exorcism. The demons had to obey him, without question. Even the disciples sent by him in his name found that the demons obeyed them (Lk. 10:17, 20).

xii) The cross was the supreme rout of Satan and his demons. This is stressed in many places in the Gospels, but Matt. 8:16, 17 are significant hints of it. The passage from Isaiah 53 "He took our infirmities and bore our diseases" is applied to the exorcising and healing work of Jesus described in the previous verse. This is undoubtedly a secondary and derived application of the prophecy. It was on the cross that Jesus fully took our sicknesses and sins and defeated our foe. But the evangelist is applying it back to the life of Jesus, because in each healing and exorcism there was, for those who had eyes to see, a miniature, a trailer of the main film to be shown on Calvary. The repulses on Satan and his demons inflicted by Jesus in the course of his ministry led up to the total rout the Enemy suffered on the cross. The cross was the critical defeat of Satan which determined the ultimate outcome of the whole conflict. Thus it became also the ground on which Christians can stand when facing the occult.

The church Father, Tertullian, maintained that any Christian who did not know how to exorcise deserved to be put to death! But that certainly does not mean that every Christian ought to be involved in this type of ministry. All can: not all should. And never look for it. If God means to use you in this ministry he will make it so painfully obvious that you can scarcely avoid it without gross disobedience.

But at the outset there is an important distinction to bear in mind, one which Michael Scanlan is at pains to stress from the Catholic standpoint in his helpful book, *Deliverance from Evil Spirits*. And that is the difference between exorcism and deliverance.

"Solemn exorcism" is appropriate only in cases of complete "possession", where Satan has so taken over the personality that the patient's free will is rendered inoperative. This rare and extreme situation may only be handled by priests specially authorised by the local bishop. The church of Rome requires that such exorcism be done in the name of and with the authority of the church.

By way of contrast, "deliverance" or what the Roman church calls "simple exorcism" may be engaged in by priests and laity alike, and is used for the relief of believing Christians. Catholic moralists such as McHugh and Callan, Tanquery and Noldin recommend some such simple formula as "In the name of Jesus Christ, unholy spirit, I command you to depart from this creature of God". The Christian who is administering this deliverance is not seen as acting in the name of the Church nor with its authority. "It is done in virtue of the name of God and Jesus Christ" (Noldin).

In short, exorcisms proper are restricted to those who have been utterly taken over by Satan, and should be attempted only by authorised priests with the express permission of the bishop in the name of the church. Deliverance for those who are troubled in some area of their lives by an evil influence beyond their control and earnestly desire to be rid of it, is open to the ministry of mature Christians, ordained or lay, and need not require particular authorisation.

If you do find yourself drawn into this work, there are three areas at least which require some attention: discernment, preparation and action.

## Discernment

If the demon inhabits a person, it can only show itself through that person's personality, through his psychological or physical expression. Therefore it is all too easy to mistake demonic for other manifestations of the body and mind. The following is only a rough guide, gleaned largely from experience. It makes no claim to be exhaustive.

One of the gifts of the Holy Spirit is called "discernment of spirits" (1 Cor. 12:10) and it refers to this very question of discerning whether or not a person is demonised. Heb. 5:14 points to the same thing and indicates that experience of discerning good from evil is something which grows in the mature Christian. I find that, quite unsought by me, I possess this gift, and it is very useful. I have never yet known it to be wrong, though it does not always operate when the demons are not manifesting themselves. It is a certain physical sensation. I felt it first in Ghana when somebody fainted right across me at the moment of commitment to Christ: a feeling of unutterable evil led me simply to call on the name of Jesus again and again. The person revived and is a bold and dynamic Christian worker today. But that person had been in touch with the demonic and the enemy was having a last fling. I think of several occasions when I have sensed it going into a house that has been used for the occult or meeting a person who is involved in it. The most sensational, and one of the earliest experiences I had was when entering a room where a possessed person was standing (and raving). The person screeched aloud and shrank to the wall at the arrival of another Christian. I felt an immediate, almost palpable, sense of evil, went up to the person and commanded the evil thing that was causing the trouble to name itself. This it did, to my great surprise. Then, having nothing but the Gospels to go on, I commanded it by its name to come out. It did – and the person crashed to the ground!

It is a curious thing, but animals are often very quick to

spot the occult. We have two dogs, spaniels, which are sensitive in this area. I do not know how widespread this proclivity is, but I imagine it is quite common. On occasion when we have been involved in the ministry of deliverance the dogs have been cowering in another room with one of our colleagues who has been praying: they were literally shivering. And I have observed the dog's hair standing on end up its back before a demonised person, only to come and fondle against the same person when they are set free. I do not understand it. I simply record it. It may help somebody.

## Diagnosis

But we do not have to rely on a sensation or hunch. It would be most dangerous to do so. John Richards has a chapter on "Deliverance" in his book, *But Deliver Us from Evil*, which is the best and most comprehensive guide I have read to the vexed question of discernment. He stresses the importance of establishing as full a case history as possible, covering medical, psychological, social, personal, psychic, religious factors, together with any note of involvement with the occult or a disturbed house. He stresses the value of the spiritual as well as the psychological and medical diagnosis. He distinguishes between the discernment of evil forces by reason and by spiritual gifts. Possession (as unsatisfactory and unbiblical a word in this connection as exorcism, but we seem to be landed with both) may come from voluntary surrender to the demonic forces, as in Satanism and some ouija board addicts; it may also come involuntarily, and this is largely through involvement one way or the other with the occult. He then gives twenty-three examples to illustrate some of the manifestations which are met with in the demonised: abnormal aggression and strength, tongues, preternatural knowledge, amnesia, violent reaction to Christ and so forth. He lightly touches on the possibility of possession by the living and the departed.

My own observations in this area are less comprehensive but in strong agreement. I suspect demonic influence when I find:

i) an irrational and violent reaction against the name of

Jesus, any mention of his cross, or being faced with the Bible, the Communion, entry into a church building (particularly towards the sanctuary), or the application of holy water or oil. The reaction may come in verbal abuse or physical violence.

ii) Violent struggles with a strength out of all proportion to a person's size, when under the influence of the demon.

iii) Any involvement in occult practice now or in the past; including Christian Science, transcendental meditation, spiritism, and all animistic Eastern religions.

iv) The possession of or exposure to any objects which have been used in the occult, emanating from a witch or medium, any occult literature, charms, amulets, bracelets, rings, especially any curios from the East which could have been used in idolatry.

v) A disturbed history in previous generations (is Exodus 20:4 relevant?)

vi) Unnatural bondage to sexual perversion or other compulsive habits, unsought blasphemy, or uncontrollable mockery of God and holy things.

vii) Strange behaviour, including sharp bursts of temper or moodiness, mutterings, frothing at the mouth, palpitations of the heart, sudden fluctuations of mood.

viii) Change of voice in speech or laughter.

ix) The grip of a nameless fear, unrelated to anything specific.

x) Compulsive inability to pray even when the person longs to do so.

xi) Something strange about the eyes. The eyes are the window to the inner man. The eyes of the possessed are often unnaturally bright, glazed, or full of manic hatred.

These characteristics are neither exhaustive nor always present. Some of them are found in Christian and unbeliever alike who are not demonised at all but have never learnt to "crucify the flesh with its affections and lusts". Some are found in common with mental sickness. Diagnosis of demonisation should never be arrived at lightly nor without consultation (with doctors and psychiatrists, preferably, as well as with spiritually competent guides and any like diocesan exorcists, specifically commissioned in this matter). Suspicion of demon infestation should be the last not the first expedient. But the fact remains that in the current situation of widespread exposure to the occult this is becoming more and more a problem Christians will have to recognise and deal with. In my experience the most palpable clues are a combination of the divided self, involvement in the occult, superhuman strength and an insensate hate against things Christian. It ought to be added that the demonic powers, like their Master, prefer to remain hidden, and normally manifest themselves most readily in a specifically Christian context – in a meeting for praise and worship, at the eucharist, in church, or in the presence of a Christian, where a similar love-hate relationship will generally occur as between the Gerasene demoniac and Jesus. The person will be drawn both because of the beauty of Christ in the believer and because of the hope of deliverance. But the spirits will be stirred into rebellion and opposition.

I think of one person I know who became uncontrollably afflicted with shaking, motor movements of the arms and grinding of the teeth during a protracted time of worship. This was the utterly unexpected evidence of demonic attack, which proved to be both multiple and long lived and went back to ancestor infestation and Hindu background and worship. I think of another who gave no sign of demonisation until during praise and worship uncontrollable mockery arose in them; with another it was inability to pray; with another it was uncontrollable laughter at holy things.

On one occasion a demonised person broke into a largish church prayer meeting: I just had time to warn them before she came. The disturbance was awful, exacerbated, of course, by the large number of people gathered to pray and praise God. Within a few minutes members were imploring me to call the police and get her committed to a mental hospital. But within an hour she was sitting, and in her right mind before the cross of Christ, praising God for her deliverance – even though it was at that stage quite incomplete.

On the whole, God gives a quiet assurance about the

diagnosis to all concerned if he wants you to proceed. All is not lost if you make a mistaken diagnosis. It is not as dangerous as may be thought, particularly if you have made the client feel relaxed and at home. Explain to him that you are not sure whether occult forces are involved, but are going to explore the situation with his cooperation. Should no evidence materialise, you and he have made an important advance, and nobody should lose any sleep about the exclusion of a false trail. But I cannot emphasise too strongly the unwisdom of young, overzealous Christians rushing to conclusions about demonisation among their acquaintances. One final word: if a person proclaims with great confidence that he is possessed, take leave to doubt it. The demons are normally in no hurry to invite expulsion.

**Preparation**

John Richards asks a shrewd question in his book, *But Deliver Us from Evil*. "Who are the casualties in warfare? The disobedient, the unarmed, the weak, the undisciplined, and those with illusions about the war being somewhere else. So too are the casualties in spiritual warfare." For it is nothing less than spiritual warfare that we are engaged in. "The weapons of our warfare are not carnal but are mighty through God to the pulling down of strongholds" (2 Cor. 10:4). Unless we recognise that, there is little hope of helping others to deliverance. Granted that recognition, here are some factors which have been found helpful in preparation for a ministry of deliverance – when there is time for preparation. Sometimes the matter is immediate and there is no time for preparation. It is then that the long-term preparedness of the Christian worker stands him in good stead.

i) He must recognise that deliverance from the demonic can be achieved only by Christ, not by any technique or ritual or achievement of his own.

ii) He must therefore ensure that there is no blockage between him and his Lord. This will involve confession to God and if necessary to somebody else. Sacramental confession can be helpful.

iii) He must be aware of and glad to use the gifts of the Holy Spirit. Unless he has allowed the power and love of the Spirit to fill him he will achieve nothing. This openness to spiritual gifts will include the readiness for God to use the gift of tongues, interpretation, insight (often through pictures) prophecy and direction (in the course of the counselling and also in direction by God to an area of Scripture that may have been quite unknown but proves entirely apt). I have written at length about spiritual gifts in *I Believe in the Holy Spirit* (and have learned a little more since then), but I am convinced that many of us Christians do not begin to possess the spiritual gifts that God wants to endue us with, through fear, prejudice, apathy or some other reason.

iv) He will naturally give time to prayer, perhaps with fasting and perhaps with friends. Study of appropriate passages of Scripture will also be natural.

v) He must claim the victory of Christ which was once and for all achieved on the cross; in that alone he will conquer. That is why he is exhorted in Ephesians 6 to put on the whole armour of God that he may be able to stand against all the wrestlings of the devil. Many people find it helpful to go through those pieces of armour one by one, claiming them in faith.

vi) He may well find it prudent to have by him a cross, material for an informal Holy Communion, holy oil for anointing as Scripture indicates, and holy water. Of the latter, more later.

vii) He will need to see that he is rightly related to and has the goodwill and support of those who are his spiritual superiors, the bishop for example.

viii) He will ensure that the session takes place in a room where one can be undisturbed and where there is ample leisure for counselling.

ix) He will ensure the support of a group to pray, if possible during the whole time of the encounter, which may well be protracted. And he will never go into such a situation alone: he will always have at least one other person with him.

x) The team for deliverance should normally include a

clergyman. The authority to bind and loose was passed down to him in his ordination, and the devil knows it.

xi) The team should go in an attitude of humility, prayerful dependence on God, confidence in his power, and deep compassion for the afflicted person.

xii) The team should never minister at the dictates of the situation. They minister to the Lord, and the ministry must reflect him, not the rush and anxiety of the emergency. If we rush into situations, our rushing reflects the disturbance of the situation, not the victory of Christ. There is much to be said for the vicar who would not engage in deliverance ministry unless the folk concerned committed themselves to six months of church attendance.

xiii) The team should never opt for the greater ministry when the lesser will suffice. There is in some circles an unhealthy interest in "spirit-language" particularly when "sin-language" is weak. One leader prominent in deliverance ministry rightly said that forgiveness would halve the number of exorcisms! Indeed, most genuine demonic disturbance is the result of sin, and needs first to be approached at that level. We should assume that counselling, prayer, confession, renewal of baptismal vows will be adequate, and only proceed to direct confrontation with the demonic should this prove, subsequently, to be necessary. I cannot stress too strongly that the Enemy of souls is delighted when those who have woken up to the existence of the demonic become absorbed in it to the exclusion of weightier aspects of their ministry. Do not get involved unless you must; but if you must, then go in believing company, at the time and place of your choosing, with no prior assumptions, and a deep waiting on God in dependence and confident assurance of his good will towards all who are in bondage of any kind.

## Action

It is extraordinarily difficult to generalise because the circumstances in which cases of the demonic present themselves differ so much, and in any event a great deal of flexibility is obviously necessary. As we have seen in Jesus' deliverance ministry, he was in no way bound to a particular technique. But certain principles may be well to keep in mind as a rough guide.

i) If you have made an appointment with the patient already, help him to relax, and gain his cooperation: without this nothing will happen. Christ can set him free, but only if he is willing to be freed. Explain to him that when under domination of the demon he will not feel willing; get that cooperation before the demon is activated. And explain to him that when challenging the demon it is the evil spirit, not him, you are coming against.

ii) His own approach is of the utmost importance. Not only must he be willing to be set free, he must be totally honest both about his condition and any sins he is aware of which may have led to that condition.

iii) This leads to a time of confession, which should be specific and include an emphatic repudiation of the devil and all his works, particularly a renunciation of any occult involvement. I found that two things are particular barriers to liberation; one is fear, and this needs to be acknowledged and handed over to the Lord in principle. The other is resentment; few things so preclude the possibility of deliverance as a grudge nursed against somebody else. "Forgive, if you have anything against anyone, so that your heavenly Father may also forgive you your trespasses" (Mk. 11:25, cf. Matt. 18:21–35). He can be sure "if we confess our sins God is faithful and just, and will forgive our sins and cleanse us from all unrighteousness" (1 John 1:9).

iv) The power and protection of the name of Jesus Christ need to be claimed explicitly by all concerned. "In my name they shall cast out demons . . . I charge you in the name of Jesus Christ to come out of her" (Mk. 16:17 and Acts 16:18).

v) The minister should then command the spirit in the name of Jesus Christ to manifest itself and to depart; to harm nobody; never to return; and to go to the Lord of spirits. It may do so at once, but the command may need to be repeated: even Jesus found that on occasion. It can be a help if the partner in the deliverance ministry prays, in the vernacular or in tongues, or sings quietly.

vi) One must be prepared for anything. Sometimes the

demon manifests itself traumatically, as with a faint on the floor or violent aggression where one may need six strong men to hold down a slip of a girl. Sometimes it is in a sly look creeping into the face, a wild look entering the eyes, a frothing at the mouth or jerky movements of the hands. Close attention should be paid to whatever happens, as it will provide a clue for proceeding.

vii) The devil usually works undercover; demons likewise love to hide. It is important therefore to be authoritative and persistent. Verses from Scripture, either prepared beforehand or else brought to mind by the Spirit are very helpful. I have a colleague who is particularly receptive to God in this matter. He finds a text becomes inscribed on his mind, often from a most obscure part of the Bible. He turns it up, and invariably it proves immensely effective in shifting the demon.

viii) In addition to Scripture there are other aids we can use. The cross of Christ is of course the great sign of demonic defeat, and I find that few things so provoke the demon to manifest itself and to leave as using a cross to hold before the eyes of the patient. They will often shut their eyes to exclude the sight. Marking the cross upon the patient's person is equally certain to provide a reaction if they are in fact possessed.

ix) The use of holy oil as instructed in Scripture is highly effective. On occasion demons emerge at once when a person is anointed.

x) Holy water is another effective symbol, and indeed agency. I discovered its value by mistake, not coming from a churchmanship where the use of holy water was common. One person under the influence of multiple demon possession crowed at me, "Ah, you haven't got any holy water." "I have," I replied, and at once consecrated some water in a glass in the name of the Trinity, and proceeded to sprinkle her. The effect was immediate, electric and amazing. She jumped as if she had been scalded. The spirit manifested itself powerfully and in due course departed. But I learnt a lesson from that. Holy water is a most valuable adjunct to deliverance. The funny thing is that if the person is not possessed, or after they have been delivered, there is no reaction whatever when the water is applied. It becomes a useful thermometer therefore.

It is interesting to reflect on the status of holy water in the church. The Catholic strand of Christendom has retained it but does not know what to do with it. It had once been dynamic in the days of faith, but became static and fossilised when men no longer believed. The Protestant churches have rejected it as superstition, seeing only its fossilised state and reacting against that. In fact we are fools not to use it both in places and with people who are or may be possessed.

xi) The Eucharist is of course the most powerful of all Christian symbols and sacraments. It is an invaluable instrument for cleansing any place affected by haunting or poltergeists, and equally so with affected persons. If the demon is manifesting itself they will be quite unable to partake. It is literally true as Paul told the Corinthians that "you cannot drink the cup of the Lord and the cup of demons" (1 Cor. 10:21). But once delivered, the Communion is the most wonderful means of consolidating what has been done. It gives a tangible demonstration of the love of God for the penitent.

xii) It is important for members of the deliverance team to be sensitive to what God is saying during the proceedings, which may be quite long (though if it goes on more than a couple of hours it may be wise to stop and return to the fray the next day). I think of one occasion when we were praying with a person and were very aware of a blockage, but neither we nor the patient were aware of the reason for it. One member of the group was given a picture of a ruined barn and a circle gathered inside it. The patient at once recognised this as an exact replay of an incident which had happened years beforehand when she had in fact gone into that ruined barn and had been roped into a circle engaged in occult practice. The thing brought to mind by this vision was then at once confessed and dealt with.

xiii) Other symbolic actions can be helpful. I know of an occasion where there was multiple possession, and deliverance came through an enacted use of Ps. 118:12 –

with the minister stamping around as if treading on bees! I know another who was greatly helped by an enactment of going seven times round the walls of Jericho until they fell with a great shout! A symbolic cutting away of all other demonic influences from outside the patient, all the principalities and powers that could conceivably render aid, is another useful preliminary and helps to concentrate attention on the matter in hand with the patient alone.

On one occasion a person who had been deep in witchcraft was having a public and powerful manifestation of the demonic in church at the end of a service, with a bishop and two clergy present. It was late at night. Her husband, himself not a Christian, was with her. She was a believer but had gone back into witchcraft under the enormous pressures brought by the coven against those who leave. We got to the point where she was almost ready to give in. Slowly the group progressed up the church and knelt at the altar rail. It was this symbolism which proved the turning-point. A message came in tongues to one of the group: the patient herself gave the interpretation, which was a wonderful message of welcome, love and forgiveness from Christ. This was accompanied by a vision she received of Jesus holding out his arms in welcome. This prostrated her before the Lord, and she came back to him at once, with tears of joy. The husband was converted on the spot, and then and there in the middle of the night he was baptised, confessing his sins.

xiv) Often during such a session one of the team, or the patient himself, will become aware of some object or book which has been a cause of trouble and needs to be burnt or smashed to pieces as soon as the session is over. It is the counterpart of the Gadarene swine being destroyed for ever in the lake. I think of one night when we had to go and smash to pieces an idol, brought from a pagan country as a curio. I think of another when a deeply disturbed woman who had kept a talisman on her person for over twenty years came to Christ finding wonderful deliverance; that talisman when taken from her neck was thrown into the river. Another person who was unable to knit except when under the power of the spirit, allowed us to take the compulsive knitting away, burn it, break the needles, and give her a fresh cardigan in return. She still cannot knit to this day!

xv) There is danger in all this, but only if you are not living close to Christ. If you are, nothing can hurt you. But on one occasion I was knocked backwards onto the floor when a spirit left, so powerful and deeprooted was it. On another occasion I sank to the floor when "disinfecting" at the Holy Table a cross which had been offered to Satan and then planted in our home. On another occasion I was attacked by a knife and by a broken glass, but on each assault I made the mark of the cross in the air and the patient simply could not pass beyond it. On another occasion a colleague who came to "disinfect" a room that had been steeped in witchcraft was so knocked up that he had to spend the rest of the day in bed. There have also been effects on children in our home, but these vanished at once when we claimed the power and protection of the blood of Christ. The moral is clear. In Christ you are safe: outside him you are in danger.

xvi) The great thing to remember is that the evil spirit will have to go because Jesus Christ is Lord. So however it dodges and evades, you can be sure of victory. Praise the Lord out loud for the deliverance he is about to bring. According to your faith it will be unto you.

xvii) If the battle is protracted, urge the patient himself to call on the Lord for deliverance. There are moments, they may only be fleeting, when you can get past the demon to the will of the person concerned but he can help himself a great deal this way. The demon cannot stay for long when it is commanded to leave by patient and minister alike, in Christ's name.

xviii) The patient knows when the thing has gone. There is a sense of relief and freedom. It may be accompanied by coughing, vomiting, or the secretion of mucus; but he is aware of a new measure of release.

xix) It is important to challenge any other spirits that may be lurking in the patient, commanding them to manifest themselves and go. On one occasion we failed to do this to

144

start with, and wondered why the patient who seemed to gain such relief after the exorcism was still in trouble the next day. It was simply because we had failed to recognise and dislodge others which were there. Challenge anything which may be there to *manifest itself and go*, in the name of Christ. It is bound to do so. Generally after the main one has been despatched the others come out speedily.

xx) The whole process is physically and emotionally exhausting for all concerned, but particularly for the patient who may well feel that he has had a major operation. Food, drink, love and rest are essential.

There are times when a very special indication is given to the patient that all is over. One such person was much troubled about the death of a fiancé, and had got involved in the occult quite deeply as a result. The session of deliverance ended with one member of the team having a vision of a young man whom she described precisely, even to the overcoat he wore and the patch on that overcoat. She saw him going out of the door. When she described this to the patient the reply was to this effect, "Oh yes, that's him all right. I sewed that patch onto his coat myself." Needless to say this was an enormous step forward and encouragement to the person concerned; an assurance that God had taken into his own hands that presence which had been haunting her.

Needless to say, after deliverance people need special pastoral care. They need deep assurance from Scripture that they are accepted in Christ. They need to be baptised if they have not already been. They need to be nourished by the Holy Communion. They need to learn to read the Scripture devotionally and to pray. They need the constant companionship of Christian friends in the aftermath of deliverance when they are very vulnerable. They need, like Jesus, to learn to use Scripture in spiritual warfare against the temptations the devil will bring to them. They need to learn from the Bible and experience how to stand in the liberty in which Christ has set them free. They need to be clothed daily in the armour of God. They need to learn the value of praise, and the need for wholeheartedness in following Christ: "give no place to the devil", "resist the devil" (Eph. 4:27, Jas. 4:7) are very necessary injunctions. They need to learn to trust the Lord and to grow daily in the faith, encouraged by one or two close companions who are more experienced Christians. Above all they need to be filled with the Spirit of God (Eph. 5:18), for an internal spiritual vacuum is a very dangerous thing. I have no hope of anyone maintaining the deliverance with which Christ has set him free unless he is prepared to allow the Lord to fill the place which had been filled by other lords. He must say with Isaiah, "O Lord our God, other lords beside thee have ruled over us, but thy name alone we acknowledge. They are dead, they will not live. They are shades, they will not arise. To that end thou hast visited them with destruction and wiped out all remembrance of them" (26:13). And in a marvellous way that is just what the Lord does. So many people who have received this ministry of deliverance are not only set free; the past seems like shadows that have flitted away. And they are often, in the mercy of God, utterly unaware of what has happened during the process of deliverance.

If all this seems like Alice in Wonderland, I can only say that it used to seem like that to me. Unfortunately I have discovered it is real, painfully real. The church of God has known it all down the ages. Only in the present century has she ceased to expect deliverance for the demonised. And the consequences of that failure are great. Many possessed people go to doctors and psychiatrists because they have no idea of spiritual healing. And when they are demonised no doctor or psychiatrist can help them. Only Christ can rid them of the invading spirit. The pastoral ineffectiveness of the church and the spiritual scepticism of the church are two fruits of the failure in much modern Christianity to take seriously the power and relevance of evil. Where the church is growing and being renewed there always dawns an awareness of spiritual battle and the power of Jesus Christ to drive out the dark forces of the enemy. Thank God that the offer of Christ to the disciples going out on their mission is still true for his followers engaged in the extension of that same mission: "Behold I have given you authority to tread upon serpents and scorpions, and over all the power of the enemy; and nothing shall hurt you. Nevertheless do not rejoice in this, that the spirits are subject to you; but rejoice that your names are written in heaven" (Lk. 10:19).

# CHAPTER 6

## *Counterfeit Religion*

THROUGHOUT HISTORY SATAN has time and time again advanced his cause through the medium of religion. Mankind is incurably religious: he will either worship God or some idol; and this is as true today as it was in the days of ancient paganism. In Israel Satan was at his most dangerous and seductive when he spoke through false prophets. In the Gospels the Pharisees were far more dangerous to Jesus than the prostitutes and open sinners. In the Epistles the writers have to warn us against the Antichrist that exalts itself into the place of God, the devil who masquerades as an angel of light and who inspires a gospel other than the one taught by Jesus. In the Book of Revelation we have already seen the devilish imitation of prophecy and of true religion. In the final discourse held with his disciples Jesus warns passionately against being led astray by false messiahs skilful enough to deceive the very elect. And Paul, in his farewell address to the Ephesian elders, warns against "grievous wolves which will come in among you, not sparing the flock". This set of warnings found an early fulfilment in the events of the second century. Montanism, Marcionism, Gnosticism and Ebionism between them, not to mention the messianism of Bar Cochba's Zionist Revolt, very nearly did away with authentic Christianity altogether.

Helmut Thielicke comments on this religious guise of the devil in his book *Between God and Satan*. The devil is a firm believer in God:

> For this reason he is so dangerous a seducer, a "teacher of error" in the church, because there his principle of taking his stand on the fact of God, on the basis of positive Christian belief, is seen at its most effective. We may well say that the most diabolical thing about the devil is that he takes this stand. That is

why he is accounted a liar from the beginning. That is why he is called the "ape" of God. That is why we can mistake him for God.

The Enemy has not lost his cunning. It would be surprising if he had. And our generation which combines such a mixture of scepticism and credulity, of materialism and religiosity, provides him with easy meat. I propose in this chapter to examine some representatives of different genres of counterfeit religion which are widespread today. They provide Satan with a garment of light. He comes to us dressed in the mantle of the new cult, of political religion, and of religion in disguise, to take three typical examples. All these garments are attractive. All are heavily infected.

## The Counterfeit of Cult Religion

Cults are proliferating very fast at present. They tend to do so in times of massive change. It was so in the religious ferment of the sixteenth century. It is so in the prevailing secularism of the twentieth century. At present there are many factors favouring their growth: the decline of orthodox Christianity, widespread ignorance of the Bible, hunger for certainty in a world falling apart, disillusionment with the church, politics and materialism. The relativism of contemporary life, in matters of truth, religious pluralism and ethics is another factor encouraging the emergence of new cults. So is the greatly increased emphasis on experience, in the wake of existentialism and the drug culture. In an age when youngsters have tried everything by the age of fifteen, the cult is a fascinating new frontier to cross, and the breakdown of the family contributes a further factor in the present cultural chaos.

The cults have many common factors. They all sound like Christianity. They offer us considerable and desirable benefits. They are generally authoritative. They are nearly always led by a personality who is dominant in the cult. They all have a new revelation additional to or replacing Scripture. They all look for total commitment. Many of them require the money of their members. Many of them have a form of initiation which is little short of indoctrination. Often they profess a secret knowledge revealed only to initiates. And they are very resentful of criticism – quick to intimidate or to sue for libel.

It is impossible to examine a variety of cults in this book. It has in any case been done elsewhere. Let us take one colourful and at present well known representative, the Moonies.

## The Unification Church

You will meet them at street corners and in the market place. They will be polite, charming, sincere and probably young. They will have an attractive gaiety about them, and look neat, well dressed, friendly and enthusiastic. They will be coy about their organisation, will claim to be Christians, but will soon prove very critical of the Christian church. They will tell you that they exist to unify world Christianity. They will encourage you to state your beliefs first, and they will harmonise their views with yours in so far as they can, as if to demonstrate their stated aim of unity among all Christians and eventually among all religions. They will stress the similarities and avoid the differences. They will testify enthusiastically to the spiritual blessings they have found in the Unification Church. And you may be invited back to a three-day workshop, followed by one lasting a week, and finally a three-week course before becoming a full member of the sect.

This movement with over two hundred different names has spread fast. It originates with the "Rev" Sun Myung Moon, born in 1920 in North Korea. He claims that Jesus appeared to him at prayer on Easter Day 1936 and revealed to him that he would complete the great mission begun by Jesus long before. He asserts that he continually receives fresh revelations, and practises "soul travel" to converse with Jesus and other religious leaders in the spirit world. The Introduction to *The Divine Principle* maintains that "with the fulness of time God sent His messenger to resolve the fundamental questions of life and the universe. His name is Sun Myung Moon" (p. 16). It goes on to assert that in 1945 "he fought alone against myriads of satanic forces, both in the spirit and physical world, and finally triumphed over them all". Ken Suto, one of the Unification Church leaders, teaches that "at that moment he became the absolute victor of heaven and earth. The whole spirit world bowed down to him on that day of victory. The spirit world has already recognised him as the victor of the universe, and the Lord of Creation" (*Master Speaks*, March 1976, p. 4f).

The "holy book" of the movement in which many of Moon's claims are embodied is *The Divine Principle*. It was developed during the 1940s and 1950s, was published in 1957, and has since undergone revision. It is an eclectic combination of Christian and Taoist thought. It is an interpretation of the Bible from a strongly neo-Confucian standpoint, seeking to combine the biblical doctrines of covenant and creation with the Confucian principle of static, unchanging creation which governs both man and the universe. In *The Divine Principle*, therefore, Moon purports to present a theological interpretation of the Bible together with many of the messages Moon received from the spirit world. The basic thesis is that the first Adam fell through the seduction of Eve by Lucifer, and so our original parents lapsed into a man-centred marriage and failed to establish God's Kingdom on earth. The second Adam also failed, for Jesus was crucified before he could get married and create the God-centred marriage from which the perfect children, appropriate for the Kingdom, could be born. The cross was not God's purpose for Jesus. Quite the reverse. It was primarily the failure of John the Baptist which led to the crucifixion. Jesus was raised from the dead as a "spirit man", and did indeed redeem mankind spiritually, but he failed to give redemption to the body, and he did not, of course, usher in the Kingdom of God on earth. His role is not to save souls, but to build the Kingdom of God on earth. A third Adam, a Lord of the second Advent is needed for this. Moon is coy, in print at least, of claiming that he is the third Adam. He merely asserts that the last Adam must be born in Korea! Doubtless the majority of Moonies believe that he is the latter day Messiah, and that his marriage is the Ideal Marriage which is essential for the founding and building up of the Kingdom. This is the reason why their own marital emphasis is so strong and so pure. Within the Unification Church they hope to discover a way of attaining a perfect marriage, and they look to other married members of the Church as examples; naturally, the greatest of all examples is provided by Sun Myung Moon and his wife.

Moon is clear that Jesus was not divine, and he does not actually claim deity for himself, through he gets very near to it. "I had to pay indemnity for what has been lost by Jacob, Moses and Jesus . . . I have paid a great amount of indemnity and because of this I have the right to forgive another's sin" (*Master Speaks*, March 1965). The same copy of *Master Speaks* says, "As Christians we prayed in the name of the Father, the Son and the Holy Spirit. Now we should pray in the name of the True Parents . . . The True Parents are now on earth."

There is no doubt that his followers accord him divine honours. Ronald Enroth, a Christian and a sociologist, gives a fascinating insight in his *Youth Brainwashing and the Extremist Cults* (p. 101ff) into the adoration offered Moon by his devotees. He quotes Shelley Liebert, a girl who was engulfed by the welcoming enthusiasm of the movement and subsequently managed to emerge. She tells of her feelings when she knew that Moon was coming to stay the night at the community house where she was stationed:

> We would conjure up his image in our minds. I knew his face better than my own, and I loved him so much. I thought about him all the time.
>
> Preparations for his coming were elaborate. The entire kitchen had to be cleaned out – everything had to be taken out. Everything had to be replaced. If you wanted to use a particular canned good you had to buy the biggest and most expensive. Even if the can was not opened you still had to buy a new one. Everything had to be completely new. After all, we were preparing it for "God".

The night of his arrival everyone was exhausted and all the members went to bed. I thought, "How can they sleep when Father is in the house?" I was the only one to stay up all night, praying and making breakfast. When he didn't eat my breakfast, I was crushed . . .

After he had left, all of the things he had used and touched were divided up among the members. They were considered to be sacred artefacts to be preserved for posterity, like splinters from the cross.

After he left I just collapsed from exhaustion. I locked myself into the library of the mansion and cried and cried for hours. I cried because I felt he was the embodiment of all the love that could possibly be. I was crying tears of joy; everything in history had been funnelled down to this one man, and I was connected to him.

Such was the messianic devotion Moon could inspire in followers, and still can, though his lifestyle does little enough to commend him. In his native Korea his stock is very low, and his opulent lifestyle alone causes many a raised eyebrow in the United States where he lives. He is reputed to have assets in excess of seven million pounds, while his devotees live in poverty and go fund-raising on the streets.

But granted the questions about his fund-raising, claims and theology – is there any harm in all this? Does it matter?

It does. A recent example, reported in *The Oxford Times* 16 January 1981, is afforded by Judith Sherwood, a local secretary who was reporting to her M.P., Mr. Tom Benyon, her experiences after spending eleven weeks with the Moonies before she made her escape. She joined the sect on the last day of her holiday in San Francisco.

"People may think I was stupid," she said "but they simply seemed like friendly people. I was invited to spend some time with them, and it seemed a good way of passing time as I was at a loose end until my flight left, but I just got entangled in it all." She did not at first realise that they were Moonies. They called themselves "creative community", but she soon found out. After being subjected to repetitive lecture sessions about Sun Myung Moon, "I felt my hold on reality was beginning to go, and I had to get away. If I had not made the break then I was afraid that I would go under and start believing everything they were preaching. I was never alone, and never given any time to think. Looking back, it all seems very sinister and secretive. I still have nightmares thinking about it even now." She eventually made her escape at night by climbing a wooden fence, wading a stream, and running through a wood to a highway. She dived into a ditch whenever a car passed from the direction of the camp. "It is an experience which will be with me for the rest of my life, and I hope my story will act as a warning to other young people to be on their guard against approaches from groups like the Moonies," she said. She has written up her experiences for a dossier on the activities of the sect being compiled by Family Action Information and Rescue.

There is much that attracts: the hero worship, the solidarity with other young people who have a clear missionary task before them that provides challenge and a task for every member. The simplicity of the lifestyle and the sexual purity which are demanded of members stand out in stark contrast to normal apathetic, self-centred, hedonistic Western life. There is much in the authoritativeness of the system that appeals to young people, as does the sense of altering history with a movement which is going to succeed.

And yet behind it all the Enemy is laughing. He laughs at the deceptions which people swallow – is he not the father of lies? He laughs at worship of a creature rather than the Creator – has he not led the way in that direction? He laughs at a man setting himself up as supreme: such is Satan's own path. He laughs at the blind irrational adulation of Moon's followers: after all, he expects it in his own principalities and powers. Most of all he laughs at the ease with which his own influence can sweep the movement. And it does so by two ways in particular.

One is by the derision in which the cross is held. The cross that is the key to Satan's own defeat is seen as the place where Satan defeated Jesus, and prevented him achieving the purpose of his ministry. Shelley Liebert, cited above, remarked on how the cross became a symbol of Satan's victory to the Moonies. "In Unification theology the cross actually becomes synonymous with Satan. I had been wearing a cross, and no way was I going to continue wearing it. We would comment, as we drove through a city, how ironic that all the churches had crosses on them, because the cross was a symbol of Satan" (*op. cit.* p. 119).

The other is by means of the spiritism in which Moon himself indulges. Clairvoyance, clairaudience and other spiritualistic phenomena are practised by him. Moon claims, "I have talked with many masters including Jesus on questions of life and the universe and creation, God's dispensation, and many other things. They have subjected themselves to me in terms of wisdom. After I won the victory they surrendered. With this foundation of victory the spirit world is responsible to teach and reply to your questions and to help you with your problems." He claimed that many mediums are now led by him: this is clearly true. Jeane Dixon and Arthur Ford, both well-known mediums in the U.S.A., have given him their backing. So for all its Christian-sounding name, the "Holy Spirit Association for the Unification of World Christianity" is not very Christian after all, and is heavily intertwined with Eastern occultism. It is under the clutches of the Satan on whom it concentrates so much, and it proves as much by its use of "heavenly deception". As they point out, if Satan deceived God's children, why should they not deceive Satan's children?

The Unification Church is just one among many cult movements, some from partially Christian roots, others not, which are such a feature of the modern religious scene. The Divine Light Mission, the Hare Krishna movement, the Children of God (now on the wane), The Local Church, Bahai, Zen Buddhism and Scientology are all very much in evidence, along with the older cults such as Freemasonry and Christian Science. Those who wish to examine them further can consult W. J. Peterson, *Those Curious New Cults*, James Bjornstad, *The Moon is not the Son*, or Ronald Enroth, *Youth Brainwashing and the Extremist*

*Cults*. Some invaluable material is put out and continually revised by the Berkeley Christian Coalition in the U.S.A. It is probably the case that most new cults can be found, if they did not originate, within thirty miles of San Francisco, and the Berkeley Christian Coalition is therefore ideally placed for monitoring and analysing new cults, as they arise, from the viewpoint of historic Christianity.

## The Counterfeit of Political Religion

In a fascinating book published recently, Jacques Ellul has maintained that far from being secularised, our society in the West is highly religious, only it idolises the creature not the Creator. This is a perennial tendency of the human heart. Paul saw it in his own day in imperial Rome. "Although they knew God, they did not honour him as God or give thanks to him . . . They exchanged the truth of God for a lie, and worshipped and served the creature rather than the Creator who is blessed for ever." (Rom. 1:21–25). The modern state, thoroughly emancipated from organised religion, has itself become the supreme religion of the age, equipped as it is with a growing power over the lives of its members, and a powerful ideology with which to interpret every aspect of life. This tendency is most obvious in the totalitarian régimes of the world, but is by no means confined to them. Democracy, if absolutised, can become just as much of an idol as Marxist-Leninism.

When we had occasion earlier on to examine the Book of Revelation and its profound insights into the extent of the demonic influence on the world, we saw that Satan, the great dragon, exercised his powers particularly through two other beasts, the beast from the earth and the beast from the sea. And we saw that the devil maintains his grip on the world through the socio-political and the religious influences represented by these two mythical beasts. There have been many historical exemplifications of this truth since the first century when the Emperor Domitian made blasphemous claims to divinity and enforced them through political persecution, economic boycott and the terrorism of sudden arrest and execution. And in our own day there

156

are plenty of clear examples of the "beast" which adopts the dress of religion in order to extinguish and replace it by the adulation of itself.

## Fascism, Marxism, Maoism
All three of the greatest socio-political movements of our times have turned into counterfeit religions.

The Fascism of Nazi Germany is a very obvious example. Nazism was not merely an economic reaction to disaster, nor the resurgence of an abashed patriotism. It was first and foremost a religious drive of enormous proportions. With its massive rallies, its fanatical conviction of the triumph of its cause, its adulation of the messianic Leader, its passion and readiness to sacrifice for the cause, its assurance of a Thousand Year Reich, it was emphatically religious. It is hardly surprising that it came into violent conflict with the confessing church.

The Communism of Marx and Lenin was no less religious. Once again the passionate adulation of the Leader when alive and worship of him when dead; once more the unquestionable dogmas such as the evolution of matter and the dialectic of history; once more the elevation of a holy book, the anticipation of a fulfilment state, the idealism of sacrifice – even the Party system was established by Lenin on the model of the Jesuit Order. As Edward Rogers points out in his *Christian Commentary on Communism*, "The problems posed by Communism are ultimately religious. The practical problems are moral, the theoretical problems are theological and the factor which cannot be ignored without disaster is sin . . . Marx set out with the intention to deduce a reasonable interpretation of existence which could take the place of – as he thought – a decaying Christianity" (p. 208). The continuous fanatical opposition of the Russian Communist Party against Christians is immediately intelligible once the religious dimension of Communism is appreciated. You cannot have two absolute allegiances.

The Chinese régime, inaugurated by Chairman Mao, has precisely the same character. "There we see the same traits as in the predecessors," Ellul remarks acutely. "A mystique, irrationality, a party of clergy, identification of the god, attributes of divinity etc., together with a dogmatic closure on all discussion, a totalitarian control over all actions and feelings to the exclusion of all other values . . . and, above all, the celebrated determination to create a new man of virtue" (*The New Demons*, p. 170).

Ellul enumerates a number of characteristics which are clearly pseudo-religious in these three massive totalitarian régimes. They are worth reflecting on, for they apply far more widely than Germany, Russia and China. In more ways than one, in more political systems than one, the Beast counterfeits the Lamb.

## Personality cult

One such characteristic is the extreme cult of personality: Hitler, Lenin, Stalin, Mao. The faithful in effect deify the Leader: he is supreme and his will must be obeyed. This imperative overrules all others supplied by family, humanity or faith. Indeed, his position corresponds almost exactly to that of the Roman emperor who exercised ultimate political control over the known world, and was worshipped (overtly in the East and with more sophistication in the West) by his subjects. Thus Hitler announced himself as the emissary of the Almighty and the founder of the Thousand Year Reich: Nazis died invoking his name: and his personality was deemed transcendent.

Stalin's propaganda was that he was the wisest, the most beloved and the most genial man the world had ever known. He was the only one to care for the poor and protect the oppressed! He was actually one of the greatest murderers the world has ever seen, and his memory is now execrated in the U.S.S.R. But while he lived, he was god.

It was the same with Mao. Chairman Mao was not just Leader; he was deity. He was worshipped. Men bowed down before him. They recited his thoughts. They believed that he healed them through the hands of the surgeon. They worked for him in the factory. He had the ultimate power: he made the ultimate claims on his people's allegiance. He assumed the place of God.

General Amin did much the same in Uganda. Despite his

Muslim orthodoxy the Ayatollah Khomeni has done something very similar in Iran, and I myself recall seeing something of the power and fear induced by the totalitarian régime of Kwame Nkrumah in Ghana shortly before his overthrow, and the blasphemous claim fixed to his statue outside Parliament in Accra,

> Seek ye first the political kingdom and all these things shall be added unto you.

Some words of St. Paul, wrongly seen as fulfilled in various particular dictatorships down history, do apply to the whole attitude of self-deification manifested in such régimes. He warns the Thessalonians against "the son of perdition who opposes and exalts himself against every so called god or object of worship so that he takes his seat in the temple of God, proclaiming himself to be God." (2 Thess. 2:3ff).

## Faith

Another mark of the religious nature of political absolutism is faith. A faith which is total commitment. A faith which, having made that commitment rejects all theories which militate against it. A faith which may be credulous, which may have to face masses of contrary evidence, but still doggedly persists. Whatever the pogroms of Lenin, Trotsky, Stalin; whatever the revelations of the *Gulag Archipelago* and the terrifying brutality of the Soviet concentration camps; whatever the rapes of a Hungary, a Czechoslovakia, an Afghanistan, the faith of the committed Russian Communist persists. All personal judgement is obscured in the name of faith; faith is absolutely essential if everything is not to come tumbling round his ears. The quality of this faith, this total commitment, is precisely analogous to Christian faith. It is no mere intellectual acceptance but total and passionate surrender. Political faith has taken the place of Christian faith in many parts of the world. And it is a sobering thought that whereas Christian faith is evoked by the Ideal, coming in love and self-sacrifice to seek us and refashion us, political faith is "incarnate only in the political power, the modern state. In that respect it is the most atrocious of all the religions humanity has ever known. It is the religion of abstract power incarnated in the police, the army, and the administration." (Ellul, *op. cit.* p. 177).

## A holy book

A holy book is another essential in most religions, and once again the political religions do not disappoint us. Hitler's *Mein Kampf*, Marx's *Das Kapital*, Mao's *The Little Red Book* have become scriptures to the faithful. They have guided the daily lives of men. Their contents have been learnt off by heart. Their precepts have been used to justify any atrocity. Their citation closes all argument. Min Ho, the Maoist leader, said of *The Little Red Book* what many evangelical Christians say of the Bible: "We must study the works of President Mao every day. If we miss only one day the problems pile up. If we miss two days we fall back. If we miss three days we can no longer live."

## A messianic leader

A messianic figure is another essential in most religions. And here again we find them in the three under review, to look no further. Hitler rescued the Aryan race from its supposedly debased and exploited state, victimised and alienated, and he turned it into the resurrection people, the Herrenvolk, the medium through which the eschatological goal of a millennial Reich would be brought about. Lenin did as much for the proletariat in Russia, languishing in bondage to the cruelties and exploitation of the Czar. So did Mao for the downtrodden peasants of China. The members of the Party already share, by anticipation, in the new age which the Leader has inaugurated, but whose fulfilment lies in the future when the obstacles have all been swept away and a new world awaits the new men. Logically, of course, there is no reason why a modern Communist should bother to work for a utopia in which he will never share: this is one of the surds in Communism. But he is inspired by the vision, attracted by the prospect, stimulated by the struggle and warmed by the companionship. The millennial utopia held out by Fascism and Communism alike is both a pale imitation of and unconsciously inspired by the Christian teaching of the Kingdom of God which is partly realised in Christ and his people now, and will be consummated at the last day, when all who have worked for it, be they living or dead, will share in its joys.

## The ideology

The faith, the Leader and the Book have led to the "theory", the dogma which is incumbent upon the faithful, and which applies to every side of life. The process of living by, revising, commentating on the sacred text on the one hand, and of rejecting and persecuting those who do not follow it on the other, is a procedure sadly familiar to the religious world. It happened in Christendom in the Middle Ages with the Crusades and subsequently with the Inquisition. It is happening with the killings, the witch-hunts and the religious persecutions in Iran as I write. It is all too familiar. And it happens when men are blinded by dogma to which all humanitarianism, all other values must be subject. It helps to explain the violent persecutions of Christians in the Soviet Union. It helps to explain the locking away of deviationists in concentration camps among the insane – they must be insane to reject the dogma of Marxism.

There are other religious characteristics which manifested themselves in the movements of Hitler, Stalin and Mao. The all-embracing philosophy of life, covering and controlling every detail of existence; the missionary determination to capture the world; the hero-cult, "Work for the Führer", "Lenin is with you", "Mao is god"; the emotional public adulation of the Leader with hymns created in his honour; all these factors make it very plain that in some of the most important political institutions of today we are in fact confronted by a counterfeit religion. Ellul's conclusion is incontrovertible:

> If there were ceremonies alone, or sacred books alone, or an organisation alone, even if that one element could be likened to a religious factor, certainly no

161

general conclusion could be drawn. It is the combination of these indices which is decisive. For what we find in the end is that, on the one hand, *everything* which goes to make up the outward appearance of Christianity, for example, is reproduced in Nazism or Communism, with nothing left out, and conversely, *everything* which goes to make up the outward appearance of Nazism or Communism has existed already in Christianity. It is this perfect correspondence which obliges us to say that we are dealing here with religions.

(*op. cit.* p. 189)

## Democracy

What appears with startling clarity in totalitarian régimes can also be found in democracies, though more obscurely. France is a democracy, yet Ellul notes tendencies in his own land which bear the marks of pseudo-religion disguised as patriotism. For many years President de Gaulle was pre-eminent, whatever the government. He could quell riots with his personal ascendency alone. Father of his country, "the god was speaking through the Father". What impresses Ellul is not the multiplication of portraits of de Gaulle, or his tomb as a place of pilgrimage: it is the dedication of votive offerings to him at cemeteries, the purchase of packets of earth from his grave, and the kissing of his tombstone.

Here we are exactly at the level of the veneration of relics, of the saint, of the sacred tomb. It is not a matter of the hero, of the "Great Man", nor of mementos, nor of expressions of gratitude, but precisely of religious acts directed towards the man who incarnated the spirit of the nation. It is an expression of the religious need of modern man, which focuses on all available objects.

(*op. cit.* p. 175)

Stringfellow makes the same point about America. He regards his own country not so much as Jerusalem, the ideal

162

community, but as Babylon, the modern embodiment of the Antichrist. His book is carefully argued and highly astringent. He sees the State as paramount among the principalities and powers, because of its authority over all other institutions within its borders. He sees the ultimate sanction of death wielded by the American State as a mark of the beast.

> Moral theology has failed to confront the principalities – institutions, systems, ideologies, and other political and social powers – as militant, aggressive and immensely influential creatures in this world as it is. We were familiar with their vital signs – the commerce of war, ecological corruption, racism, urban chaos, manipulation, coercion, practised deception in government, intimidation, intransigence to change, recourse to violence by agents of conformity and advocates of repression as well as some revolutionaries. Yet we remain gullible and ingenuous in the face of their usurpation of human life and domination of human beings.
>
> (*An Ethic for Christians and Other Strangers in a Strange Land,* p. 17)

Such is his theme, and he warns against absolutising democracy, against giving higher obedience to patriotism than to anything else, and being uncritical of the State and the other institutions within it. "These same principalities threaten and defy and enslave human beings of other status in diverse ways, but the most poignant victim of the demonic in America today is the so-called leader" (*op. cit.* p. 89).

### The demonic powers

Stringfellow gives an apt and up-to-date restatement of what the New Testament solemnly asserts: namely that the usurper prince of this world is the devil, and that his princes seek to dominate both men and nations. According to the most probable interpretation of Romans 13, the demonic powers may well operate in and through the authorities which hold sway in the State. That exegesis sprang from the horrors of the Second World War, and the sense of tragic inevitability at that time when good men were swept aside by forces too great for them to resist. Who can look back at those years of phenomenal destruction, the deaths of more than fifty million people, the genocide of the Jews, and the unbridled reign of evil in Germany, and *not* believe that there was something more at work than mere human beings? Who can regard the thrones and dominions and principalities mentioned in Colossians as merely names for theological non-entities, rather than mighty forces of evil active in the world of real men and nations?

To turn the religious instincts of men towards the political arena exclusively – this is part of the strategy of "the new demons" as Ellul calls them. And significantly enough there are signs of explicit reaching out to the dark powers in both Fascist and Communist camps. The link between a violent anti-God philosophy and recognition of the suzerainty of Satan is not fortuitous.

Richard Wurmbrand in *Was Marx a Satanist?* has gathered together the fruit of research into the early Karl Marx. He was, in his early teens, an enthusiastic Christian. Suddenly he changed round. It is not possible to demonstrate conclusively that he formed part of the highly secret Satanist cult, but they are known to have been operating near his home, and his early poems give considerable evidence that he became involved with them. He wrote a drama, 'Oulanem' which is an inversion of the name Emmanuel (God is with us). Inversion of prayers, holy words, crosses and so forth is a well attested Satanist practice. In this drama he pictures the abyss yawning in darkness, and himself wishing to draw the whole of mankind after him into this pit designed for the devil and his angels.

If there is something which devours,
I'll leap within it, though I bring the world to ruins,
The world which bulks between me and the abyss
I will smash it to pieces with my enduring curses.
I'll throw my arms around its harsh reality

Embracing me, the world will dumbly pass away
And then sink down to utter nothingness
Perished, with no existence; that would be really living.

He was only eighteen when he wrote thus. Already some crisis seems to have taken place in his life, in which he renounced his Christian faith and became filled with hate. In 'The Fiddler' he writes:

The hellish vapours rise and fill the brain
Till I go mad and my heart it utterly changed
See this sword? The prince of darkness
Sold it to me.

In a letter to his father he said, "A curtain had fallen. My holy of holies was rent asunder and new gods had to be installed." To which his father replies that Karl will only be happy "if your heart remains pure and beats humanly, and if no demon will be able to alienate your heart from better feelings".

Circumstantial evidence, and no more. But it is fairly strong. Marx did not become an atheist, but a God-hater. "I wish to avenge myself on the One who rules above," he cried. And in his poem "The Pale Maiden" he writes

Thus heaven I've forfeited,
I know it full well.
My soul once true to God
Is chosen for hell.

Engels too began as a Christian. After his first meeting with Marx he wrote of him as "a monster possessed by thousands of devils". But Engels also moved in Satanist circles, and it is not improbable that Bruno Bauer, the Tübingen professor who lost his chair for heresy, and was close to both Marx and Engels, was himself involved in occult practices. At all events this man, whose preposterous views of a second-century origin for Christianity became – and still remains – official Communist teaching, wrote to his friend Arnold Ruge on December 6, 1841:

I deliver lectures here at the university before a large audience. I don't recognise myself when I pronounce my blasphemies from the pulpit. They are so great that these children, whom nobody should offend, have their hair standing on end. While delivering the blasphemies I remember how I work piously at home writing an apology of the Holy Scriptures and of the Revelation. In any case, it is a very bad demon that possesses me as soon as I mount the pulpit, and I am so weak that I am compelled to yield to him . . . My spirit of blasphemy will be satisfied only if I am authorised to preach openly as professor of the atheistic system.

*(Marx-Engels*, 1927 edn. 1. 1.)

The occult links that are highly probable in the genesis of Communism are certain in the case of Hitler's National Socialism. Dr. Rollo May in *Love and Will* and Professor Hugh Trevor Roper in *The Last Days of Hitler* show how Hitler, Hess, Goebbels and Himmler were all fully involved in occult practices. But then so was much of Germany between the wars. In his book *We Have Seen Evil*, Rom Landau describes the country as riddled with all kinds of psychic currents, astrologers, fortune-tellers and the like. Christian beliefs, if held, were intellectual and emotional rather than life-changing. The precariousness of the present and hopelessness for the future led to an upsurge of occult questing: "Communication with 'the other side' was almost as common as that with a friend next door." It is perhaps a salutary warning to recall that a society so impregnated with the occult was unable to discern the dark influence in the Nazi leadership, at all events in its early days.

The principalities and powers, whether or not overtly recognised through occult worship, are active in every state, and none more so than the totalitarian, where the checks and balances of power have been removed. In Domitian's Rome, Hitler's Germany, Stalin's Russia or Mao's China the state becomes a pseudo-religion, and the Beast apes the Lamb. Happy the nation that perceives this, and acts before it is too late.

## Transcendental Meditation

Before me as I write are two documents. One is a newspaper, with the information that the Maharishi Mahesh Yogi's Transcendental Meditation movement is proposing to buy up the Meccano factory in Liverpool. If they do, the 930 workers will be required to meditate for two hours a day, though this need not involve the lotus position but can be done sitting in an easy chair. The article (*Daily Telegraph*, Jan 17, 1980) repeats the claim of the movement that when one per cent of the people in an area practise transcendental meditation crime is reduced and a state of general harmony is advanced.

The other is a lavishly produced journal, sent to the Education Office in Oxford "Making Education Ideal Through the Transcendental Meditation Programme and the Science of Creative Intelligence". As if that were not enough it has a subtitle, "A Proposal to Governments for a Complete System of Education". It claims that now there is overwhelming evidence that the Transcendental Meditation Programme not only produces the state of enlightenment in individual life – the realisation of man's full potential – but also structures the qualities of an ideal society, thus bringing invincibility to the nation and peace to the world. Needless to say, the document pleads that T.M. be introduced into education at every level. I was intrigued to see a map with the claim that world peace had been achieved in South-East Asia, Iran, the Middle East, Central America and South Africa after the Maharishi sent teams to teach T.M. there! What is this remarkable panacea, and what does it offer?

## The Maharishi

Transcendental Meditation, as taught by India's Maharishi Mahesh Yogi is making considerable advances all over the world. People in every spectrum of society are beginning to practise T.M. as a means of mental and physical relaxation which brings relief from stress and an expansion of awareness. Housewives, businessmen, scientists, senior military men, prisoners, students and even young children are all "meditating". T.M. has recently been taught in many schools and colleges, prisons and business houses as a required part of the curriculum, not least in the U.S.A.

Maharishi was born in India in 1918, graduated in physics from Allahabad University, and thereafter became a favoured disciple of "His Holiness Swami Brahmananda Saraswati Jagadguru, Bhagwan, Shankaracharya of Jyotir Math" (Shri Guru Dev for short), who was at that time one of India's four greatest Hindu teachers. Just before Swami died, he commissioned Maharishi to evolve a simple form of meditation which anyone could learn and practise. Maharishi agreed, went into the Himmalayas for a couple of years of reflection, and emerged with a yoga technique he called Transcendental Meditation. He made little progress in India: religious Hindus despised his adulteration of their ethnic faith. So he decided to bring it to the West. He sought recognition in both America and Britain, but first achieved fame when he became the guru of the Beatles. Now, despite their rapid disillusionment with him, his movement is reputed to have taken root in nearly a hundred and fifty countries, and was at one stage growing at a rate of forty thousand a month. This has however sharply decreased since the Supreme Court judgement in the U.S.A. found against the movement.

### A meditative technique
T.M. like other forms of yoga, is portrayed as a harmless non-religious means to relaxation and the attaining of at least "the fourth state of consciousness". This lies beyond waking, sleeping and dreaming: you are totally aware of your surroundings, and yet you gain relaxation more satisfying than can be had from a good night's sleep. The advertisements in the streets tell you that T.M. is so simple that it can be learned by anyone, that it demands no more than two sessions of twenty minutes a day, that it develops creative intelligence, and ensures freedom from stress and full development of the individual's powers. If you practise it you will be less liable to psychosomatic ailments like heart disease and ulcers.

168

## Attractive goals

It has further attractions. You are not presented with any dogma, at all events to begin with. You are not required to make any change in religion, philosophical tenets, moral stances or commitments for the future. No asceticism is required in this easy-going opiate from the East (greatly to the annoyance of other Hindu teachers). It offers to the individual peace of mind, consciousness of bliss and absence of stress, for the price of half an hour or so twice a day putting the mind into neutral and reciting the sacred mantra. It appeals quite overtly to the selfishness which wants to have your cake and eat it. Happiness and material prosperity are quite compatible in the Maharishi's teaching. It is hardly surprising that this has a considerable pull in the materialistic West.

Shrewdly, therefore, the Maharishi has promoted his meditative techniques in as neutral a guise as possible, appealing not merely to the longing in the individual for fulfilment but to the need for integration in society. The seven goals set forward in *An Address to Governments* are as follows:

1. To develop the full potential of the individual
2. To improve governmental achievements
3. To realise the highest ideal of education
4. To maximise the intelligent use of the environment
5. To solve the problems of crime, drug abuse, and all behaviour that brings unhappiness to the family of man
6. To bring fulfilment to the economic aspirations of individuals and society
7. To achieve the spiritual goals of mankind in this generation

Pretty comprehensive goals, are they not? They cover the personal, political, educational, ecological, social, economic and spiritual aspects of life. Naturally, the spiritual goal is soft-pedalled in much of the West, and the whole thing presented in terms of scientific technique as an educative device which is essential for the fulfilment of men and nations.

## A branch of Hinduism

What you are not told is that T.M. is essentially a branch of Hinduism. All pretence that it is non-religious is a deception. T.M. stems directly from the Shankara tradition within Hinduism. The Maharishi himself acknowledges the tradition which maintains that the practice of T.M. passes through cycles of decline and revival following its initial revelation to the warrior Arjuna by Lord Krishna some five thousand years ago. One such revival took place under the Hindu philosopher Shankara and now another under Guru Dev. T.M. is, in fact, a revival of ancient Indian Brahmanism. Its origins lie in the sacred texts of the Vedas, Upanishads and especially the Bhagavad-Gita. And when the teachers of T.M. claim that there is a field of Creative Intelligence underlying all life, they are merely expressing in other words the impersonal Brahman or "Being" which, in the monism* of Hinduism, is presumed to underlie all existence. T.M. is absolutely steeped in Eastern monism or pantheism. And if you worship all being, and confuse the creature with the Creator you are in serious danger of falling under the influence of the principalities and powers which owe no allegiance to the God and Father of Jesus Christ. C. S. Lewis issues a shrewd warning on pantheism in *Miracles* (p. 84 f).

> Modern Europe escaped it only while she remained Christian . . . So far from being the final religious refinement, pantheism is in fact the permanent natural bent of the human mind; the permanent ordinary level below which man sometimes sinks . . . but above which his own unaided efforts can never raise him for very long . . . It is the attitude into which the human mind automatically falls when left to himself. No wonder we find it congenial. If "religion" means simply what man says about God and not what God says about man, then pantheism almost *is* religion.

* "Monism" is that philosophical theory, common in the East, which resolves all individuation into one. It solves the problem of unity and diversity by subordinating all diversity to a supposed underlying unity in the universe.

And "religion" in that sense has, in the long run, only one really formidable opponent – namely Christianity. Modern philosophy . . . and modern science . . . have both proved quite powerless to curb the human impulse towards pantheism . . . Yet, by a strange irony, each new relapse into this immemorial "religion" is hailed as the last word in novelty and emancipation.

Despite this manifestly Hindu background to the movement, it comes to us in secular guise denying its spiritual origins. And it does this in order to gain adherents in the secular cultures of the West.

## Initiation ceremony

The Hindu background of T.M. is emphasised not only by its origins but by its initiation ceremony. You become a member not merely by paying a substantial sum of money and attending a short preliminary instruction. You also have to undergo the initiation ceremony of Hindus following the tradition of the Shankara, and bring offerings of six flowers (representing life), three pieces of fruit (representing the seed of life) and a white handkerchief (representing cleansing). You remove your shoes and are led into a small incense-filled room lit by candles. There is a table holding a picture of the Maharishi's teacher, Shri Guru Dev. The initiate is placed before an altar and the teacher begins to sing in Sanskrit the *puja*, a Vedic hymn of worship acknowledging Hindu deities. This is, not unnaturally, never translated for the initiate. However in 1975 the Spiritual Counterfeits project of Berkeley, California obtained T.M.'s own translation from an ex-teacher. According to this version, the *puja* consists of three parts.

Part one is a recitation of the names of gods and masters through whom the secret knowledge of the mantras has passed: each one is worshipped. Part two consists in the offering of the sacrificial gifts to the feet of Shri Guru Dev, accompanied by the words "I bow down". Part three is an overt act of worship to Shri Guru Dev who is identified with the three gods of the Hindu Trimurti, Brahma, Vishnu and Shiva, as the "personified fulness of Brahman".

When the *puja* is completed, teacher and initiate are encouraged to kneel at the altar and the newcomer is given his *mantra*, the secret Sanskrit word(s) to be used only in his meditating and to be repeated continuously. The mantra sounds meaningless and you are told that it is personal for yourself alone, having been specially chosen in the light of your own needs, character and so forth. In point of fact the mantra is either the name of a Hindu deity or is designed by its vibrations to invoke one. And there appear to be only sixteen of them, not an infinite number – but since you are sworn to secrecy, this is not something you are likely to find out!

In a word, the whole ceremony is explicitly idolatrous, but since it is conducted in Sanskrit most initiates do not realise what is happening.

**Religious character**

The Hindu nature of T.M. comes out clearly enough in other ways. The Maharishi's analysis of consciousness into seven states, ranging from sleeping, dreaming, waking, through to Unity-consciousness is quintessential Hindu monism. The fact that the only scriptures cited by the movement are the Bhagavad-Gita, and more especially the Maharishi's translation and commentary on those scriptures, points in the same direction. So does the fact that those authorised to teach T.M. have all been initiated into the beliefs and techniques of yoga; the very word means "union" in Sanskrit. Yoga offers man union with Brahman. It is hardly surprising, therefore, that when the T.M. movement was charged in the U.S. Federal Court with unconstitutionally teaching religion in the public schools (despite their claim to be non-religious), they lost. After careful scrutiny of the evidence, the Court concluded that T.M. was religious and therefore could no longer be taught under the umbrella of State Schools and Institutions in America. T.M. appealed against this decision to the Federal Court of Appeals, where they lost again. This was obviously a very serious setback to the T.M. movement in the U.S.A., and may well have provided an added incentive to the penetration of Britain.

## Eastern monism
If Transcendental Meditation is clearly religious, it is equally clearly incompatible with the claims and the message of Jesus Christ. A few examples of the Maharishi's teaching should suffice to demonstrate this. Naturally, coming from a monistic background, he denies a personal creator God. "With the dissolution of creation, the almighty, personal God also merges into the impersonal, absolute state of the Supreme" (*The Science of Being and Art of Living*, p. 277). Man, to the Maharishi, is basically good and his failings can be solved through meditating. "Simplicity and innocence are already deeply rooted in the very nature of each individual," he maintains (*op. cit.* p. 104). "Each individual is, in his true nature, the impersonal God. That is why the Vedic philosophy of the Upanishads declares, 'I am That, thou are That, and all this is That'" (p. 276). This is Eastern monism again: all men partake in the Brahman – what they need to do is to realise it. Thus "all suffering is due to ignorance of a way to unfold the divine glory which is present within oneself" (p. 81). I doubt whether that would have been much consolation to the victims of Hiroshima.

## Consequences
Once you grant the premise of monism, there is no basic distinction between good and evil: the universe consists in one basic stuff. So there can inevitably be no code of morality or goodness. This is part of the charm of T.M. for modern hedonistic men. It makes no moral claims. But this is one of its most sinister facets, in which, despite apparent similarities, it is totally at odds with Christian mysticism. The Christian mystical tradition, starting with the New Testament, has always insisted that you do not become absorbed into the One: you have deep relationship with the personal source of life, Almighty God. And this relationship does not leave you unchanged. It rebukes your moral evil, transforms your desires and issues in love to others,

173

including the hungry, needy and unattractive. You need only contrast the impact of the Maharishi and Mother Theresa, both of whom live in Calcutta, on their city of appalling need, to see the difference. If you believe that suffering is an illusion, that "the basic premise in every religion should be that man need not suffer in life" (*op. cit.* p. 260), it will drive you in a completely different direction from the belief that "he who does not love his brother whom he has seen, cannot love God whom he has not seen" (1 John 4:20). The criterion of authentic mysticism must always be ethical. And this is where the teachings of T.M. fail disastrously. It does nothing to challenge the wickedness or transform the way of life of its practitioners. It merely enables them to relax and do their own thing, whatever it may be, better. The Maharishi has himself put it with admirable succinctness. "The path of enlightenment is, we could say, a path of self-hypnotism" (*Transcendental Meditation*, p. 279). Absorbed in self-fulfilment and the quest for bliss, the meditator hypnotises himself by means of his mantra and is oblivious to the needs of others. It is essentially egocentric. All Eastern monism must be. Believing that every man has the divine spark within him, they devote their attention to realising and liberating that element for absorption into the One. Inevitably, therefore, there is some self-deification in the process. Meditation enables us to realise our real selves. "Although we are all 100 per cent divine, consciously we do not know that we are divine," writes the Maharishi (*The Science of Being*, p. 81). Hence the need to meditate. But this self-deification is exceedingly dangerous. It not only confuses the Creator with the creature, but blinds man to his own wickedness and sin whilst fostering his arrogance and self-esteem.

R. C. Zaehner, Professor of Eastern Religions and Ethics at Oxford, in his book *Hindu and Muslim Mysticism* sharply criticises this tendency to self-deification with Hinduism:

> In Hindu terminology he (Abu Yazid) sees himself not only as Brahman but as Isvara too, so he has no scruple in exclaiming, "I am the Lord Most High" or more

preposterously still: "Verily, I am – there is no God but me, so worship me"

(op. cit. p. 114)

T.M. makes great claims, as we have seen. It is set out as the panacea for ignorance, drugs, environmental pollution, incompetent government, personal frustrations and crime. It backs up its claims with a mass of "scientific proof". However, most of the experiments are set up by the proponents of the movement, and those that are not show conflicting results. A careful analysis of some of the major research in this area is to be found in *T.M. Wants You* by Haddon and Hamilton (Baker). It seems clear that while many of the claims are fraudulent or open to question, the practice of meditating for forty minutes a day does relieve strain and tension: but so would lying relaxed on your bed for half an hour after lunch.

### Dangers

The dangers of T.M. have not escaped notice. Repetition of the mantra with its attendant self-hypnotism tends to break down the barriers between the conscious and subconscious mind. In some people this leads to psychological disorders. T.M. frequently, for the same reason, produces in its practitioners a sense of separation from the material universe, leading to depersonalisation and loss of individual identity. This is to be expected, granted the premise of Hindu monism which underlies the whole procedure. Moreover, whilst removing some of the strain and stress in life, T.M. does not and cannot touch the deeper underlying causes of that stress, and so does not deal with the roots of the problem. Accordingly, it may well remove any motivation to work through and resolve personal problems. It is a psychological aspirin.

### The demonic factor

But much the most serious danger in T.M. is exposure to the possibility of negative spiritual forces: in a word, the Satanic. You have only to believe that there is no essential difference between good and evil; you have only to open yourself up entirely to admit the forces of the universe – and the possibility of influence by the forces of evil is obvious. Self-emptying without any ethical or spiritual criteria is at best undiscriminating and at worst disastrous. How the Enemy laughs at man's naïveté!

Moreover, as we have seen, the whole world view behind yoga is monism, dedicated to breaking down the differentia between conscious and subconscious, good and evil, joy and suffering, the divine and the human. The basic philosophy is fallacious, and it is not surprising that deception marks the methodology of the leadership of this movement. The "deceiver of the brethren" is delighted.

The motivation for yoga is self-improvement. It is to deliver the self from its supposed imprisonment and release it by the self-redemption of meditation to discover its true deity. This makes the practitioner of yoga utterly self-centred. He is taken up with his own betterment. And the supremely selfish Enemy of souls is gratified by this reproduction of his likeness.

The mantra itself may appear to be prayer. Maharishi refers to T.M. as a "form of prayer", but what he means by this seems to be a kind of ritual invocation of certain spiritual entities and an opening of oneself to receive a communication of non-cognitive spiritual energies from these beings. There is no I-Thou relationship, but rather self-hypnotism and magic. The mantra, steeped in Hinduism, is not only a repudiation of the interpersonal and rational: it is an opening up to the heathen and the occult. "The fact that mantras are kept secret from the public in general and that the powers behind them are kept secret from the beginner confirms that the mantras are not to be compared with a prayer or meditation in the biblical sense. Mantras are magic words or formulae. They can most readily be compared with the gnostic Abraxas." So Ernst Gogler, a Swiss specialist in Indian culture, in the periodical *Kirchenboten*, September 1974. Yoga practices have, of course, long been connected with occult powers. Mircea Eliade writes, "In India a yogi was always regarded as a mahasiddha, one who possessed occult powers" (*Yoga* p. 97) and these supernatural powers, *siddhis*, are still held

176

out as an inducement to the advanced yoga student. These same *siddhis* have also been made an integral part of the T.M. package in the last three years. The Satanic handiwork is obvious.

## Lit-sen Chang

Finally, the devilish origin of Transcendental Meditation, at first sight so harmless not to say beneficial, is emphasised by those who have emerged from its clutches into Christian faith. Professor Lit-sen Chang, a distinguished Chinese academic, was deep into mantra-meditation for over fifty years: indeed, he was on his way to India to promote a resurgent movement of Buddhism, when he was converted to Christianity in Indonesia. He is emphatic about the demonic nature of what he once practised. "The mantra is an active symbol of a particular deity, and if a person meditates and repeats a mantra enough whilst making the effort to identify himself with it, the meditator becomes one with the deity . . . But according to the Bible the gods worshipped by the Hindus are false gods – actually they are demon spirits. In Ps. 96:5 (LXX) there is a definite statement concerning pagan gods: 'All gods of the peoples are demons.' So the pagan gods of the Hindu faith are Satan's counterfeits, demons in God's clothing. The essence of the mantra is an invitation to a demon spirit to take control of one's faculties." (*Transcendental Meditation*, p. 21). He tells of his own deep involvement both in T.M. and Zen, the healings and séances he experienced, and his recognition of these spiritual forces as demons since his conversion to Christianity. He pleads with "the West who are 'under the control of the evil one' (1 John 5:19) in the disastrous trend of T.M. craze – 'Do not believe every spirit, but test the spirits to see whether they are from God, because many false spirits have gone out into the world' (1 John 4:1)".

## Vail Hamilton

By way of cultural contrast, Vail Hamilton is an American girl who became a teacher of T.M. She writes:

177

The first effect of meditation was a calming of my mind and an altering of awareness, which gradually got better than being high on marijuana, so I discontinued smoking pot. As my consciousness changed, I began to become aware of the presence of spirit beings sitting on either side of me when I was meditating . . . I did not consider the possibility of Satan or his demons at the time but just accepted it as a really weird trip . . . After four years of meditating . . . I awoke one night with a sense of fear and apprehension because a spirit was putting pressure all over my body and head in an attempt to enter and take possession of my body. I commanded it to leave, and resisted it until it left. I did not fully realise the implications of this oppression until later. I began to experience other supernatural sensations – ESP and clairvoyance, telepathy, and the beginnings of astral travel.

> (*T.M. Wants You*, David Haddon &
> Vail Hamilton, p. 67f).

She had this to say after her conversion:

Since becoming a Christian I have encountered the same kind of spirits I used to experience during T.M. The Lord has given me discernment, and I now see that they are demons. Before I became a Christian the demons seldom bothered me, and I even mistook them for guardian angels at times. But after I was born again in Christ, they became very hostile and tried to overpower me on several occasions. They always had to leave when I commanded them to go in the name of Jesus. The Bible says that Satan often comes as an angel of light to deceive people.

> (*op. cit.* p. 73).

**Rabindranath Maharaj**
The third testimony I wish to adduce for the demonic element within Transcendental Meditation is both explicit and moving. It comes from yet another cultural scene, and

is contained in Rabindranath Maharaj's book, *Death of a Guru*. It tells of how Rabindranath, descended from a long line of Brahmin priests and trained as a yogi, found his way to liberation in Christ after many inward struggles and much disillusionment. It gives a very honest and clear description of Hindu life and customs in Trinidad, and the sense of struggle against principalities and powers of darkness is paramount. His father was a distinguished yogi, hailed by many as an *avatar*. Early on in the book there is a terrible description of Rabi's inconsolable grief at his father's cremation; then of the assiduous attentions of palmists and astrologers predicting for him a bright future as a spiritual leader. But as he practised his yoga he began to have terrifying encounters with the spirit world. The house became haunted by the spirit of the dead Nana. Members of the household sensed the activity of Shiva, the Destroyer, in such incidents as being slapped by invisible hands and knocked over when studying late at night. Rabi found himself at times possessed of a supernatural strength and occult powers. But when faced by imminent death in the bush through a great black snake, Rabi in terror called on the name of Jesus for help. He suddenly recalled his mother saying years beforehand, "If you are ever in real danger, and nothing else seems to work, there's another god you can pray to. His name is Jesus." So he cried "Jesus, help me", and at once the snake turned round and wriggled away. This incident had a profound impact on him and he began his search, which culminated in his conversion some time later. Meanwhile he wrestled with questions like these: "Who were these gods and spirits and forces that I invited to come into me through *nyasa* and yoga and meditation? Were they evil or good, or both – or was everything *maya*, and I insane to try and make sense of it?" (*op. cit.* p. 108). Such things brought him to the verge of suicide, and it was at this juncture that he found forgiveness and release through the gospel of Jesus Christ, of which he later became an effective preacher. "Astral travel to other planets, yogic visions and higher states of consciousness in deep meditation – all these things, once so thrilling and self-exalting, had become dust and ashes. What I was experi-

179

encing now was not just another psychic trip. I was sure of that . . . I knew He had made me a new person on the inside. Never had I been so genuinely happy" (p. 137). So without anybody suggesting it to him, he made a pile of amulets, fetishes, pictures, lingams and other heathen paraphernalia and burnt them publicly, a thing he would never have dared to do had he not come to know the love and liberation of Christ. Needless to say, he had to face a lot of persecution, but it did nothing to lessen his faith. He came to the West, and his assessment of the whole deceptiveness of the monistic background in which he had been nurtured seems to me to be worth repeating. He was struck by the fact that a Cambridge student friend of his, a musical genius deep into the drug culture, had without any exposure to Hindu philosophy come to precisely the same views of the world as Rabi himself had espoused when a yogi:

I began to ponder and to pray earnestly about the fact that so many addicts – though not all by any means – had the same experience as yogis: what one got on drugs the other got through Eastern meditation. I learned that drugs caused altered states of consciousness similar to those experienced in meditation, making it possible for demons to manipulate the neurons of the brain and create all manner of seemingly real experiences that were actually deceptive tricks played on the mind. The same evil spirits that had led me ever deeper into meditation to gain control of me were obviously behind the drug movement, and for the same diabolical purpose. I began to see that the same Satanic strategy lay behind drugs, meditation, free sex, and the rebelliousness of youth expressed in the hippie movement that was just beginning in those days, and embodied in certain music like that of the Beatles and the Rolling Stones. I remember a Rolling Stones concert where about 250,000 gathered in Hyde Park after the death of Brian Jones from a drug overdose. There were as stoned on the music as they were on hash and LSD.

As he reflected on his own future in the light of his background and conversion he continues:

It startled me most of all to discover the philosophy behind the whole counterculture of drugs, rebellion and rock music was basically Hinduism: the same lies about the unity of all life, vegetarianism, evolving upward to union with the Universe, and doing one's own thing. I discovered that young people by the thousands were not just dropping out to turn on with drugs; they were taking up Transcendental Meditation and various other forms of yoga. Their whole way of thinking became clouded by Eastern mysticism. Nearly all began to accept reincarnation, which ended any belief in Christ's resurrection: the two were absolute opposites.

Slowly, and with a growing sense of alarm, I became convinced that Satan was masterminding an invasion of the West with Eastern mysticism. I could see that few Christians really understood his plan and were prepared to combat it. Could it be that God was preparing me, an ex-Hindu, to sound a warning alarm to millions in the West who were falling for an Eastern philosophy that I knew was false?

(*op. cit.* p. 169f)

False religion, particularly when skilfully disguised, remains an invaluable strategic tool in the hands of the Enemy. "Even Satan disguises himself as an angel of light . . . We are not ignorant of his designs" (2 Cor. 11:14, and 2:11).

### Marks of Counterfeit Religion in Colossians

We have looked at three representative examples of counterfeit religion; overt false religion, heathen religion masquerading in educational and scientific guise, and an ideology opposed to religion but exercising "religious", because total, claims on its adherents. None of these three manifestations of the Satanic is new. We are warned of all of them in Scripture, and one of the most illuminating places is the Epistle of Paul to the Colossians. It offers us at least eight indicators of counterfeit religion.

## Counterfeit religion at Colossae

All heresy has some truth admixed with its error, and the Colossian heresy was no exception. But it was dangerous because it was syncretistic, and Christianity is the declared foe of syncretism. There were Jewish elements at Colossae: sabbaths (2:16) and circumcision (2:13) for sure; and perhaps a false philosophy (2:8) and a new cultus (2:18, 21) though these may just as easily have come from pagan sources. For Colossae, situated as it was in the Lycus valley in Asia Minor, was just the place for a cultural and religious *pot-pourri*. Cthonic deities like Attis, Sabazius and the age-old fertility goddess Cybele were worshipped in this area. Thales of Miletus, situated nearby, had centuries before Christ declared that the whole world was alive with spirits and full of "daimons", while Heraclitus had asserted that all things were in a state of flux. It was a natural place for heresy in the church to breed.

Nobody knows precisely what the Colossian heresy was, because we can do no more than listen to one end of a telephone conversation about it, Paul's end. However it is sufficiently clear that salvation was being advocated by means of a philosophy which Paul saw to be empty and counterfeit. It included the mediation of angelic spirits of some sort or other. It involved either the "elemental spirits" of the universe or else "basic teachings" of Judaism, depending on how you understand *stoicheia* (2:8). There was undoubtedly a spiritual élitism of the sort later found among the Gnostics, suggesting that salvation lay in the knowledge which they alone possessed (3:11). And there was a combination of the paradoxical extremes of asceticism and sensuality (2:21–23 and 3:1ff). How did Paul handle such a farrago? What can we learn from his treatment of the nature of false teaching generally?

## 1. A false philosophy (2:8)

Paul is not against philosophy: no lover of God could be opposed to the pursuit of wisdom. But he is opposed to that philosophy which is empty deceit. It is not entirely clear what this philosophy was at Colossae, but it probably fell into one or other of these two broad categories, which remain dangerously common today.

The first is monism. This is the view, to which we have already devoted a good deal of attention in the previous pages, which obliterates the distinction between God and his world. It is one of the classic ways of resolving the problem of the one and the many, a quest which had a perennial fascination for Greek philosophy. The answer given at Colossae may well have been to lose the many in the one. Hence the network of intermediaries they relied on, the thrones, dominions, principalities, and authorities alluded to in 1:16. Whatever the case at Colossae, monism is today one of the major intellectual forces in the world. It underlies most Eastern religions and cults. "There is only one without a second," says the Vedanta. And that is typical. All that differentiates us is due to depart. We shall be absorbed into the one. There is no real creation, only the illusion of it in a soul overpowered by ignorance and in desperate need of the illumination afforded by monism. Men are constantly deceived by *maya*, illusion. Neither the world around us nor ourselves have substantive reality. The only reality is Brahman, ultimate Being.

This is the outlook underlying Hinduism, Buddhism, Islamic Sufism and Eastern thought at large. It has enormous consequences. Naturally it tends to break down the divide between perceiver and object, between the human and the divine, between flesh and spirit. Naturally it is uninterested in natural science – for this belongs to the world of illusion. And naturally, too, it does little to try to assuage suffering or to promote love. In the long run, neither are important, for our human individuality is not important. It is due to be absorbed into the Absolute.

The second broad philosophical category which may have given rise to the Colossian heresy is dualism. This is the view which solves the problem of the one and the many by

183

absolutising the division between the two. The barriers between God and his world are absolute. God is spirit and the world material. Therefore the world must be the product of some inferior Workman (or demiourge), and the good spiritual God is only remotely linked to the evil, material world by means of an ever more crass line of intermediaries (? thrones, dominions, principalities, authorities). The world of time and sense is an evil thing, imprisoning the soul whose destiny is to escape from the material prison to the divine. How is this escape ensured? By a secret knowledge available to the few. How should one then live? It does not matter. You can either live it up in luxury and lust: nothing merely material can affect your immortal soul, that chip of the heavenly block within your mortal body. Or else you can don the hair shirt and sleep on beds of nails and meditate until you are a walking skeleton. In this way you will minimise the shackles of the material and facilitate the return of the soul to God.

This view, like the monistic, has a horde of followers. It was very popular among the Gnostics of old, and remains popular among their modern counterparts like Christian Science and Theosophy. It has a strong hold on the Christian tradition, both in the Manicheans of old and in those today who set Satan up into an equal and opposite power to God, or who put all their eggs in the heavenly basket, neglecting socio-political obligations on earth.

Monism and dualism are the only two logical views you can hold of the relation between finite and infinite, God and the world, good and evil. The only two, that is, outside the Judaeo-Christian revelation. This does not come from "the traditions of men", but by revelation from the God who discloses himself as both Creator and Redeemer, as both spirit and the source of all life, as both transcendent and immanent within this world in the person of Jesus Christ. The Judaeo-Christian alternative to monism and dualism has great power. It gives a real meaning to the world and to our human bodies: for God made our world, then shared our human state. Both are therefore important, to be rejoiced in, and yet not ultimate. Suffering is neither illusion nor retribution: it is, corporately and individually, one face of a fallen world – a world which is not as the Creator made it or as the Redeemer will refashion it. The relation between the one and the many is neither absorption nor eternal counterpoint. It will be the relation of love between the Creator who redeems and the redeemed who respond. Such a philosophy of life is coherent and profound. There is no need to combine it with that philosophy which is empty deceit, according to human tradition. For that human tradition, be it dualistic or monistic, is in bondage to the elemental spirits of the universe and not to Christ.

## 2. A broken bridge (2:9)

How can finite and fallen man have dealings with an infinite and perfect deity? That remains one of the fundamental questions of mankind. What is the bridge over the troubled water of sin and finitude? The mediators espoused at Colossae were ineffective. They were either so human that they were not divine, or the reverse. They either crowded round one end of the bridge or the other. But they did not span the gulf. That was achieved only by Jesus Christ, firmly anchored on both sides of the divine. He was one with God and one with us. In him the whole fulness of deity dwells (2:9).

Many cults today will allow some place to Jesus Christ, but not the supreme and only place. They wish to supplement him in some way or other. Almost all serious heresy has a defective Christology. He is either seen as so divine as not really to be part of our world (Docetism) or so much one of us that he is not really divine (Ebionism). The pendulum has swung between these two possibilities throughout the ages, and often in Christian circles. Much Roman Catholic teaching, much Evangelical teaching has presented a Christ so beyond us that it is hard to identify with him: and in some Roman Catholic theologies there is therefore a chain of mediators between us and Jesus, consisting of the Virgin Mary and the saints. By way of contrast, much modern theology, including the "Death of God" and "Myth" theologies of recent times, react against the transcendence of Jesus, and make him so much one of us that he is just that and no more. The cults, for their part, make him part of a scenario whose chief figure lies elsewhere – Jesus Christ *and* Mary Baker Eddy, for instance, or Jesus Christ *and* Mr. Moon.

Jesus is *the only* and *the sufficient* bridge between God and man. Examine any suspected cult by its Christology. Does it present us with the Word made flesh? Does it maintain that "in him dwells all the fulness of the godhead in bodily form" (2:9)? Every word of that sentence is polemical. "In him" – and in no one else. "Dwells" – that is, "has its permanent abode": Paul uses the strongest of the Greek words for "to dwell". "All the fulness": the heretics used this word "fulness" to describe the divine attributes, and they seem to have distributed them among a variety of mediators, the thrones and principalities of which Paul speaks. The apostle asserts that "all the fulness" has its permanent abode in Jesus, and in him alone. There are in Greek two words for deity: and when Paul writes "godhead" here, he is deliberately using the stronger word. The final thrust of his claim comes with the last word, as provocative in Greek as in English, *bodily*. He is maintaining that not in some ideal, ethereal Christ, but in the human Jesus who walked the streets of Palestine, the fulness of God was permanently located, and in him alone. It is a mighty claim of the sufficiency and uniqueness of Christ. "He is the image of the invisible God, the firstborn of all creation. For in him all things were created, in heaven and on earth, visible and invisible, whether thrones or dominions, or principalities or authorities – all things were created through him and for him. He is before all things, and in him all things hold together. He is the head of the body, the church . . ." (1:15f). In this amazing passage Paul presses his Christological point. Christ is the visible representation of God in the only terms we can take it in, the terms of a human life. Whatever other spiritual beings there may be (even if they have, like Satan, become rebel spirits), they derive their life from him who shared in creation with his Father. He is the source of all things in heaven and earth. He is the goal of all things in heaven and earth. He is the principle of coherence of all things in heaven and earth.

And it is this cosmic Christ, and none other, who is the head of his body, the church. There is no other bridge between the finite and infinite, between God and man, than he. But that is a great stumbling-block to the cults.

### 3. A ring road round Calvary (1:20, 2:13f)

It seems that at Colossae the false teachers were neglecting or denying the significance of the cross. This is hardly surprising if the person of Jesus was inadequately perceived. Paul insists that the bridge between God and man is cruciform. There full reconciliation was made, and in no other place. You were spiritually dead, and there at Calvary he brought you to life (2:13). You belonged to the uncircumcised outsiders, and there at Calvary you received the spiritual circumcision which brought you into God's household (2:13). You were in debt to God with all your sins, and there at Calvary he cancelled the debt, nailing it to his cross (2:13f). You were under the power of forces you could not conquer, and there at Calvary Christ disarmed those powers and triumphed over them (2:16). You were hostile to him in your mind, hostile and estranged, and there at Calvary he made peace by the blood of his cross and reconciled you in order to present you blameless before the Father (1:20ff). Christianity can in no way tolerate a ring road round Calvary. If the incarnation is the revelation of God to man, the cross is the reconciliation of men to God.

But counterfeit religion finds the cross a scandal. It seeks to evade it, by one expedient or another. The two most common are to say "Forgiveness – naturally, that's God's job!" or to say "Forgiveness – that's a beggar's refuge. We must work our passage." The former is the way of monism. Nothing, including sin, will eventually be able to keep the many from the one. The latter is the way of dualism. The divide is real: you have to do your best to bridge it. And doing your best is the key to this false philosophy. It is essentially anthropocentric.

Examples of the monist and the dualist abound. The Divine Light Mission, Zen and Bahai, like most Eastern faiths, refuse to take evil seriously: forgiveness is not really a problem, for there is no personal God whose holiness has been affronted, merely an Absolute into which we shall eventually be merged, as all rivers eventually flow into the sea. Jehovah's Witnesses are a good example of the second position. They are taught that the judgement at the end of the thousand years will depend entirely on their works. Unitarians believe that their salvation lies in "moral values and spiritual insights". Theosophy teaches that man is saved by working out his own *karma*. All such avenues lead to despair or delusion. No partial reconciliation by mediators angelic or human can suffice; only total reconciliation through the cross of Jesus who is both human and divine. Christ is indispensable both to revelation and to redemption. He alone spans the gulf between the infinite and the finite, between a holy God and sinful men.

### 4. A bogus ceremonialism (2:11, 21)

"Touch not, taste not, handle not" were the parrot cries of the false teachers. They clearly insisted on certain external behaviour patterns. They fussed about drink, food, the correct festivals and the observance of new moons (2:16). There were manifestly certain legalistic tests for belonging to their company. Indeed, a recently discovered inscription has given the clue to the strange phrase *ha heoraken embateuōn* (2:18). It probably means "taking his stand on the visions he received during his initiation".

There were many such cults in antiquity, notably the Eleusinian and other Mysteries. Their modern counterparts are movements like the Masons, comparatively secret societies placing a lot of emphasis on cultic initiation and advancement. The same is, as we have seen, true of T.M. and it is a common feature in the cults at large. It is interesting to see how Paul handles this overemphasis on the ceremonial. He takes both baptism, the initiation mark of the New Covenant, and circumcision, which brought men into the Old Covenant, and relates them to Christ (2:11, 12). Christ is the reality to which the initiation rites point, because he alone is the mediator between God and men. No mythical dying-and-rising ceremonies of the Eleusinian Mysteries or the Adonis cult could do for man what Christ had achieved through his incarnation and atonement. To be sure, the cults speak of brotherhood and initiation for their members. But if you are a Christian, and have been initiated into Christ through his death and resurrection, marked upon you in baptism, what more do you want? It is the most marvellous and all-embracing family on earth. Any other initiation or fellowship (if regarded as essential) is both a slur on Jesus Christ and a diminution of the brotherhood he came to bring.

### 5. A shallow moralism (2:20–3:11)
If the body is theologically indifferent, you are at liberty either to mortify it or abuse it. It seems that both courses were being adopted at Colossae. In 2:16–23 Paul attacks the mortification brigade; in 3:1–11 the licentious. It is obvious enough why he is unhappy about the "fornication, impurity, evil desire and covetousness" of the latter. On no showing could such a life pass as Christian; though it is salutary to remember that all down the centuries this sort of behaviour has followed, as surely as night follows day, from the premise that God is only interested in our souls and not in our bodies.

More surprising at first sight is why he should attack those who restrained their natural desires, and were very careful about what they ate, drank, looked at and did. Actually his assault was very shrewd and very necessary. He mounts it partly because external restraints and legalistic rules are powerless to curb the "flesh", that strong fallen self which is part of us all. Indeed, in the original Greek there seems to be a bitter satire at the end of 2:23, indicating that far from checking indulgence legalism often leads to it, as the pent-up waters inside a dam sometimes burst over the top. But at a more profound level Paul attacks legalism because of its basic assumption that the body is evil and the spirit good. That he knows to be sheer self-delusion. In fact, the body is neutral and the spirit corrupt. It needs to be put off (3:9). It needs to be taken to the cross with Christ and put to death so that his risen life can flood the personality of the believer (3:1, 3, 5, 12).

It is because the Colossians adopted this wrong view of

matter that Paul deals so uncompromisingly with legalism here, in contrast to his liberal approach in Romans 14. There is no harm in renouncing certain actions for the sake of Christ and out of love for him. We should respect one another in this matter even when we do not feel drawn to the same sort of action as other Christian brethren. This is the message of Romans 14. But when legalism is advocated as a necessity for belonging to the movement in question; when the freedom of the individual's conscience is over-ridden by the leadership who demand a certain set of behaviour patterns, especially when there is the underlying implication that the spiritual is all that matters and the physical is either vaguely reprehensible or at best of no consequence – then beware. The sectarian tendency is not far away. You find fierce legalism like this in some of the Jesus Movements, such as the Children of God reacting as they do against the extreme permissiveness in other parts of the counter-culture. You find it in the enforced abstinence from meat, alcohol, sex and drugs among the "premies" who have received the guru's "knowledge" in the Divine Light Mission. Many of the house church movements are extraordinarily legalistic and display nothing of the liberty of the children of God in which St. Paul wanted Christians to rejoice. Paul affirms that the way is the same for legalist and licentious alike. They must die with Christ instead of mortifying some of their passions – or else indulging them. They must rise with Christ and set their affections not on earthly precepts or enjoyment but above, where Christ is. Only then will the image of the Creator, lost at the Fall, and embodied in Christ, be renewed within them (3:10).

## 6. An undiscriminating mysticism (2:15, 18f)

As we have seen in examining T.M., mysticism which does not focus on and come through Christ is dangerous. The meditator opens himself to forces over which he has no control. At worst he is prey to demonic influence which could be destructive of his whole life. At best he is caught up in an activity which is selfish and does nothing for anybody else. Only in Judaism and Christianity is mysticism inescapably linked with love and compassion. After all, you cannot relate in depth to a loving personal God without some of his characteristics making themselves felt in your subsequent attitudes. But a mystic approach to the impersonal "One" has absolutely no necessary link with ethics. I have no doubt whatever that spiritualism, no less than witchcraft, can induce healings. But that does not mean we should follow these avenues. I have no doubt that meditation through yoga and Hinduism can bring tranquillity. But that does not mean these paths are unexceptionable. Mysticism is very attractive. It appeals to an age which is for ever restlessly activist. It is glitteringly attractive to seek power over men through spiritual exercises. It is appealing to gain an esoteric knowledge through initiation into some mystery, particularly if it goes beyond death. But all such quests are forbidden in Scripture. God has given us the veil of death for good reasons, and the only way through which he offers us is the one which is totally adequate, communion with Christ who transcended death by his resurrection and is Lord of the dead and the living.

At Colossae some were clearly taking their stand on mystical experiences which gave them a sense of superiority over other believers. They had a private revelation which they were flaunting in the face of less fortunate brothers. And herein lies one of the foremost marks of counterfeit religion. It lays pretentious claims to new revelation. Jesus Christ is often recognised, in a patronising way, but what is *stressed* is the new revelation. That is the case with Jehovah's Witnesses, with Mormonism, with Christian Science. If God spoke fully in Jesus Christ he can have no further revelation up his sleeve, waiting to be disclosed through whoever the next cult leader may be. God's last word to man is the Word who became flesh. Any pretended revelation through angel or vision, through mystery or new enlightenment must square with him if it is to have any hope of making headway in authentic Christian circles. In him dwells all the fulness of the godhead bodily, and all "Jesus plus . . ." cults are, by that very token, deceived.

## 7. A hateful exclusivism (3:11, 1:28)

Once again we can only read between the lines, but the

message seems clear enough. Those who claimed to have gained exclusive knowledge, to having attained to new mysteries, were not very loving towards their less enlightened brethren in the church at Colossae. That is why Paul makes such play with the universality and unrestricted offer of the gospel of Christ. "Here there cannot be Greek and Jew, circumcised and uncircumcised, barbarian, Scythian, slave, free man; but Christ is all, and in all." (3:11). He continues "Put on therefore, as God's chosen ones, compassion, kindness, lowliness, meekness and patience . . . And above all these things put on love, which binds everything together in perfect harmony." By way of contrast, exclusiveness is a characteristic of counterfeit religion. The non-member is not loved: he is generally rejected as beyond the pale. The Maranatha movement, the Children of God and many modern cults show this distressing tendency to denounce and exclude other believers. Alas, it is often a failing in orthodox Christian circles too: and there is no excuse for it. The Lord who has accepted me with all my failings has accepted you with all yours, and it ill befits us to carp at one another. Whenever you get unhealthy emphasis on any one leader, such as Mary Baker Eddy in Christian Science, Ron Hubbard in Scientology, Meher Baba of the Bahai faith, Joseph Smith of the Mormons, Sun Myung Moon of the Unification Church, there you have the mark of the sect. The God and Father of our Lord Jesus Christ does not give glory to men, and when men arrogate it to themselves counterfeit religion is at work. In the Christian family there is no room for pride, or for distinctions between believers who have and believers who have not. There are no second-class citizens. There is no room for discrimination on the grounds of enlightenment, financial standing, colour or class. That is why Paul stresses an *open* mystery (1:26) teaches wisdom to *all*, and seeks to present *every man* a *mature initiate* in Christ Jesus. Each word must have cut like a whiplash to the arrogant sectaries who were sure that they had arrived, and that the ordinary run-of-the-mill Christian had not. Indeed, the whole of the latter section of the Epistle on the relationships of love and respect and openness between parents, children, masters, slaves and the like may all be governed by Paul's determination to root out this sectarian attitude in gnostic circles at Colossae which saw wisdom and comradeship as the perquisite of the few who were initiates. In Christ all are initiates, and nothing must be allowed to separate those whom God has united in the one family of his Son.

## 8. A spiritual blindness

Once again, we have to read between the lines. But in the Colossian Letter there is a great deal of emphasis by the apostle on "knowledge". It is more than likely that he is taking over one of the key emphases of the sect and throwing it back in their teeth. One of the marked characteristics of the developed Gnosticism of the second century, to which the Colossian heresy appears as a precursor, was a failure to understand the seriousness of sin. To them it was primarily ignorance. And such seems to have been the case at Colossae. Their stress on knowledge (cf 1:9, 10, 2:2, 3:10) perhaps implies a Platonism which believed that nobody willingly errs: we are all good at heart. Now this is totally incompatible with the Christian doctrine of indwelling sin, and with the profound sensitivity of the man who wrote the Epistle to the Romans. Salvation by knowledge remains one of the hallmarks of the cult mentality, and naturally it fails to plumb the depths of the human situation.

It is not merely the Eastern cults such as the Divine Light Mission that make this fundamental error (which, in his later years Plato discovered to his cost), but many of the perfectionist cults of the West. Some of the charismatic splinter groups so common today throughout the world are confident that sin is a thing of the past for such as they – have they not been baptised with the Holy Spirit and thus entered on a new plane of spirituality? Paul is ruthless in attacking this dangerous misconception. He stresses the need for Christ, his cross and resurrection (2:14f, 3:1f). He needs to enter their lives (1:27) redeem them, forgive them, and transfer them from the kingdom of darkness into the kingdom of his dear Son (1:13f). Nothing less will suffice.

Spiritual regeneration is his medicine, not intellectual enlightenment; conversion to Christ, not membership of a cult; a new birth, not a new insight.

Christ himself is the apostle's answer to counterfeit Christianity at Colossae. It was a dangerous heresy, always liable to recrudesce. "In Christ dwells all the fulness of the godhead bodily, and you are complete in him." From such a secure vantage point the Christian when faced with any specious new teaching will ask:

1. Is it a merely human philosophical system, or does it accord with the revelation in Scripture?
2. How does it account for the good and the evil, the infinite and the finite?
3. How does it attempt to bring together a holy God and unholy men?
4. What emphasis does it lay on ceremonial and initiatory rites?
5. Does it offer new power or old rules?
6. Does it offer a fresh revelation, or seek to bypass Jesus in reaching to mysteries beyond this world?
7. Is it an open secret or an exclusive club?
8. Does it offer new knowledge or new birth?

Counterfeit religion is one of the strongest weapons in Satan's armoury. Hence the warning of Jesus Christ: "False Christs and false prophets will arise and show great signs and wonders, so as to lead astray, if possible, even the elect. Lo, I have told you beforehand" (Matt. 24:24).

# CHAPTER 7

## The Defeat of Satan

ONE OF THE remarkable things that meets us in the Gospels is the flurry of demonic activity. Satan and his minions are more in evidence than anywhere else in the whole Bible. This is not accidental. If Jesus Christ came primarily to destroy the works of the devil, if his arrival on the scene was the signal for the final battle to begin, then it is not so surprising that Satan should be stirred to wrath.

### The Life of Jesus

The life of Jesus was attacked from the start. We have already seen in the Book of Revelation a striking picture of Satan anticipating the birth of "the man child", the woman's seed who was destined to bruise his head. He stands, that ancient dragon, watching the pregnant woman, and waiting for the birth of the child. But he is frustrated. "The dragon stood before the woman who was about to bear a child, that he might devour her child when she brought it forth. She brought forth a male child, one who is to rule the nations with a rod of iron, but her child was caught up to God and his throne." (Rev. 12:5). In that evocative flash the story of Jesus and his defeat of the Enemy is summarised with superb artistry. The initial reference is, no doubt, to the attempt made by Herod to have Jesus killed: the slaughter of the innocents of Bethlehem did not achieve Herod's purpose of safeguarding his kingdom – nor Satan's of safeguarding his. But it has also a much wider reference to the total victory achieved over the devil by Jesus in the course of his life on earth, before he was triumphantly snatched up to God and his throne.

### The wilderness temptations

The classic passage dealing with Jesus' temptations comes in Matthew 4 and Luke 4, the wilderness battle. The

195

account could only have reached the early church through Jesus himself, and while the story was clearly used to help Christians face temptation themselves (the different order of the temptations in Luke and Matthew shows that the stories circulated independently for the teaching and encouragement of Christians going through rough times) its primary reference is to Jesus himself and the temptations to which he was particularly prone as Messiah. No doubt those temptations recurred throughout his ministry. Indeed we know they did. But here they are graphically brought together in one initial onslaught of aggressive guile, right at the beginning of his ministry. If Jesus could be made to fail there, he would fail comprehensively.

## The timing

The timing of this acute period of temptation is very interesting. It came when Jesus had just been baptised. This had been a moment of great elation for him. He had stooped to identify himself with sinful men needing to repent, though he himself had done nothing to repent of (and Matthew's account highlights the fact, 3:14, 15). That was an anticipation of the way he would stoop to identify himself more profoundly with sinners in the greater baptism of Calvary. At his baptism he had seen a vision of the Spirit of God coming upon him in power like a dove. He had heard a voice from heaven, "This is my Son, my beloved, in whom I am well pleased." His knowledge of the Old Testament Scriptures must at once have led him to see a deeper significance in that encouraging voice than is immediately apparent to us. Psalm 2:7, a royal psalm, addresses the king as God's son. That destiny was about to reach a fulfilment it never had under David or any other Old Testament monarch. But the phrase "in whom I am well pleased" would take Jesus' mind back to that mysterious yet magnificent figure of the sinless sufferer, the Servant of the Lord celebrated in four songs in Isaiah. The first of them begins, "Behold my servant whom I uphold, my chosen, *in whom I am well pleased*, I have put my Spirit upon him." Jesus would have seen in that message from heaven a combination of two very different rôles. He was to be God's Son, exercising his kingly rule: but he was to do it as the Servant of God and men, in dependence on his Father, in utter obedience, through undeserved suffering, and through death. Isaiah 53 would have sprung to his mind as the climax of those Servant Songs, and the horror of suffering for the sins of the world if the world was going to be rescued from its sins would begin to dawn upon him. It was after this shattering revelation that the temptations came.

## The setting

The setting of the temptation was equally significant. Jesus went into the wilderness. It lies a stone's throw from Jerusalem, this shimmering, solitary, burning wilderness of Judea. Almost all the great men of God in the Old Testament had been through testing in the desert: Moses, Joshua, Elijah and many others. It was in the wilderness that Israel tempted God once and again by complaining against his providence and grumbling at what he allowed them (Psalm 95:8). Their failure in the desert receives a lot of attention in the Scriptures (Ex. 17:5–7, Num. 20:2–5, 1 Cor. 10:6ff, Heb. 3:7–4:10). It was in the desert that Jesus faced his test. Mark tells us that it was among the beasts. This is perhaps not only a reminder of the physical danger which forty days in the deserts involved, but a hint of the last Adam succeeding where the first Adam fell. For Adam, too, was involved with the beasts. He had named them all in those far-off days in the Garden. And now in their company Jesus sets out to win where Adam lost.

There is another important aspect to this temptation. All three accounts stress the fact that the Spirit drove him into the wilderness (Mk. 1:12, Matt. 4:1, Lk. 4:1). Jesus overcame the Tempter not by the exercise of innate deity but by dependence on the Spirit of God to strengthen him – just as we have to do. He was in no privileged position. His rôle as God's king-servant, of which he had become deeply aware at his baptism, did not exempt him from temptation: it drove him all the more towards it. The Spirit was not there to give him an easy time, but to equip him for battle. And so it is still. There is a very strong emphasis in these accounts of the temptation on the humanity of Jesus. God as such cannot be tempted with evil (Jas. 1:13), but Jesus was not God as such. He shared God's nature, it is true, but not God's privileges of immunity from temptation. For he shared our nature just as much as he shared God's. And the victory he won here in the wilderness he won as our representative, endued with our humanity, relying on the same Spirit who is given to strengthen us.

## Stones into bread

The first temptation, as in the Garden of Eden, came through his body. He had not eaten for forty days. Now many men have done that, but they are not usually subject to the burning days and cool nights of the desert while undergoing their ordeal. This simple detail shows both how tough Jesus was and how exhausted and emaciated he must have become. Satan then begins his assault by taking the obvious opening. Actually, he takes two obvious openings. He leads with an appeal to meet the excruciating pain of extreme bodily hunger. And he leads by building on the fact that Jesus is the recently acknowledged Son of God. "If you are the Son of God" may have a touch of cynical doubt about it, but is probably to be taken in the sense of "Since you are the Son of God . . ." He invites Jesus to go up to the God level, since that is what he is. God feeds the hungry. God can turn stones into bread. Right. Let Jesus use his divine powers to satisfy his obvious need. Our Lord's reponse to this subtle temptation is profound.

First, he makes use of Scripture. He meets the devil's attack by quoting Deut. 8:3. In each of these three temptations Jesus quotes the Old Testament. This is highly significant, and the higher your Christology the more significant it is that the Son of God himself should rely so heavily upon the armoury of the Scriptures. He could not regard them more highly than he does. And this attitude is maintained throughout his ministry, after the resurrection as well as before it. It is maintained whether he is seeking light on his own destiny, settling a moral issue, or disputing with the Pharisees. I have tried to show the cumulative force of this appeal to Scripture in my small book, *The Authority of Scripture*. It has been done at much greater depth by R. T. France in *Jesus and the Old Testament*. ✓

There is surely a message for us here. If Jesus Christ needed to have recourse to the Scriptures as the "sword of the Spirit, the word of God" (Eph. 6:17) it is certain that we do. Actually, I think we can make an inference which takes us further. All three of the quotations which Jesus uses here come from the same part of the book of Deuteronomy. Is it a wild flight of fancy to suppose that Jesus had recently been reading that book devotionally, and had committed to memory verses from it which stood him in good stead when the test came? It is a practice which many Christians have found invaluable.

Second, Jesus emphatically ranges himself on the side of man in this temptation. He could have exercised that divine prerogative which was his. He could have gone up and used God's power. Instead he chose to stay down alongside man, and be subject to man's limitations. "If you are the *Son of God*," purrs the Tempter. "*Man* shall not live by bread alone," replies the Saviour. It was as man, as one of us, that he lived and suffered and died. Allotted the rôle of the suffering Servant at his baptism, he employs it now at the outset of his ministry by taking the lower place: and he maintains that rôle until the bitter end, death on a cross. That is why he tells his followers on the night before his passion that they were to take their pattern of leadership ✓ from him, not from the world. "Let the greatest of you become as the youngest, and the leader as one who serves" (Lk. 22:26).

Third, Jesus as man displays the most marvellous trust in his heavenly Father. Satan had fallen by grasping. Jesus overcame by trusting. God might seem ungracious to allow his Son to suffer such anguish. But "though he slay me, yet will I trust in him" might have been Jesus' motto. He refused to use God's power to enable him to do what God did not direct. He was willing to starve if it was the Father's will. That is how deep his trust went. It is not that to supply food supernaturally to meet human need was wrong. He did so when wine ran out in Cana of Galilee. He did so on the hillside when he fed the multitude from a boy's picnic basket. The wrong thing was to do good at the devil's instigation, to listen to any suggestion, however good and admirable in itself, that sprang not from his heavenly Father but from his Enemy. Jesus was determined to live a life totally pleasing to his Father, and nowhere is that attitude more clearly exemplified than in dealing with these temptations. Where Eve fell, Jesus overcame. The attack on his bodily appetites was triumphantly rebutted. At once the quotation from Scripture silences the Tempter and causes him to give up . . . for the moment. He then comes up with a fresh form of attack.

## A jump to fame
Jesus has shown that he trusts the Father implicitly, has he? Right, let there be a religious form to the next temptation. Let us see if he will trust the Father enough to throw himself off the highest pinnacle of the Temple. Once again the pattern of Eden is being repeated. Once again Satan attacks through the mind. He follows Jesus' example and quotes Scripture, a marvellous psalm celebrating the safety of the man who really trusts in the Lord. He quotes it while tempting Jesus to do just the opposite, and make a public exhibition of himself as he undoubtedly would if he jumped off the top of the Temple, which towered four hundred feet above the valley of Hinnom below. He would either be killed, and that would suit Satan admirably: or else he would become a five-minute wonder and win the temporary adulation of the masses while their hearts and attitudes remained firmly in the devil's camp. Either way Satan would be well pleased. But the subtlety of the temptation came in the approach to his mind. Would God really take care of him? Would that jump exhibit filial trust in God – or naked showmanship? Would the plaudits of the crowd (if he landed unharmed) turn into anything deeper? Doubt and confusion of mind: these were the weapons Satan was using.

Jesus' response was short and sharp. "You shall not tempt the Lord your God" (Deut. 6:16). I do not think he was laying claim to deity, assenting to Satan's sardonic, "If

thou art the Son of God." He was reflecting on the temptation which Satan was suggesting. It would not be to trust
God, as it was being represented. It would be to tempt
God, to put him to the test, attempt to force his hand. And
that is the ultimate in disobedience and distrust. The Deuteronomy verse mentions the way the Israelites had
tempted God at Massah, "because they put the Lord to the
test by saying 'Is the Lord among us or not?'" (Ex. 17:7).
That is precisely what Jesus was being tempted to discover:
to walk by sight would be the very antithesis of the trusting
walk of faith to which God's Messiah, along with all men,
was called. He overcame in the realm of the mind no less
than of the body. He was repairing the ravages caused by
the first man.

### Shortcut to world dominion
The third temptation assailed his ambition. This must have
been particularly congenial to the Tempter, for it was
through ambition that he fell. His own ambition was so
overweening, so selfish that it led him into total revolt.
Perhaps an assault on ambition would work on Jesus. So he
showed him "all the kingdoms of the world and the glory of
them", perhaps in a vision conjured up by the vast panor-
amic view over much of Palestine that can be had from one
of the mountain peaks in the desert. He offers them all to
Jesus, if only he will fall down and worship him. We see
here to the very heart of the Tempter. He is the usurper
prince of this world. He knows it, and Jesus knows it. There
is no argument on that matter. But the whole purpose of
Jesus' coming into the world was to reverse that situation.
He was proposing through obedience and trust to repair the
ruin of Adam's unbelief and disobedience. He constituted
a massive threat to Satan's fancied hegemony. The devil
had to win over the allegiance, break down the single-
minded trust and obedience of Jesus if he was to have any
hope of gaining the whole world for himself. The temptations in the wilderness, and particularly this crucial one,
were absolutely necessary to the Evil One if he was to make
any headway against God's last Adam. This temptation,
then, takes us to the very root of Satan's ambition.

But did he really think he had a hope of getting Jesus to bow down and worship him? Did he think Jesus would take the kingdoms of the world as the bribe for filial disloyalty? Well, it had worked in Eden. It was worth trying. What that temptation was really saying was "just a little compromise. Bow to the inevitable, be willing to shelve those principles of yours for a moment, and great good will come. Did you not come to gain the leadership of this world? Well, you shall have it. Have you not at your baptism had grim forebodings of a rôle as Son which involves the fate of the Suffering Servant? Is that how much your boasted heavenly Father cares? Listen to me. Let us go into partnership together. Nobody need know. It will be only a momentary deviation. And look at what will ensue. You shall have the kingdom you came to found. You shall have the hearts of men. And you will achieve it all without having recourse to that way of suffering your Father seems to have delighted to map out for you."

The glittering goal of world dominion: the petty price of compromise: the powerful inducement to take a short cut and bypass the way of the cross. Some temptation!

Once again Jesus did not toy with it. He gave it short shrift. A decisive reply. A brief command, "Begone, Satan". And a clinching verse from Scripture. Again the unfailing trust. Again the implicit obedience. Again the utter opposition to evil in all its forms.

### Lessons from the desert
Leaving aside the particular messianic significance of those temptations, what can we learn from the way Jesus met the devil as to how we can hope in a measure to share in his victory?

Jesus shows us that the most powerful preparation for meeting temptation successfully is a life without sin. Satan had only once previously met a life like that, in the Garden of Eden. A sinless life like Jesus' was a novel and threatening experience for him. Now of course we cannot mirror that quality. But we can start each day accepted in the Beloved; with no condemnation against us, with our conscience right with our God. And that is the best protection

202

against falling into sin. We may well be tempted fiercely, but if we have that singleminded attitude towards God we shall increasingly be able to discern his whisper from the devil's amid the conflicting calls and clamours of each day.

Jesus shows us that temptation can best be met in the power of the Holy Spirit. He was, Luke tells us, full of the Spirit, and as such he was tempted. That is the way to face temptation, with the Spirit guiding us through the whole operation. Only a power greater than ours can overcome Satan. And God has provided one.

Jesus shows us that trust and obedience are are the twin pillars of a successful operation against the devil. However the Tempter twisted and turned, and sought to dazzle him, Jesus never wavered in his trust in the Father, and never swerved from obedience to him. Satan bent all his wiles to achieve a millimetre of disobedience, of deviation from the true. He failed with Jesus, where he had succeeded in Eden.

Jesus shows us that unselfishness is decisive in warfare with Satan. Satan could not understand one whose ambition was entirely for Another. Yet that was the case with Jesus. His meat and drink were to do the will of the Father who sent him. In a life where self-seeking, self-assertion, self-pity are predominant characteristics you cannot expect victory over the Tempter. He has too large a landing ground.

Jesus shows us that the use of Scripture in temptation is a powerful weapon. The devil is not afraid of us. He is afraid of all that speaks of God. The scriptures do just that. If you want to overcome temptation regularly, habitually, I know of no weapon sharper than the Word of God, studied, learnt by heart and used with confidence in the moment of attack. Nor is this any mere matter of proof-texts. The way Jesus handles the devil's quotation of Scripture shows how the context was uppermost in his mind. He was not going to base his action on a verse from the Old Testament ripped carelessly from its context.

Jesus shows us that we have no need to be afraid of Satan. Jesus went into the battle with confidence of victory so long as he remained trusting, obedient and dependent on the Spirit. We can go in the same fearlessness. We need only fear the devil when we cease fully to oppose him. At heart he is a coward. At a firm rebuttal backed by the word of God, he flees. But he is always dogged, and soon there will be a new attack.

Jesus shows us that we have to be decisive with Satan. No playing with the temptation. No parleying with the Tempter (that was where Eve made her mistake). Jesus' contact with him was reduced to the minimum. He did not ask him to go. He told him to go. There was an aggressiveness about Jesus' response to temptation which has a lot to teach us. It was the aggression of love in the face of hate and destruction.

**Temptations throughout the ministry**
If I have spent a good deal of time on the Temptation in the wilderness it is because that story tells us most of what we need to know about the way Jesus overcame Satan throughout his life. Temptation did not cease during his ministry. Indeed, these same temptations came up afresh in different guises. When the multitude after the feeding wanted to make him king, or when the crowd shouted hosanna as he entered the temple, it was the old messianic temptation of crowns without thorns, control through exhibitionism, which he had rejected in the wilderness. The thought that he could ask his Father and receive legions of angels to save him from the cross: or, as he hung there, the jeers that invited him to come down from the cross if he was what he claimed to be, were both galling, agonising assaults by Satan along the lines explored in the wilderness. Jesus' refusal to give the crowds a compulsive proof of who he was (when they had already had plenty of signs – and attributed them to Satan) was a reaffirmation of the victory he had won in the desert when he refused to jump off the pinnacle of the temple.

It is noticeable throughout his career how often temptation came to him under the cover of other people about whom he cared deeply. One occasion, which all the Synoptists record, is the time when his mother and his brothers came to the house where he was teaching and wanted to get through the crowd and see him (Mk. 3:31–35, Matt. 12:46–50, Lk. 8:19–21). The scribes and Pharisees were nettled by his success, and were pressing all the more insistently around him. We already hear allusions to a plan that was being devised to kill him (Mk. 3:6). It could be that the religious leaders were trying to get his family to dissuade Jesus from what they saw as his mistaken course. At all events, Jesus saw their intervention as a serious interruption of his work. He was entirely single-minded. In the context he had in effect charged Satan's kingdom with going Pharisee (3:23–30).* His passion was to do the will of God, and not even the ties of family were going to deflect him from it. "Who are my mother and my brothers?" he asked. And looking around on those who sat about him, he said, "Here are my mother and my brothers! Whoever does the will of God is my brother, and sister, and mother."

Another such occasion I have alluded to above. It comes in John chapter six. Jesus has compassion on the multitudes. He teaches them and feeds them. Then he goes into a mountain apart to pray. Why? Because "they were about to come and take him by force to make him king" (6:15). Maybe the disciples were in cahoots with the multitude: in Matthew's account of the incident Jesus had to force them to get into a boat and row across the lake while he sent the crowds away (Matt. 14:22). But whoever was behind it, it was the old temptation of popular appeal, of rejecting the path of the Servant, to which he had been prey ever since the wilderness temptation. And once again, he rejects it decisively.

A third such occasion was the celebrated one at Caesarea Philippi. Jesus was seeking to find out who they really thought he was. They stumble into confession that he is the Messiah. But that word had all the wrong connotations for Jesus, true though it was in some sense. It smacked of military prowess and earthly success. Read the 17th *Psalm of Solomon* and see for yourself what the expectations were

* The derivation of the word Pharisee means "separated" or "divided ones". Jesus puns on the word.

205

for the Messiah in Pharisaic circles only a few years before Jesus was born. So he transposed "Messiah" into another key. It was the lesson he had learnt at his baptism: that the highest Son needs to take upon him the lowest rôle, that of the Servant, if he is to be truly great. So he begins to tell his disciples that the Son of Man (his favourite self-designation, both because of its ambiguity and its covert allusion to the glory of Dan. 7:14) must suffer. He must take the destiny of the Suffering Servant and go the way of Isaiah 53. Simon Peter takes him in hand. He says "God forbid, Lord! This shall never happen to you" (Matt. 16:22). But Jesus rounds on Peter in startling tones. "Get behind me, Satan. You are a hindrance to me; for you are not on the side of God, but of men." Staggering, especially when Jesus had commended Peter just beforehand for his insight into who he was. But there was no doubt about it. If Jesus had done as Peter suggested, there would have been no cross, no redemption, and the ploy of the Tempter back in the wilderness would eventually have come off, as the old serpent tried once again, this time through the agency of a trusted friend and colleague.

A fourth instance of subtle temptations from Satan, coming through apparently innocent suggestions from those for whom Jesus cared, comes in John chapter twelve. Some Greeks expressed the desire to see Jesus. They found two Greek-speaking members of the circle of disciples, Philip and Andrew, and sought an introduction. How Jesus must have longed to widen his ministry to include folks like this. Here were men who seemed to have been genuine seekers after truth, at the very time when Israel had turned decisively against him and even the raising of Lazarus produced a hornet's nest. What a sore temptation it must have been to welcome this approach from the wider world he came to win. Instead, he set his face to the cross, so that by dying he might win that wider world. He realised that only if he were lifted up on the cross would he be able to draw all types of men to himself. He knew that only when it fell into the ground and died would the corn of wheat be able to produce much fruit (12:24, 32). But the decision to decline their request was extremely costly to him. "Now is my soul troubled. And what shall I say? 'Father, save me from this hour'? No. For this purpose I have come to this hour. 'Father, glorify thy name'" (12:27f). Once again we see him treading with wonderful trust and obedience the path the Father had given him, attractive though the temptation undoubtedly was to him of avoiding the cross, going to where he would be appreciated and doing much good – yet it would not be the Father's way for him.

## Gethsemane

These four incidents give us, in many ways, the story of his life. It was subject to temptation at every level, and throughout its duration. One of the fiercest battles was when he really came face to face with the horror of what the cross would mean, not just in its physical barbarity, unthinkable though that was, but in the inner task of sinbearing and dying under the curse of God that it brought with it (Gal. 3:10, 13). In the Garden of Gethsemane he battled it out. In the full light of what would happen on the morrow unless he changed direction, Jesus faced the temptation: it was quite literally hell for him. He sweated blood in the intensity of the fight. His closest friends could not keep awake in prayer to support him, so he had to face it alone. One of his intimates was even then on the way to betray him. Another on whom he had placed such high hopes would deny he knew him before the night was out.

It was a lonely battle. "In the days of his flesh" writes the author to the Hebrews, "Jesus offered up prayers and supplications with loud cries and tears to him who was able to save him from death, and he was heard for his godly fear" (Heb. 5:7f). He was indeed heard, but his prayer that the cup might pass from him was not given an affirmative answer. In his heart of hearts he knew that this must be so. He had been living the life of a Servant long enough to know that the rôle would not be taken from him at the last. Had he not told his disciples repeatedly that he came to give his life a ransom for many, and that he would be mocked, spat on, scourged and killed? But life is sweet at thirty-three. And the hope that "it may not be as bad as that" springs eternal. So he prayed and sweated over the tempta-

207

tion to take the short cut. It would have proved as fatal as it was attractive.

When we look at the life of Jesus, assailed as it was at every point by temptations of which we can have only the slightest understanding, those words of the author to the Hebrews come home with new force: they almost seem an understatement. "He was in all points tempted as we are, yet without sinning" (4:15). He was indeed. As a result, those other words of Hebrews can be true for us, "Because he himself has suffered, being tempted, he is able to help those who are tempted" (2:18).

### Temptation, disease, and demons

In the course of his ministry Jesus met the Tempter head on in three ways. In the first place he overcame every temptation thrown at him, and thus not only thwarted the Enemy but gave hope and an example to those who follow him.

But he also repulsed Satan in the whole area of disease. As we have seen, disease and death are all part and parcel of the spurious deal the devil gave in return for primal man's "Yes" to temptation. In some mysterious way sin, disease and death are all part of the heritage of disobedience. Throughout his ministry Jesus preached the "salvation" or "wholeness" which God intends for his people, and he backed that up with appropriate action. His healings and his raisings from the dead are all part of that salvation. They are only the tip of the iceberg, so to speak, of God's saving activity, but they are the firstfruits of the eventual harvest. The restoration of health to diseased limbs, sight to blind eyes, speech to dumb lips, hearing to deaf ears, strength to palsied arms all speaks of one aspect of the wholeness which God in his love plans for man. And thus his miracles of healing are an integral part of the salvation he proclaimed. Equally, those forays into the realm of death, when the widow of Nain's son, Jairus' daughter and then Lazarus were brought back to life for a while, were all anticipations of the final resurrection to a new quality of life that he would make possible through his death and resurrection. Then it would be no temporary resuscitation, but the raising of man to a new quality of life which would last for ever with the Lord. The healings and the raisings were both acted parables, implicit claims of who he was and what he was achieving.

Then there were the exorcisms. Those, too, were an integral part of his ministry. For he came to rectify not only sin, not only disease and death, but the demonic forces that invade and spoil men's lives. Throughout his ministry he cast out demons and drove back the power of the Enemy in the lives of those who came to trust him.

## *The Death of Jesus*

### The achievements of Calvary

But the climax of it all came at the cross. That was the fixed battle between Christ and Satan. That was the turning-point of the whole war. When the victors in the Book of Revelation are exulting in the power they have over the Evil One, it is "the blood of the Lamb" which is the ground for their triumph. His cross is the supreme example of his trusting obedience, and the supreme humiliation of the Enemy.

What happened on Calvary? How did Jesus win that last and greatest battle with Satan? We shall never know the full answer, but what we do know is profoundly wonderful.

### The fruit of obedience

In the first place Jesus won the battle by continuing his obedience to the very end. That has never been done before or since. But it broke the spell of constant failure. It snapped the entail of disobedience that was deep in our race. Paul revels in this truth. He quotes what may well be an old Aramaic hymn, dating from the very earliest days of the church. "Have this mind among yourselves which was also in Christ Jesus", he writes:

Though he was in the form of God
He did not count equality with God a thing to be
    grasped,
But emptied himself,

Taking the form of a servant,
Being born in the likeness of men.
And being found in human form he humbled himself
    and became obedient
Unto death, even death on a cross.
Therefore God has highly exalted him,
And bestowed on him the name which is above every
    name,
That at the name of Jesus every knee should bow,
In heaven and on earth and under the earth,
And every tongue confess that Jesus Christ is Lord,
To the glory of God the Father.

(Phil. 2:5–11)

Satan, though not in the form of God, strove to achieve it. Instead of humbling himself he made his status a thing to be grasped. He became the embodiment of disobedience, and as a result he is destined for eternal ruin. The contrast with Jesus is complete. Adam, too, rejected the form of a servant. He grasped at a status now bestowed on him. He gave way to disobedience which had cosmic repercussions. Where the first man failed, the last man won. Obedience, right up to the most ghastly death a man can die, characterised the Lord of glory who chose the path of the Servant for us. Could any truth be more sublime, more worthy of God? And were it not for his sinless life of perfect obedience he could never have offered his life for the life of the world. "Although he was a Son," muses the author to the Hebrews in wonder, "he learned obedience through what he suffered; and being made perfect, he became the source of eternal salvation to all who obey him" (5:8ff). The primacy of obedience could scarcely be put more powerfully.

### The sin of the world
In the second place Jesus won the battle by taking upon himself the sin of the world. He saw his life and death in the light of the Songs of the Suffering Servant, particularly Isaiah 53, which influenced his famous ransom saying: "the Son of man came to give his life a ransom for many" (Mk. 10:45). Peter came to see the cross as a fivefold fulfilment of

Isaiah 53, as he reflected on what his Lord achieved for him and others upon that cross (1 Pet. 2:21–25). "All we like sheep have gone astray. We have turned every one to his own way. And the Lord has laid on him the iniquity of us all" (Isai. 53:6) summarises the achievement of Calvary in this respect as few other verses do. Jesus willingly took upon himself on that cross the guilt and the failure of a world that had gone astray. Paul goes so far as to say that the curse for breaking God's law, which rightly belonged to us, fell on him, and he was exposed in the place of the curse, "for cursed is every one who hangs upon a tree" (Deut. 21:23, Gal. 3:10, 13). In another place he says that Jesus became sin for us, though he knew no sin, that we might become the righteousness of God in him (2 Cor. 5:21). In words like this the New Testament writers struggle to express their gratitude and exhilaration that God had done for them in Christ what they could never have done for themselves. He has put them in the right, justified them, by taking responsibility for all the sin and failure. And thus the devil is robbed of his power as "Satan" or "Accuser". For "there is now no condemnation for those who are in Christ Jesus" (Rom. 8:1).

The classic passage on this subject is Romans 5. In the first half of that chapter Paul argues that we sinners are justified through the blood of Christ shed for us on the cross. "God shows his love for us in that while we were yet sinners Christ died for us . . .". No wonder then that "we rejoice in God through our Lord Jesus Christ through whom we have received our reconciliation" (5:8, 11). In the second half of the chapter we have an obscure but equally important truth. Paul compares the achievement of Christ's rescue with the extent of Adam's fall. The two representative men are compared and contrasted. Now is not the moment to study it in detail, but the thrust of what he is saying is this. Christ utterly righted Adam's wrong. I am in the wrong with God both because I am "in Adam" (that is to say, part of the corporate humanity of which he is the progenitor and fount) and because Adam-like, I have done wrong things. That is my fallen state. But my Christian state reverses that situation. I am accepted, justified, acquitted both because of what Christ did for me in his life of perfect obedience laid down in self-oblation on the cross, and also because I am "in Christ" (that is to say, part of the corporate redeemed humanity of which he is the progenitor and fount). That is my restored state. And it was brought about on Calvary. That cross spells the downfall of the Accuser. "If God is for us, who can be against us? Who shall bring any charge against God's elect? It is God who justifies. Who is to condemn?" (Rom. 8:31, 33).

## The defeat of death

In the third place Jesus won the battle by taking on himself the death of man and snapping its power. Our life, be it short or long, is always bounded by death. The warning that disobedience in our first parents would produce death has come true at several levels. We noted that spiritual death occurred with the rupture of relationships with God. Physical death, when it comes upon us, seals and finalises all the other aspects of death we have already begun to taste. "The wages of sin is death. But the gift of God is eternal life through Jesus Christ our Lord" (Rom. 6:23). The unimaginable generosity of God offers us a new life when ours had become forfeit. Whether or not Matt. 8:17, applying Isaiah 53 to the healing ministry of Jesus, indicates that in some mysterious way he took our sicknesses with him to the cross as well as our sins, I do not know. But he certainly took the death which ends our lives be they healthy or sick. He dealt with the last enemy, death (1 Cor. 15:26). What he did was to rise again. Not like the resuscitations that he achieved during his lifetime: Lazarus had to die again. But "Christ being raised from the dead will never die again. Death no longer has dominion over him" (Rom. 6:9). "In fact Christ has been raised from the dead, the firstfruits of those who have fallen asleep. For as in Adam all die, so also in Christ shall all be made alive . . . The first man, Adam, became a living being: the last Adam became a life-giving spirit . . . Death is swallowed up in victory. O death, where is thy victory? O death, where is thy sting?" (1 Cor. 15:20, 22, 45, 54f). Or, as the majestic words of the risen Christ in the Apocalypse put it, "Fear not, I am the first and the last, and the living one. I died and behold I am alive for evermore, and I hold the keys of Death and Hades" (1:17f). Could any words express greater confidence that the last enemy had been routed? Of course, men still have to die. But as Paul explained in 1 Cor. 15:56, "the sting of death is sin," and that sting has been drawn. Death for believers is no longer the finalising of our state of alienation. It is moving from one room in the Father's house to another. Accordingly it shrinks in significance, particularly as we go to meet the Risen One who has gone to prepare a place for us.

## The harrowing of hell

There is a long tradition in Christianity that the death of Christ constituted the harrowing of hell. And that is a true insight, alluded to rather cryptically in several parts of the New Testament: the best known comes in 1 Pet. 3:18–22. No sooner has Peter spoken of the death of Christ, in perhaps the simplest and most moving terms in the whole Bible, than he goes straight to this consequence, the harrowing of hell. "Christ also died for sins once for all, the just for the unjust, that he might bring us to God, being put to death in the flesh but made alive in the spirit; in which he preached to the spirits in prison, who formerly did not obey, when God's patience waited in the days of Noah . . ." The passage ends with a confident assertion of the ascension and reign of Jesus, "he has gone into heaven and is at the right hand of God, with angels, authorities and powers subject to him." This is a notoriously difficult passage, and there is an enormous literature on the subject (see the commentaries, especially Selwyn's great commentary on the Greek text). But the main point is fairly clear. Peter is asserting that the death of Christ ravaged the inmost dungeon of hades. The sinners who were disobedient in the days of Noah are referred to in Genesis 6:1–4, fruit of the illicit union between "the sons of God" and "the daughters of men". These *nephilim*, however we construe them, were giants in sinning as well as size, and the intertestamental books are full of the horror of their fate. They are the archetypal sinners, and they await the judgement with foreboding whilst they exist in the nethermost hell. This is how the Jews would think of them. Well, says Peter, Christ's death was of such cosmic significance that it pierced even that innermost dungeon. We are not to assume that when Christ "went and preached to the spirits in prison" Peter is talking about some sort of wider hope or universalism. He is doing nothing of the kind. Peter is very precise whom he is talking about, the sinners of Noah's day. Nor are we to think that Jesus preached the good news of salvation to these spirits. A very different word is used in the original, *ekeruxen*. This means that he heralded his victory over all the powers of evil, and that this news percolated into the depths of hell.

2 Timothy 1:10f puts the whole matter in a nutshell: Paul revels in the "grace which God gave us in Christ Jesus long ago and has now manifested through the appearance of our Saviour Christ Jesus, who abolished death, and brought life and immortality to light through the gospel." It was this new quality of life, enjoyed with God now and to be enjoyed hereafter, which was such a completely fresh dimension in the ancient world, racked as it was with doubt as to whether there might be a life after death or not; and if there was, whether it would be a shadowy copy of this earthly existence or else perhaps the alternatives of feasting with the immortals in Olympus or agonising with the lost in Tartarus. And Christianity maintained that in the cross of Christ the poison of death had been neutralised; Hades had become occupied territory, and the incarnate, crucified and risen Jesus Christ was the personal demonstration both of the quality of life beyond the grave and of the defeat of death and hell. In that conviction Christians lived and died. It made an enormous impression on the watching world.

### The conquest of Satan
Finally, Jesus won the battle by inflicting a mortal wound on Satan. The whole chilly area of the occult and the demonic was robbed of its power by Calvary. Christ is the conqueror over all the power of the Enemy, and on the cross he inflicted such a crushing defeat on the devil that whenever his name is named in faith, Satan is bound to flee.

214

I have seen this time and time again in lives afflicted by demonic possession. The demons have to leave when commanded to do so in the name of the Victor. That theme of Christ the conqueror is one of the major ways in which the cross is seen in the New Testament. It is cardinal to St. John's understanding. The triumph of Calvary is not *after* the humiliation but *in* the humiliation. John stresses this by the word "lifted up" which he uses time and again in the Gospel with a double meaning: Christ is lifted up from the earth on the cross, and only so is he lifted up in glory (3:14, 8:28, 12:32, 34). His triumph is complete. He is King of kings and Lord of lords.

Professor Gordon Rupp catches something of the extent and significance of Christ's victory in a delightful personal reminiscence.

> Most of us can still shudder when we remember how in 1940 it seemed far from fantastic to think with Hitler of a Nazi empire which might last for centuries. But I shall never forget a few weeks after the end of the war walking almost in awe down the shattered ruins of the Wilhelmstrasse past the German war ministries riven into giant pieces, to the Cathedral of Berlin where the bombs had penetrated through the dome and down into the crypt – the very place of the tombs of the Prussian Kings who laid the foundations of German militarism.
>
> And then I walked along to Hitler's Chancellery where hardly one stone was left upon another and saw there a mother sitting to rest after standing in the queue for potatoes, while across the very doorstep of Hitler's Chancellery a baby lay, sprawled out kicking and laughing at its mother. So another mother and Baby lie across human history as the empires rise and fall.
>
> (Principalities and Powers, p. 49)

The Book of Revelation has its unique way of expressing Christian exultation in Christ's triumph over Satan. The seer is wondering who is worthy to take the scroll of human destiny from the hand of God and open it. Nobody was worthy, and he wept. Then one of the celestial beings round the throne of God said to him, "Weep not. Lo, the Lion of the tribe of Judah has conquered, so that he can open the scroll." Looking round for the Lion, with consummate artistry and use of surprise, the seer continues, "I saw a *Lamb*, as though it had been slain . . . And he went and took the scroll from the right hand of him who sat on the throne." At this the redeemed in heaven broke out in a song of pure worship:

Worthy are thou to take the scroll and open its seals
For thou wast slain and by thy death didst ransom men
    for God
From every tribe and tongue and people and nation
And has made them a kingdom and priests to our God
And they shall reign on earth.

And again:

Worthy is the Lamb who was slain
To receive power and wealth and wisdom and might
And honour and glory and blessing.

(Rev. 5:1–12)

The conqueror of Satan gets his due through the worship of his redeemed and grateful followers.


### The Destiny of Satan

The Bible does not have a lot to say about the final destiny of Satan. What it does say is wrapped in the imagery of the Apocalypse. It is short, but sufficiently clear.

Satan, like the rest of the world, lives between the times. He has already suffered decisive defeat, but at present he is still allowed some rein. One day that defeat will be finalised.

He is rather like the Axis forces in Europe during the Second World War. The Normandy landings and the battle of Caen to which they led proved utterly decisive for the outcome of the war. There was no denying that the critical battle had been won. The Axis forces could look forward to nothing but final defeat. But the war went on. They refused to accept defeat until they had to. Sometimes considerable success attended their struggle. Often the appearances looked favourable for them. But nothing could alter the fact that they were doomed. The ultimate Victory Day would dawn, as it did in 1945. That is how it is with Satan.

We have had occasion to turn more than once in this book to Revelation chapters 12 and 13, full as they are of prophetic insight into the mystery and outcome of evil. We left "the great dragon, that ancient serpent, who is called the Devil and Satan, the deceiver of the whole world" with his two bestial allies, personifying corrupt political power and corrupt religion, continuing the war against God and his people. Satan, foiled in his attempt to prevent the birth and then the ascent of "the Manchild", turned his attention to "the Woman". But the woman fled into the wilderness, which was a place prepared for her until the Return of Christ. The dragon poured water like a river out of his mouth after the woman, to sweep her away with the flood – but he was foiled again. Then the dragon was angry with the woman and went off to make war against the rest of her offspring, those who keep the commandments of God and bear testimony to Jesus (12:4–17).

He has been doing that ever since. "Woe to you, O earth and sea, for the devil has come down to you in great wrath, because he knows that his time is short!" (12:12). Satan, like the church and the world, lives between the Advents. The first coming of Jesus spelt his defeat. The second coming will confirm his doom. Just as Jesus' reign has been inaugurated but not consummated, so it is with the defeat of Satan. Until then he prowls around seeking whom he may devour. Until then he attacks the children of God relentlessly.

There are only two further references to him in the Apocalypse. One comes in chapter 16:13ff when the ungodly trio of the dragon, the beast from the sea, and the beast from the earth (or false prophet) are preparing for the final battle at Armageddon. Armageddon, the narrow pass

217

at Megiddo on the Carmel range, had been the site of many a crucial battle in Middle-East history. It was here that Josiah was killed by Pharaoh Necho. It was here that Elijah defeated the prophets of Baal. So Armageddon is a fitting emblem of the final great battle when false political systems and false religions will be defeated, and the devil's fate settled. He still deceives the nations. He still sends forth "demonic spirits, performing signs" (16:13) but his time is short. In chapter 17 we are reminded that the forces of evil are playing in extra time. Their impact is strictly limited. "The ten kings (allies of the satanic trio) are to receive authority *for one hour*, together with the beast . . . They will make war on the Lamb and the Lamb will overcome them, for he is Lord of lords and King of kings." And then it goes on to make a perfectly astounding claim, but one which we saw in the Book of Job and which is implied throughout the whole Bible, namely that God is in control of the evil in his world. It will not ultimately thwart his purposes of good. John claims that "God has put it into their hearts (i.e. the hearts of the rebellious forces) to fulfil his royal decree" (17:17). Could anything express more clearly the conviction that the Lord God Omnipotent is reigning?

The end draws near, as Christ returns this time not to suffer but to reign. The false prophet, the beast from the sea and the dragon are dismissed in the opposite order from that in which they came upon the stage. They are cast into the lake of fire (19:20, 20:10). This whole concept is clothed in mystery, and we would be foolish to build a theology upon the apocalyptic imagery of a book like Revelation. We are very squeamish about the ideas like the lake of fire, but that may be because we have become very indifferent about any ultimate distinction between right and wrong. At all events, two factors may help us here. The lake of fire does not necessarily carry the implication of conscious unending torment for those consigned to it. You don't tend to last very long in a lake of fire! The imagery probably denotes final and irreversible ruin and annihilation rather than endless torment. The other factor which may help us is that all three, the devil, corrupt political power and false religion, are principles rather than people. The cosmic forces of evil are annihilated for ever from God's world. And supremely that means the archetypal spirit of evil, Satan himself. He chose isolation from God, and ultimately he will get what he chose. Whether the language of Revelation 20:1–4 implies a final short burst of Satanic activity before the Return of Christ or after it, or whether the "thousand years" is a symbol for this present age, has been endlessly discussed, and I do not wish to add to the millions of words about it. I am convinced that the Bible is not a book to answer speculative questions like this. I recall that none of those who thought they knew the details of the first Coming got it right, and I am prepared to leave the millennial question to God alone. Whatever the rights and wrongs of that issue (and it is one on which we ought not to excommunicate one another, for the whole idea is based only on one small figurative and highly imaginative passage in this complex book, the Apocalypse), the ultimate outcome is not in doubt. Satan will be defeated and abolished. Eternity will not be disfigured by the self-seeking, deceit, hatred and accusations of the Adversary, but God will be all in all and the redeemed will be for ever satisfied with their Lord, who has turned Paradise lost into Paradise regained.

## CHAPTER 8

## *The Overcomers*

### Overcoming: a study in contrasts

ONE OF THE most exciting parts of being a Christian is to realise that we are called to share in the victory of Christ. He is not merely an ideal who lived and died. He lives within the believer by his Spirit, and therefore "I can do all things in him who strengthens me" (Phil. 4:13). Indeed, "We shall overcome" might have been written as the signature tune of the New Testament.

In those days there seems to have been little of the moralism so common nowadays: sin was not a matter of do's and don'ts but a dynamic power whose nerve had been cut by Christ and whose domination would not be tolerated by his followers. The Christian message was not to be conformed to the contemporary syncretism which was even more a mark of first-century life than of our own: the gospel stood out in stark and joyous contrast to the relativism of the day. Not for them our preoccupation with the minutiae of church government and forms of worship: the early Christians were confident that they belonged to a movement which nothing could halt, and in obedience to Jesus they went out and made disciples. I do not see in the writings of the New Testament and early Fathers the modern theologian's tendency to ethical compromise which not only tolerates but sometimes even advocates the practice of fornication, homosexuality, euthanasia and abortion. I do not notice any tendency in those days to surrender to the spirit of the age – and that is just what I do notice in the presuppositions and outworkings of much modern theology. There was a confidence, a joyous abandon about the early Christians which had the flavour of adventure and gallantry. They were clear where they stood, they knew where they were going. How many modern theologians could follow Paul in the claims to victory, decisiveness, and

220

divine commissioning that we find in, for instance, 2 Cor. 2:14–17? It is worth allowing the force of the passage to make its own impact on us.

"Thanks be to God" he says (after forgiving someone, and thus ensuring that Satan got no advantage over him) "who in Christ always leads us in triumph, and through us spreads the fragrance of the knowledge of him everywhere. For we are the aroma of Christ to God among those who are being saved and among those who are perishing; to one a fragrance from death to death, to the other a fragrance from life to life. Who is sufficient for these things? We are not, like so many, pedlars of God's word; but as men of sincerity, as commissioned by God, in the sight of God we speak in Christ."

Now I ask you. Would a typical modern Christian leader realise that failure to forgive a member of another congregation gives Satan an advantage? Would he begin to think in these terms? Would such a man see his ministry as an experience of God's power triumphing in his life and circumstances, hard though these might be (and for that, see 2 Corinthians chapters 4, 6 and 11)? Would he see himself and his total lifestyle as a pleasing smell suffusing the landscape, as the aroma from the Hot Bread Kitchen gently pervades central Oxford? Would he have clear views about being saved and perishing, know the difference, and care enough to labour with all powers at his command "by all means to save some"? Would he see himself as speaking and teaching the word of God, not peddling some relativistic opinions to pass on to gullible buyers? It is impossible to miss the note of confidence and victory in a passage like that, which is only one of many. What explains it?

The answer is simple. These early Christians really did believe that Satan was a defeated foe; that no weapon formed against Christ, and therefore derivatively against them, could ultimately prosper. They were prepared to follow him to the cross if need be, confident that they would share in his resurrection – that astounding new thing which had happened in their time: the king of death had had his domain ravaged, and the gates locked since the dawn of time had been thrown open by Jesus of Nazareth. Defeatism never crossed their minds. They were expectant, confident, not in themselves but in him.

## Confidence in the cross

If we asked those early Christians for the secret of their confidence and expectancy, they would take us back to Calvary. There all the forces of evil had concentrated their assault on the Son of God, and had been broken by his obedient and sacrificial death. In four great chapters of Romans (5–8), Paul exults in the way the cross of Christ has broken the back of four great tyrants of the Old Age – wrath, sin, law and death. No more condemnation: Christ has borne it in our place. No more inveterate bondage to sin – in Christ's risen power it could be broken. No more hopeless subservience to a written code but rather the glad obedience of a living Lord and the guidance of the interiorised *torah*, the Holy Spirit. No more fear of the anonymity of *sheol*, but the assurance of being with Christ in his risen life. "To me, to live is Christ and to die is gain" (Phil. 1:21). Who, in the whole of pre-Christian civilisation could have written that? None before could have exulted like the same writer in the eighth chapter of Romans:

> I am persuaded that neither death nor life
> Nor angels nor principalities
> Nor things present nor things to come
> Nor powers nor height nor depth
> Nor anything else in all creation
> Shall be able to separate us
> From the love of God in Christ Jesus our Lord.

Yes, their confidence sprang from a firm grasp of the defeat of Satan on the cross. It was there, as Aulen saw so clearly in his book *Christus Victor*, that Jesus won the critical battle. It was precisely there, in the nadir of his exposure and weakness that he showed the acme of his glory and power. "He cancelled the bond which stood against us with its legal demands; this he set aside, nailing it to his cross. He disarmed the principalities and powers and made a public example of them, triumphing over them in it" (Col. 2:15). As F. F. Bruce puts it in his *New London Commentary* on that passage, "He grappled with them and mastered them, stripping them of all the armour in which they trusted, and held them aloft in his mighty outstretched hands, displaying to the universe their helplessness and his own unvanquished strength." It was in that unvanquished strength that the Christians went out to do battle. They never tired of reminding Satan that he was a beaten foe. "The God of peace shall bruise Satan under your feet shortly" (Rom. 16:20) was their confident conviction. They knew that God was well able to deliver the righteous from temptation (2 Peter 2:9) and that they were being "preserved by the power of God through faith for a salvation which was waiting to be revealed" (although they rejoiced in its foretaste now, 1 Peter 1:5).

I remember years ago reading some sound advice on what to do if you should find yourself in the Canadian wheat-belt with a prairie fire bearing down on you. The advice was this. You should light a fresh fire at your feet, allow the wind to drive it away, and then stand on the burnt ground as you begin to be enveloped by all the savagery of the prairie fire. The early Christians did not flinch in the face of all the problems and forces unleashed against them. They stood on the burnt ground of Calvary, and the fire could not touch them there.

## Confidence in the Spirit

These early overcomers seem to have been habitually filled by the Holy Spirit. This was not a continuous state, needless to say. We find rows between Peter and Paul, deceit by Ananias and Sapphira, immorality at Corinth and the like. They were frail and human. And yet when Paul wrote to the Ephesians, "Be filled with the Spirit," they must have sensed what he meant. It was in Ephesus that the Spirit had come in power on disciples of John the Baptist who previously had merely his proclamation and ethics to go on; their lives were changed, they spoke with tongues and prophesied (Acts 19). It was in Ephesus that the Spirit of the Christ so filled Paul that he packed the school of

223

Tyrannus daily and led many pagans to the faith. It was in Ephesus that the Spirit of the living God drove many who had been gripped by the occult arts to confess their sins, divulge their practices and burn their expensive books. It was in Ephesus that the sons of Scaeva were so impressed by the name of Jesus and the lifechanging power of his Spirit that they attempted to use his name in an exorcism. It backfired. "The evil spirit answered 'Jesus I know and Paul I know, but who are you?' And the man in whom the evil spirit was leaped on them, mastered them all, and over-powered them, so that they fled out of that house, naked and wounded." This sort of Christianity was a talking point in town. Many were annoyed by it. Many wanted to lynch the Christians. There was a riot. Political and economic domains were invaded by these uncompromising Christians, full of the Holy Spirit. It is a far cry from the normal effect of Christianity in Western Europe, is it not? But not too unusual in Latin America, much of Africa or areas of South-East Asia such as Indonesia.

## Confidence in the Word

A third characteristic of the whole Christian movement in early days seems to have been their confident belief in the Christian message. They used "the Word of God" both for the Old Testament message, and for the message about Jesus. Indeed they used it for the person of their Lord himself; was he not the very expression of the invisible God? They could write like this: "You received the word in much affliction, with joy inspired by the Holy Spirit, so that you became examples to all the believers in Macedonia and Achaia." Again, "We also thank God constantly for this, that when you received the word of God which you heard from us, you accepted it not as the word of men, but as what it really is, the word of God, which is at work in you believers" (1 Thess. 1:6, 2:13). More than thirty times in the Acts alone we read of the progress of "the word", when what the author means is that the Christian cause grew. See, for instance, Acts 13:26, 15:7, 17:11, 20:32 and ask yourself how their confidence in the clarity, inspiration and reliability of God's message of salvation compares with the uncertain notes of many a modern trumpet, which is unlikely to stir anybody much to the battle.

## Obedience

A fourth notable feature of this remarkable saga of the overcomers, where a handful of peasants in a tiny corner of the Roman map changed the face of history within a couple of generations, was their straightforward obedience. Jesus had told them not to leave Jerusalem but to "wait for the promise of the Father" (Acts 1:4). So they stayed in Jerusalem and waited. Jesus had told them that "you shall receive power when the Holy Spirit has come upon you; and you shall be my witnesses in Jerusalem and in all Judaea, and in Samaria, and to the end of the earth" (1:8). They did receive power, and they did go, in those ever-widening circles of witness.

I find myself amazed that a man like Philip the evangelist should be prepared to heed the quiet inner voice of the Spirit and leave Samaria where a revival had broken out under his leadership, in order to go down to the highly unpromising desert of the Gaza strip where the odds were that he would meet nobody (Acts 8:9–12, 26). It was sheer obedience. I am dumbfounded to reflect that the first missionary journey arose out of a service of worship where the people had the conviction (probably through a prophetic utterance) that Saul and Barnabas, their two most talented leaders, should leave them and go to pastures new. So "after fasting and praying they laid their hands upon them and sent them off" (13:3). Perfectly astounding. What modern church would show such obedience to the prompting of the Lord? We would rationalise our disobedience, would we not? We would argue that the speaker was probably not inspired by God, that it was not safe for the men to go, that it would leave the home church thin on leadership, that the time was not ripe, that a committee should be set up to look into the matter. But these men had a simple faith in God, and it made them obedient.

That obedience was a very costly thing. It involved great single-mindedness: "And now, behold, I am going to Jerusalem, bound in the Spirit, not knowing what shall befall me there; except that the Holy Spirit testifies to me in every city that imprisonment and afflictions await me. But none of these things move me, nor do I account my life of any value to myself, if only I may accomplish my course and the ministry which I received from the Lord Jesus, to testify to the gospel of the grace of God" (Acts 20:22f). That attitude is typical. That is why these men were unstoppable. They had the living Christ with them. They knew it. Naturally, they were overcomers.

## The Overcoming Life in the Individual

After each of the Letters to the Seven Churches in Revelation 2 and 3 there comes a haunting refrain from the lips of Jesus: "To him who overcomes I will give . . ." He expects Christians to overcome.

### Three dangers
There are three preliminary dangers to avoid if we are going even to begin to match up to the Lord's expectations. All three have had a lot of mileage in the history of the church. The first is defeatism, the second activism and the third quietism.

Defeatism is out because Jesus Christ has conquered Satan. No matter what besetting failure has gripped us in the past, it need not continue to do so. The power of Jesus is greater than the power of sin. We have only to want the liberation and ask him to achieve it: then the change begins.

Activism has a long history on the fringes of Christendom, and sometimes more centrally too. The impression is given that it all depends on us: our efforts to improve, our stiff upper lip when suffering comes, our resignation in the face of death. But that is Stoicism not Christianity. To be sure, there is a battle to be fought; there is an enemy to be resisted. But he is not impressed by our strength; only when we are "strong in the Lord and the power of his might" will the Tempter turn tail.

For a century and more in Christian circles that have concentrated on holiness of life, the impression has gained ground that victory is achieved by "letting go and letting

God". This quietism is a dangerous half-truth, at best. Of course, the victory is won as we abide in Christ and find his strength in our weakness. But there is an enemy to be fought. There is a battle to wage. There are evil habits to put off. There is a stand to take. There is vigilance to guard.

Victorious living is something of a cliché. It gives the dangerous impression that it is a talisman some people possess and others do not. Asked if I am enjoying victory in my Christian life, my mind immediately moves to certain areas in which I have experienced failure in the past and I hastily check up on my current performance! But that was far from the mind of Jesus when he called for overcomers. It is not deliverance from a small circle of particular private sins, but an increasing Christlikeness. That is possible as we keep in touch with him; therefore there need to be no defeatism. But it is also a battle, and will require us to engage wholeheartedly in the fight of faith. What is this going to mean for the individual Christian?

## Realism

First, as we have seen in a previous chapter, we are called to "put off" the old nature and its works. This repudiation of the claims of our fallenness is an act of will that needs to be repeated daily. We have to put off the old nature and put on Christ, renouncing the one and claiming the other by faith. This is cool and deliberate; it will also be costly.

That is why Paul emphasises that we must put to death what is earthly in us, fornication, covetousness, idolatry and the like (Col. 3:5). These things have got to go. They go to the cross where Jesus dealt them their death-blow in principle when dying as our representative. "We know that our old self was crucified with him so that the sinful body might be destroyed, and we might be no longer enslaved to sin," wrote Paul, and follows it with a challenging call to act on that knowledge. This is a very practical matter. So "you must consider yourselves dead to sin and alive to God in Christ Jesus. Do not allow sin to hold court within your mortal bodies. Do not yield your members as instruments for sin" (Rom. 6:6ff).

In other words I must put my sinful propensities where

227

Jesus put them, on the cross. That is where they belong. That is where one by one they must be nailed back, however hard and often they seek escape. "Those who belong to Christ have crucified the flesh with its passions and lusts" (Gal. 5:24). Thus, if I have a foul temper I must realise it was dealt with by Christ on the cross, be willing to put it there, and deliberately ask him to deal with it in the light of Calvary and himself reign in my body. It is as practical and challenging as that. The devil has got to be resisted and the flesh has got to be crucified. No cheap victory is possible in this war.

### Resistance

Provided we are prepared to "mortify" or "crucify" our evil passions on that cross where Jesus defeated Satan, we shall be in a position to "stand against the wiles of the devil . . . to withstand in the evil day, and having done all to stand" (Eph. 6:11ff). We shall be in a position to resist the roaring lion who prowls around seeking someone to devour, but we shall only do so as we are "firm in faith", for the power is Christ's and not ours. Firm resistance, which in the case of youthful lusts, paradoxically means running away from their entanglements (2 Tim 2:22) is required. No half measures. But it works. "Submit yourselves to God: resist the devil and he will flee from you" (James 4:7).

This matter of resisting only in the power which Christ gives is so important that Paul devotes half a chapter to it, and develops the theme under the imagery of donning armour for legionary warfare. Ephesians six is a chapter which has attracted enormous attention. John Stott in his recent commentary entitled *God's New Society* notes that William Gurnall's *The Christian in Complete Armour* runs to "three volumes, 261 chapters and 1472 pages, although it is an exposition of only eleven verses", while Dr. Martyn Lloyd-Jones' two volumes of the same eleven verses clocks up 736 pages. I do not propose to enter into competition! I wish to draw attention to only two things.

First, the armour imagery is used again in 1 Thess. 5:8 where the items have different significance, so it is doubtful if too much ought to be made of breastplate, helmet, shield and the like. Second, "the armour" is single in Greek: we are not to take our pick or don it piece by piece, but as an entity, literally, a panoply. "Put on the Lord Jesus Christ," as Paul says in Romans. *He* is the armour of God. He is the one in whom we must be clothed if we are to win the battle against Satan.

## Prayer

Two characteristic and most important words come at the end of the list of armour: pray and watch. Both are vital in Christian warfare.

Paul realised that prayer is the supreme expression of our dependence on God. And if his is the power and not our own, then it is impossible to exaggerate the need for prayer. He certainly stresses its all-pervading need. We are to pray at *all* times, with *all* prayer, with *all* perseverance, and for *all* saints. An immensely challenging command. I do not find it comes at all easily to me. But of one thing I am painfully convinced, from much experience. When I do not pray I do not enjoy the victory over the Enemy which I am intended to experience. I go under. Indeed, there are times when that prayer needs to be intensified by fasting. Jesus certainly practised fasting and intended his followers to do the same, not as if it possessed some inherent power, but secretly before God to show him our utter dependence on his power and our singlemindedness in his service. Once again, I have discovered its power in spiritual warfare. According to some texts of Matt. 17:21, Mk. 9:29 certain acts of deliverance are only possible after prayer *and fasting*.

## Watchfulness

Prayer, then, is essential, but so is watchfulness. It is constantly enjoined upon Christians in the New Testament. We are to watch out for the devil's assaults: "Be watchful, stand firm in your faith, quit you like men, be strong" (1 Cor. 16:13, cf. 1 Peter 5:8 1 Thess. 5:6). We are to be watchful in prayer, staying awake and concentrating on the one hand (Mk. 14:37f) and, on the other, looking for answers for which to praise God and for opportunities to use for God (Col. 4:2). We are invited to remain watchful against heresy in the church – this was a major concern of Paul's towards the end of his life (Acts 20:31). We must watch against the tendency to "sleep" or remain oblivious to moral failures in our own lives: self-examination is required in those who follow Jesus Christ (1 Thess. 5:6, cf. 2 Cor. 13:5). Time and again we are told to be watchful for the return of Christ at the end of history – not in overheated apocalyptic speculation, but in that quiet attitude of expectancy, holiness of life, faithfulness in our work which would give us reason not to be ashamed before him at his coming (Matt. 24:42, 25:13, Lk. 12:37). No wonder Sardis, the city that was twice captured as she slept, is held up to us as a warning of what can happen to those who do not watch (Rev. 3:2). Appropriately the last reference to watchfulness in the Bible runs like this: "Lo I am coming like a thief! Blessed is he who is watchful, keeping his garments that he may not go naked and be seen exposed!" (Rev. 16:15).

It is significant that Jesus' combination, "Watch and pray that you may not enter into temptation," (Matt. 26:41) became the foundation for an early Christian catechism, as Carrington, Selwyn and Hunter have shown. The themes of the new birth, putting off the old nature, putting on the new, watching and prayer, and standing fast or resisting the devil are present, and in that order, in James, 1 Peter, Colossians and Ephesians. In modern Christian teaching I wonder whether any of those priorities, apart possibly from prayer, find a place.

### Scripture

Another important weapon in spiritual warfare is the use of Scripture. In the passage on the Christian armour it is called "the sword of the Spirit, the word of God", and just as a sword is both an attacking and a defensive weapon, so is the sword of the Spirit. Time and again Jesus clinched his arguments with the Jews by citing Scripture: "It is written" or "Have you not read?" And as we saw in the last chapter, in his own battle with the Tempter he three times quoted verses from Deuteronomy. It was the same on Calvary, where word after word from the cross was either a direct quotation from or a reflection of the Old Testament. Time and again in the ministry of deliverance we have found that the Spirit would suddenly lead us to a passage of Scripture which opened up the whole problem and pointed the way to release. Time and again in personal counselling a passage from Scripture has brought light and comfort where my words had conspicuously failed.

### Spiritual gifts

As I have sought to show in *I Believe in the Holy Spirit*, part of the work of the Spirit from the very beginning in the church has been to make available gifts to be used in the prosecution of its mission and the building up of its members. These gifts, unlike many of his other gifts, are not an intensification of qualities he has implanted in us naturally, but something fresh from outside.

The most obvious and widespread in recent decades is the revival of the gift of tongues within every denomination of the church. For a discussion of it I would refer the reader to my previous book. The point here is that these gifts are intended to be used. God can guide a congregation with immediacy through a message in tongues that is then interpreted. God can use tongues as a spiritual weapon in dealing with occult forces. Personally, I should hesitate to engage in deliverance ministry without it, although I am aware that there is no scriptural basis for this.

Prophecy is another of God's gifts through the Spirit to be used in Christian warfare. Often the church becomes stale and slack, or slips into a bypath from which it needs to be recalled by prophetic utterance through some member of the congregation. Sometimes such a message is predictive, sometimes hortatory, sometimes analytic. One of the great needs today is for the church at large to recover a prophetic stance for the nation. Prophecy was prized in the early church above all other gifts: through it the Lord could direct his people. It has fallen into widespread desuetude. The very word is devalued. Yet it remains an important weapon in the spiritual arsenal. It is of great value in ministering to those who are gripped by the occult. It is of great value in guidance and direction for the congregation.

231

And at times it can be of significance for the nation. The most astonishing example of prophecy of this widespread predictive type that I have come across was given to a Russian monk, Seraphin, in 1911, six years before the Revolution. It was brought to the West by Mother Barbara, who now lives on the Mount of Olives and gives herself daily to intercession for the world.

> An evil will shortly take Russia, and wherever this evil comes, rivers of blood will flow because of it. It is not the Russian soul, but an imposition on the Russian soul. It is not an ideology, or a philosophy, but a spirit from hell. In the last days Germany will be divided in two. France will just be nothing. Italy will be judged by natural disasters. Britain will lose her empire and all her colonies and will come to almost total ruin, but will be saved by praying women. America will feed the world but will finally collapse. Russia and China will destroy each other. Finally, Russia will be free, and from her believers will go forth and turn many from the nations to God.

Whatever we make of something like that, enough of it has already taken place to make one think twice before rejecting it. Did not the Old Testament give fulfilment as the acid test of predictive prophecy?

Healing is, of course, another of the gifts of the Spirit which we are increasingly seeing not only among members of the churches but among those who are not yet Christians. This at once gives palpable assurance of the Lord's living reality, and predisposes them to be receptive towards the message of the gospel. Such however is the hardness of the human heart that some people who are filled with awe at the hand of God in rescuing either themselves or a close relation from immediate death as a result of the Spirit's healing ministry, then turn their back on God and refuse to allow him access to their lives. For others, however, healing is the gateway to Christian faith.

It is important, I believe, that the gifts which the Spirit has been renewing in the church in this generation are seen

232

as a sacred trust – not to be used selfishly and internally within the church for its gratification, but to be exercised outside the church for the service of mankind. And this holds good not only for the three gifts I have just mentioned, but for gifts of knowledge, wisdom, hospitality, administration and so forth. All God's gifts are intended not for self-congratulation but for the edification of the church and the service of the world. They are meant to furnish spiritual equipment for overcomers.

## Positive thinking

A great deal of exaggerated emphasis is being given these days to the power of positive thinking, particularly in America. By itself it is no match whatever for Satan; nevertheless it has an important subsidiary role to play. Paul tells the Philippians, in the verses before his celebrated claim to be able to face anything through the Christ who strengthens him, that they need to fill their minds with what is good. "Finally, brethren, whatever is true, whatever is honourable, whatever is just, whatever is pure, whatever is lovely, whatever is gracious, if there is anything worthy of praise, think about these things" (Phil. 4:8f). Such positive thinking is part of feeding the new nature and starving the old. It supplies the support forces, so to speak, behind the shock troops in battle.

## Faith

And when the assault is on, there is one weapon above all others that we must take. It is the shield of faith. This means calling out, as we feel ourselves beginning to sink, "Lord, save me" (Matt. 14:30). That look of faith sufficed to rescue Peter from drowning. That look of faith, "Jesus, remember me when you come into your kingdom", brought the penitent thief to paradise (Lk. 23:43). It can do the same for any of us. The point is well made in 1 Cor. 10:13. "No temptation has overtaken you that is not common to man." That is an encouragement. My temptations are not of a unique difficulty. Others are in the same boat. The verse continues: "God is faithful and he will not let you be tempted beyond your strength." That is even more encouraging: to dwell on God's reliability in his promises and succour, and to be assured that he will temper the winds of temptation to the shorn lamb. "But with the temptation he will also provide the way of escape, that you may be able to endure it." So ends the verse, and the way of escape is always available. It is the way of calling to the Lord out of our extremity and weakness and humbly trusting his power to have its way. Then "my God shall supply every need of yours according to his riches in glory in Christ Jesus" (Phil. 4:19), and you shall be "strengthened with might through his Spirit in the inner man, that Christ may be at home in your hearts, through faith" (Eph. 3:17).

The overcoming life is progressively possible for us as Christian believers. God has already "blessed us with all spiritual blessings in the heavenly places in Christ", and he longs to open our eyes to the possibilities of victory, to "the immeasurable greatness of his power in us who believe" (Eph. 1:3, 19).

### The Overcoming Life in Society

**The two dimensional struggle**
Dr. Visser 't Hooft at the Uppsala Assembly of the World Council of Churches made the point well when he declared:

> A Christianity which has lost its vertical dimension has lost its salt, and is not only insipid itself, but useless to the world. But a Christianity which would use the vertical dimension as a means of escape from responsibility for and in the common life of men is a denial of the incarnation of God's life for the world manifested in Christ.

The struggle against Satan has often been seen in either solely supernaturalist or solely personal terms. This is quite wrong. As we have seen in chapter four, the principalities and powers have invaded the very structures of society. Jesus came not merely to save individuals and put them in a right relationship with God, but to found a kingdom which was the embodiment and pledge of the Kingdom of God on earth. The spiritual and social aspects of the gospel of Christ are inseparable. The Christian is in an ambiguous position. He is a member both of "this passing age" as the Bible calls it, and of "the age to come". He lives in the overlap between the ages. He is subject both to God and to Caesar. He lives in this age but not according to this age. He owes allegiance provisionally to the family, society, state and world in which he lives now, but ultimately to "that kingdom which cannot be shaken". How is he to confront the devil in the principalities and powers of modern life? How is he to live as an agent of God in the kingdom of Caesar?

## The survival of man

Our society and our world are facing problems of a magnitude never paralleled in the history of mankind. The threats to the future of man arising from famine, overpopulation, the ravaging of non-renewable resources, the energy and environmental crisis, and the ever-increasing possibility of thermonuclear, biological and germ warfare pose global problems which no man or nation has been able to solve. Professor Robert Heilbroner, one of the leading economists in the U.S.A., published in 1974 *An Inquiry into the Human Prospect*. His opening sentence concluded with the question "Is there hope for man?". On the whole, his conclusion was that in the light of the enormous problems facing mankind and our extreme reluctance to face up to them, there could be little hope. The book had an enormous impact and created sharp division of opinion in the Western world. In 1980 it was issued afresh, updated and reconsidered. The main thesis is unaltered. Heilbroner takes no joy in predicting the collapse of industrial civilisation. "Am I not the child and beneficiary of this civilisation? Can I discuss its deaththroes unaware that I am talking about my own demise?" (p. 174). A similar conclusion is reached in Ronald Higgins' book, *The Seventh Enemy* to which we referred in chapter one. Behind six appalling threats overhanging mankind lies a seventh, apathy; the feeling both on the individual and the political front that nothing can be done. Neither book is written from a specifically Christian perspective. Both books are

235

persuaded of the existence of forces beyond human control gripping our institutions and our world. In the light of this predicament, more threatening now than at any time in history, what are Christians to do?

## Watchfulness

First, we are commanded by our Lord to watch. The word means to be on the alert, to keep awake, to be perceptive. And in a world where clichés are replacing thought, where surrender to the spirit of the age is increasingly common, where the media have a dangerously dominant role in opinion-forming, and where a false security – or perhaps opiate – is provided by the modern equivalents to the "bread and circuses" which masked the collapse of the Roman Empire, it is critical for Christians to watch. If Christians who are, or should be, aware of the superhuman forces which lie behind our fallen institutions do not perceive what is going on and speak out, the human prospect is bleak indeed.

William Stringfellow in his book *An Ethic for Christians and Other Aliens in a Strange Land* transposes the multifarious biblical titles such as principalities, powers, rulers, gods, elements, dominions, lords and the like into contemporary terms.

> They include all institutions, all ideologies, all images, all movements, all causes, all corporations, all bureaucracies, all traditions, all methods and routines, all conglomerates, all races, all nations, all idols. Thus the Pentagon or the Ford Motor Company or Harvard University or the Hudson Institute or Consolidated Edison or the Diners Club or the Olympics or the Methodist Church or the Teamsters Union are all principalities. So are capitalism, Maoism, humanism, Mormonism, astrology, the Puritan work ethic, science and scientism, white supremacy, patriotism, sports, sex, any profession or discipline, technology, money, even the family. The principalities and powers *are* legion.
>
> (*op. cit.* p. 78)

236

He goes on to show the fallenness as well as the grip of these principalities and powers.

> Specific illustrations of it from the contemporary American scene abound – in the precedence, for example, of bureaucratic routine over human need in the administration of welfare; in the brutalisation of inmates where imprisonment is really a means of banishing men from human status, hiding them, treating them as animals or as if they were dead as human beings; in the separation of citizens in apartheid, enforced, as the case may be, by urban housing and development schemes, by racial limitations or access to credit, or by the militia; in the social priorities determined by the momentum of technological proliferation, regardless of either environmental or human interests thereby neglected, damaged or lost; in genocide practised for generations against Indian Americans; in the customs of male chauvinism; in the fraud and fakery and the perils to human health sponsored by American merchandising methodology.
>
> (*op. cit.* p. 83)

Fortunately, Stringfellow is not a lone voice. Others are coming to recognise the demonic in human affairs. Jacques Ellul in his book, *The New Demons* unmasks some modern myths, uncritically accepted by the majority of educated men, such as "science", "history", "the revolution" and "progress". He also unmasks some modern religious substitutes, such as the occult explosion, the hippie cult, the orgiastic delirium of violence, the worship of movie or sports stars, and the cult of sexuality. Most dangerous of all is political religion, the ascription of supreme worth to the state or the system: we have already considered this in chapter six. They all present a tremendous challenge to vigilance.

René Padilla, perhaps the ablest representative of the new genre of radical biblical theologians from Latin America, sees one of the most threatening manifestations of the principalities and powers in an increasingly "urban civilisation whose defining feature is the all-importance of technological products". The city gradually presses men into a materialistic mould, "a mould which gives absolute value to 'things' because they are status symbols, a mould which leaves no room for questions about the meaning of work or the purpose of life." "In the first revolution man's work was replaced by that of the machine; in the second, man's very thinking is being replaced by the machine. The era of automation and cybernetics is beginning."

What is happening on a global scale? Man is becoming merely a cog in the machine which operates on the laws of supply and demand and is the principal cause of environmental pollution. Man's quest for continued growth will probably bring world economy to a halt by the end of the century (see the arguments in Heilbroner, *op. cit.*, chapters three and four). Meanwhile the gap between the haves and the have nots yawns ever wider. The rich nations refuse to recognise the relationship between their own economic development and the underdevelopment of the poor nations. Consumerism, aided by advertisement's creation of bogus needs, is rampant. Padilla rightly observes that behind the materialism which deifies consumption lie the powers of destruction to which the New Testament refers. The demonic powers enslave mankind through the structures and systems he treats as absolute, and Padilla interprets Gal. 4:8 and 1 Cor. 10:20 against this background. Paul is warning his readers against a return to bondage of spiritual powers by worshipping what in reality is not worthy of worship, that is to say, by absolutising the relative. He quotes C. K. Barrett to the effect that for Paul idolatry was evil "primarily because it robbed God of the glory due to him alone . . . but it was evil also because it meant that man, engaged in a spiritual act and directing his worship towards something other than the one true God, was brought into intimate relation with the lower, and evil, spiritual powers" (*The New Face of Evangelicalism*, ed. René Padilla, p. 208–212).

No wonder we are bidden to keep alert, to watch.

## Prayer

But the Christian man in such a world must also pray. He must pray for "kings and for all who are in high positions". This must be no perfunctory prayer. "I urge that supplications, prayers, intercessions and thanksgivings be made," says the apostle (1 Tim. 2:1f). This is perhaps the greatest thing we can do for our country, to pray earnestly, regularly, persistently for those in the corridors of power whether in government, the media, industry or education. Daniel was placed by God in a situation where he was called to live a godly life in a position of great responsibility among a society which was absolutely in the grip of the principalities and powers. His priority? Prayer, three times a day, with his face turned to Jerusalem – and he did not mind who knew about it (Dan. 6:10).

Paul stresses the intense spiritual battle involved in such a prayer when he tells us that we do not wrestle against flesh and blood but against principalities and powers of darkness. Generally we take that to mean "We do not wrestle *only* against flesh and blood". But he does not say *only*. The staggering truth he had perceived and wants his readers to understand is that we do not wrestle against flesh and blood *at all*. It is in prayer that the battle is won. It is in prayer that the principalities and powers are defeated.

I used to think that the prayer attributed by Luke to the apostles when released from prison in Acts 4 was very strange. They took no social or political action. They simply had recourse to a prayer meeting. And even in that prayer meeting they scarcely made a request of any kind, except for boldness to speak the word of the Lord. No, they used that time of prayer to lay before the "sovereign Lord who didst make the heaven and the earth" those secondary powers which were seeking to exercise absolute power – the confederation of Herod and Pilate, the Gentiles and the leaders of Israel. But now I see that they were doing the most effective thing open to them. They were ascribing glory to Almighty God in the face of all pretended claims from other sources to exercise power over them. No wonder the place was shaken where they were assembled, and they were filled anew with the Holy Spirit. They had

239

taken on the principalities and powers in prayer, and had prevailed.

## Boldness

Watchfulness and prayer should lead Christians in society to speak out. It is interesting that the humanist Utopia and the Communist "dictatorship of the proletariat" assume that in the end all will be well in the best of all possible worlds. The Christian can never be so gullible. But he tends either to keep his own counsel, or else to surrender to the quietism that politicians wish to see in the church: "we can't have religion interfering with politics!" But unless religion does interfere in politics, God help politics. Unless the salt does influence the rotting meat, God help the rotten meat. The church needs to say, and to say loud and clear, that there is a choice at the end of the road. All will not necessarily be well. In the Book of Revelation, that most political of all the books in the New Testament, we are faced with Babylon as well as Jerusalem. Babylon the harlot: Jerusalem the bride of Christ. Babylon the man-made domain of alienation, greed, persecution, and war: Jerusalem the God-given home of sanity and freedom, of love and self-giving, of beauty and fulfilment. Between those visions, and the steps which lead to them, men and nations must choose.

There is a terrible passage in Revelation 18. It is a funeral dirge on the Babylon type of power. Babylon is highly contemporary: a land of trade and consumer goods (v. 11), a land of spendour and delicacies (v. 14), of fine clothes and costly ornaments (v. 16), of great merchant navies (v. 19) and elegant culture (v.22f). That is the fine outward impression of the city.

But what does God see? A land that feels secure in its wickedness (v. 10). A land that deifies knowledge and technology (v. 10). A land mad on pleasure and self-gratification (v. 8, 12). A land that has become a haunt for the demonic (v. 2). A land of wantonness and fornication (v. 3), of sorcery and persecution (v. 23), of rape of the earth for her own selfish greed (v. 3, 11ff), and a land of astonishing arrogance. "Since in her heart she says, 'A queen I sit, I am no widow, mourning I shall never see' – so shall her plagues come in a single day, pestilence and mourning and famine, and she shall be burnt with fire, because mighty is the Lord God who judges her." (v. 7).

The whole passage is fascinatingly up to date, both in its analysis and its warnings. Famine, plague, earthquakes, destruction are indeed awaiting this Babylon society in which we live, if it does not repent. Its fornications, its murders, its wars, its injustice towards the poor, its sorceries and its insensate pride are a stench in the nostrils of Almighty God.

> So shall Babylon the great city be thrown down with
>     violence,
> And shall be found no more.
> And the sound of harpers and minstrels, of flute
>     players and trumpeters
> Shall be heard in thee no more.
> And a craftsman of any craft shall be found in thee
>     no more.
> The light of a lamp shall shine in thee no more;
> And the voice of bridegroom and bride shall be heard
>     in thee no more.
>
> (19:21ff)

Christians in society ought to be giving warning to the nation, whether the nation will listen or not. On the whole, however, it is humanists, not Christians, who have been foremost in the ecology and nuclear, the peace and liberation movements of our time. I have not noticed the church leadership making any serious impact on the greed of our pleasure-mad, consumer society. I suppose the fear of being thought a Jeremiah or the sheer lack of influence which the church now wields in society acts as a dissuasive. But should it? The prophets were called to speak on political and social issues to their countries "whether they will hear or whether they will forbear". These men of God were always in a tiny minority: but that did not embarrass them.

But if there is anything more forbidding than the call to speak out in such situations, it is the implication that we should rejoice at the downfall of Babylon even if Babylon happens to be our own civilisation. I find it most astonishing, and most threatening, that the fall of Babylon in Revelation 18 is succeeded immediately by a paean of praise to God for her destruction.

> After this I heard what seemed to be the mighty voice
>     of a great multitude in heaven, crying,
> "Hallelujah! Salvation and glory and power belongs to
>     God,
> for his judgements are true and just;
> he has judged the great harlot who corrupted the earth
> with her fornication;
> and he has avenged on her the blood of his servants."
> 
>                                                    (19:1ff)

Does this seem an affront to our patriotism? Think of the alternative – the deification and absolutising of Babylon in all its fallenness. No, the Christian in society will rejoice and praise God when any contemporary manifestation of Babylon is thrown down, even if it be his own country. For only the Jerusalem polity can last. Only that deserves to last.

Such warnings, such rejoicing is bound to be costly. It will lead to great unpopularity. But it is incumbent on the Christians in society who are determined in the strength of Christ to overcome the principalities and powers.

### Resistance .

There are times when the Christian man will have to resist the pressures put upon him by society or state. He is called to resist the devil, in whatever form the devil comes against him. When Nebuchadnezzar made totalitarian and idolatrous claims, the faithful Jewish exiles, Shadrach, Meschach and Abednego registered their silent protest. They refused to bow down to the monstrous statue of the tyrant and do it obeisance, even though their resistance might lead to death (Dan. 3:1–30). In point of fact their faithfulness broke the power of the evil spirit that had gripped Nebuchadnezzar, and he did obeisance to their God and promoted them in Babylon.

Faithfulness does not always have such a happy ending. In the Book of Revelation we are told of "Antipas my faithful martyr" who refused to bow to Caesar's image in Pergamum, refused to take the way of compromise advised and practised by the Nicolaitans, and perished for his pains (2:13). But his name lives on, and his influence has been a spur to the church more than all those compromising Nicolaitans could ever be. He overcame the principality of Caesar worship, though it cost him his life.

These passages, among many that could be cited, show the need for Christians to expose and protest against abuses in society. Abortion, euthanasia, and homosexuality are current issues in the West where the principalities and powers have gripped men's thinking and the flow of public opinion is sharply at odds with the explicit teaching of the Bible. It is the duty of Christians to protest, to oppose and to resist such things, not because they are reactionaries (Christians follow a revolutionary Jesus and have no right to be reactionaries) but because, for all that is said to the contrary, such things spoil the dignity and freedom of man, made in the image of God.

But equally Christians ought to be aware of and resist the pressures of multi-national corporations, the exploitation of labour, the lies in advertising, the disaster of continued economic greed. And Christian voices are far less commonly heard on such issues. We have lost the passionate Old Testament concern for the poor and needy, the oppressed, the underdog. We are strong on the need for salvation but weak on the need for justice. I do not now propose to go into the vexed question of whether Christians should engage in armed rebellion on behalf of the oppressed. You have a Camilo Torres on the one hand and a Martin Luther King on the other. Judge which has had the greater influence. But both were in deadly earnest. Both were prepared to die for the cause of the oppressed. Both were passionately inflamed with a hunger for justice. Are we?

243

**Involvement**

The Christian will not merely protest about the abuses in society. He will get involved in society and work for their removal. It is no good complaining of the effect of the principalities and powers in government, world trade, entertainment, industry and television if Christian men with unblinkered eyes, resolute wills and humble hearts do not get involved and get their hands dirty. The devil has got to be resisted, not merely deprecated. That requires action.

The Bible gives us a lot of precedent for this. We see Joseph, Daniel, Isaiah in places of major political influence. They remained men of God. God blessed the nations they governed for their sake (cf. Gen. 39:5). It can be done today, and there are many men in the highest échelons of power who are there because they are seeking to influence affairs for good. They are the salt that refused to stay in the salt cellar. Sometimes they get abused by the godly who throw up pious hands in horror at their fancied compromise. Opposition springs also from many who, as Revelation puts it, bear the mark of the Beast in their foreheads. But they are obeying their Lord. They are opposing the devil. And such men and women deserve the greatest backing the church can afford them in encouragement and prayer. To be sure, they are in a dangerous place. They are in constant danger of slipping under the control of the principalities and powers. They are under constant pressure to compromise and deny their Lord. Frequently they are tempted to imagine that they can, by their own political efforts, build the Kingdom of God. But danger should be no dissuasive to the Christian. He is called to be involved.

This involvement will take many forms. Individuals can take pains to become better informed, and can write letters to the newspapers and to their representatives in government. They can stand for office in local and national elections. Parents can discuss television programmes of a global nature with their children and help form attitudes in the next generation; something to which teachers can contribute a great deal by teaching not only the history, culture and geography of other lands, but also the social and economic factors that diminish life in those countries. Clergy also have a role, not merely by preaching boldly on social and political issues, as the Old Testament prophets did so powerfully, but also by encouraging the involvement of the congregation in appropriate pressure groups to change public opinion. Students can travel in Third World countries and can see conditions for themselves. Those in business and government can consider long-term justice and the wellbeing of the people concerned, rather than short-term expediency and profit. Morality applies to government and business no less than to individual relations. If we are vigilant and prepared to become involved there is a great deal that can be achieved, even by individuals.

Sometimes this involvement will take the form of a television director's quiet influence behind the scenes. Sometimes it will be seen in the small group of Members of Parliament or Congressmen meeting in each other's rooms to pray about the political work on which they are involved. Sometimes it will take such a form as the Prison Fellowship in America, and now in England, creating cells of Christian activists in prisons, and so bringing hope, reformation, and new life in Christ to those who were hopeless and brutalised by the system. Sometimes it will involve a bold break with traditional postures, as shown in the fearless stand for justice taken by Archbishop Helder Camara in Brazil. Sometimes it may embroil Christians in armed revolt, as it did Bonhoeffer. In this extreme case, wise Christians will know, as Bonhoeffer knew, that violence is in the end self-defeating; they will know that to take the sword will probably mean to perish by the sword. But they will go ahead because they believe (rightly or wrongly) that the régime is so evil, so much under the control of the devil, that to allow it to remain in power would be greater treason to God than to attempt to overturn it by force.

Whatever our level of involvement, the Christian cannot duck out of responsibility. He is called to live out, so far as in him· lies, the life of the kingdom of heaven here on earth – and that goes for social change as well as personal holiness.

## Humanity and Scripture

William Stringfellow has a moving passage in his book where he recounts two important lessons he learnt from the leaders of the Resistance Movement at the conclusion of the Second World War. They are two lessons which provide invaluable guidance to Christians wherever they may be, who seek to confront Satan and the demonic in the structures of their society. These Underground leaders – what nerved them to resist and to take such enormous risks? What kept them going in trivial, haphazard, puny acts of daily resistance against a régime that was oppressive, monolithic and all-pervasive? "In the circumstances of the Nazi tyranny, *resistance became the only human way to live*" (*op. cit.*, p. 119).

Padilla sees it in much the same way. "The church of Jesus Christ is engaged in a spiritual conflict against the powers of evil entrenched in ideological structures which dehumanise man" (*op. cit.*, p. 213). Both men are saying a most important thing: that one of the major criteria for our aims, our protest and our involvement is the liberation of man to be what God intended him to be. The Christian is called to be willing to give himself, to death if necessary, for the sake of what is authentically human – not man as he is, necessarily, but man as God meant him to be and man as potentially he could become.

The other thing that fascinated Stringfellow in Europe among the Underground leaders after the War was the prevalence of Bible study. These men met to study the Scriptures. It was there that they found the stimulus and the guidelines for their service to their fellow men. There was nothing academic about this:

> The Bible became alive as a means of nurture and communication; recourse to the Bible was in itself a primary, practical and essential tactic of resistance. Bible study furnished the precedent for the free, mature, ecumenical, humanising style of life which became characteristic of the confessing movement . . . In Bible study within the anti-Nazi Resistance there

was an edification of the new life to which human
beings are incessantly called by God.

(op. cit., p. 120)

What does humanity demand? What does the Bible say?
These are two fundamental questions for any Christians to
keep asking themselves as they seek to confront the devil
and all his works in today's world.

### The Overcoming Life in the Church

#### Defeatism

The whole idea of the church as overcomer is faintly ludicrous. Not only is the church fairly ineffective, by and large,
and a minority interest in Western society, but it seems to
like things that way. Maybe this has something to do with
rationalising failure, but undoubtedly the church is nowadays so suspicious of its triumphalism in the past that it
almost glorifies failure. It has, quite properly, developed a
theology of the victim and of powerlessness. After all, we
follow one who was victimised, despised, and utterly
powerless: one who had no authority but himself; one
whose power was suffering love alone. That is an important
modern insight. It is a valuable corrective to the days when
the church spoke from an extrinsic authority, when it expected patronage and protection, and played the grandee.
But to interpret the role of the servant as the glorification of
failure is a perspective that is nowhere to be found in the
New Testament.

Many churches these days do not expect to see lives
changed. They do not expect to grow. They do not look for,
or get, conversions. They have surrendered to defeatism.
But as we have seen, the call and the promise of Jesus is to
the overcomers. The Letter of one so gentle as John is full
of it. "I am writing to you, young men, because you have
overcome the evil one . . . Little children, you are of God
and have overcome them (i.e. the antichrist spirits) because
he who is in you is greater than he who is in the world . . .
Whatever is born of God overcomes the world; and this is
the victory that overcomes the world, our faith . . . We

know that any one born of God does not sin, but He who was born of God keeps him and the evil one cannot touch him" (1 John 2:13, 4:4, 5:4, 18). Is that the characteristic flavour of the modern church? If not, what is needed for a recovery of that buoyancy in conflict with the world, the flesh and through it all, the devil?

## Spiritual Warfare

First, the church needs to recover the dimension of spiritual conflict. If you do not believe in Satan, how can you fight him? I hope I am wrong, but I do not see the modern church, in the West at any rate, as a body which is alive to spiritual warfare. It seems to be preoccupied with its own survival, its petty concerns, its tradition, its canons and its revised worship books – or else coming out with dicta about many of the contemporary problems of our society without getting to the heart of the matter. It scratches at the spots caused by measles without getting down to the disease itself. The disease, of course, is sin and Satan, and I do not hear a great deal about these in the contemporary church. I do not find that much emphasis is placed on prayer, on the power of the Holy Spirit, on the need for watchfulness and fasting, on the need for spiritual gifts, on the importance of the Christian mind not being conformed to the spirit of the age.

The church at large seems to have lost the recognition that there is a war on. "Church" is a place to go on a Sunday once a week – or once a month – not a corps of battle troops under a Commander against a skilful, powerful, ruthless foe. Camouflage is one of the basic arts of warfare. If the Enemy has managed to camouflage himself so well that most churchmen do not notice he is around or even believe he exists – well, that suits him admirably. Such a church is easy prey for him. But the early Christians were under no illusions. They believed in a devil who was like a roaring lion, like an angel in disguise, like an experienced wrestler, like the best soldiery known to antiquity.

248

**Truth**

Second, the church needs to pay the utmost attention to truth. Wherever you look in the New Testament there is a strong emphasis on truth. The God of truth has revealed himself in Jesus who embodies the truth. Back to John's First Letter, and its concluding words. "We know that the Son of God has come, and has given us understanding to know him who is true, and his Son, Jesus Christ. This is the true God and eternal life. Little children, keep yourselves from idols." But that is just what contemporary Christianity does not do. It is very unsure whether Jesus is more than one aspect of the truth. It does not shrink from saying that he was wrong on many things. It does not believe his words – indeed, it believes that very few of the words attributed to him were spoken by him at all. Some of its theologians believe almost nothing about him. Doctrinal laxity has reached an all time low. You can be an ordained cleric in most of the main denominations without believing that Jesus is the Son of God, without believing in his birth from a virgin, his healings, his exorcisms, his teachings, his resurrection or his second coming.

Far be it for me to advocate uniformity in doctrinal formulation. That would be impossible and undesirable. There were different doctrinal emphases in New Testament Christianity. But there was a common core of belief. There was a common conviction of the essential matters of the incarnation, miracles, atonement, resurrection and the coming of the Spirit before the end of the age. And there was a strong conception of "the word of God" and its opposite, heresy. Today the idea of "the word of God" I found to be literally meaningless when I served for some years on the Doctrinal Commission of the Church of England. The Reformation may have argued about what it consisted of – Scripture, or Scripture and Tradition. But for our Commission there was no conviction that "the word of God" *meant* anything at all. How can a church which is so unsure of its charter begin to overcome anything or win over anyone? There is not likely to be a renewal of Christian faith and life until the Bible comes into the forefront of the church's life again.

I do not for a moment wish or expect every Christian to become a Catholic or an Evangelical. I feel that would be a great impoverishment of the variety within the Body of Christ. But I do look for the day when Christians of every hue will return to the Bible as the source of their inspiration and the guide of their lives. It is time to believe and declare the uniqueness of Jesus. It is time to revel in the justification only possible through him. It is time to receive and be filled with his Spirit. It is time to abjure syncretism and "contend for the faith which was once for all delivered to the saints" (Jude 3).

At present the church in this country would seem to be some distance away from such clarity of conviction. On Whitsunday, 1980, the Cathedral Church of the first British martyr, St. Alban, celebrated the faith he died for as follows. Backed by distinguished churchmen, a gathering in association with the World Congress of Faiths took place, not only for dialogue, but for combined worship. They included Jews, Christians, Moslems and others, notably the Dalai Lama, who believes and proclaims that he is divine. Their motto was "My house shall be called a House of Prayer for all the Nations" (Jesus did not say "for all religions"). It was essentially syncretistic. It remained for the local press (rather than the local Christians) to label the whole enterprise as "Blasphemy". This is just one example of the relativism that is strangling truth. But we are becoming so acclimatised to it that we barely notice its growth.

Jacques Ellul, at the end of his book on the modern myths and religions which the church absorbs without even realising that she is doing so, says somewhat sardonically, "The fight of faith lies ahead of us. It is necessary, if we believe that there is truth in the revelation of God in Jesus Christ, as set forth in Scripture. Surely that implies that the modern religions and the modern sacred are errors or lies. Of course, if we feel it necessary to reject all distinction between error and truth, that is our privilege; but then, for goodness' sake, let's stop talking about Jesus Christ who is designated as the Truth" (*op. cit.*, p. 228). Unless the church recovers an assurance that in Jesus Christ and the Scriptures which tell of him she has a true revelation from

God, there is no possible chance of overcoming the Father
of lies.

## Unity
Unity is another indispensable spiritual weapon with which
the church must be equipped if it is to make any significant
inroads into the realm of Satan. "Divide and conquer" has
been his policy, and it has been effective. To reflect that the
greatest split in Christendom concentrated on one word,
*filioque*, is nothing short of tragic. There were many differences between Jerusalam Christianity, Antioch
Christianity, Roman Christianity, Samaritan Christianity
in the early days, but the New Testament shows the extra-
ordinary lengths to which the believers went in order to
ensure that these differences did not take them out of
communion with each other. And nowadays, when the
Spirit of God falls upon Christians in any area, renewing
and transforming them, he always binds them together in a
fellowship of love. The coming together of Roman
Catholics and Protestants in the renewal in Ireland or Latin
America or South Africa is eloquent. So long as we repeat
the ancient formulas of discord, so long as we refuse to
believe God can change either us or the other party, we will
not and cannot see any unseating of Satan. I do not believe
it is essential to have organisational unity first. Indeed, if we
have to wait for that, it may be like *Waiting for Godot* (I
speak from the experience of having served on the
Churches' Unity Commission!). But it is essential for us to
repent of our doing apart what we can with perfect integrity
together do; to come together at the level of ministers and
congregations for prayer, common action, joint evangelism
and an assault on whatever are the main principalities and
powers in our area. But we are all too busy doing our own
thing. Or the other churches would not want it. Or they are
not sound. Or . . .

## Mission
All of which leads on to the question of mission. The early
Christians were a threat to Satan because they were always
reaching out in service and evangelism making Christ

known in the very strongholds of the Enemy. They were confident of the gospel. They expected conversions. They would have been amazed at many modern churches who have never seen anyone turn from unbelief to faith, do not expect it, would not welcome it, and would certainly not know what to do with such a person if it happened! Of course, when a church does believe the New Testament message, and does rely on the Spirit of God; when it does repent of any known disunity and when every member sees it as his responsibility to make Christ known as best he can at home, at work, at the sports ground, in the pub, at the Adult Education Class or whatever – then you see growth. You see conversions. You see a dent being made in the principalities and powers. There will be many problems in such a church, no doubt; but they will be the problems that spring from life.

Truth, unity and mission: those are the aims of the World Council of Churches. Alas, currently they fall far short of achievement. But they point the way to the overcoming life for the church.

### St. John's last word

Perhaps the essence of the matter has already been given us, in Revelation 12:11. We have had occasion to look at it more than once, for it is crucial. John is describing in apocalyptic terms the primal theomachy which turned into a Christomachy and then an ecclesiomachy. "The great dragon was thrown down, that ancient serpent who is called the Devil and Satan, the deceiver of the whole world – he was thrown down to the earth, and his angels were thrown down with him. And I heard a loud voice in heaven, saying, 'Now the salvation and the power and the kingdom of our God and the authority of his Christ have come, for the accuser of our brethren has been thrown down, who accuses them day and night before our God.' And they overcame him by the blood of the Lamb, and by the word of their testimony, for they loved not their lives unto death." There you have the secret of a church which overcomes the Evil One.

You will notice the prerequisite. He is recognised and

fought, not demythologised and neglected. But how was he overcome by those early followers of Jesus? How is he overcome by the church today where it is alive and well?

The answer is threefold. First, they conquered him by the blood of the Lamb. That is to say the secret of their victory lay in depending on and applying the victory won by Jesus Christ over Satan on the cross.

> That victory of Christ is not nearly a drawn game; it is total victory. It is like the tremendous picture by Albrecht Dürer of the "Harrowing of Hell". There stand hell gates, gates of impregnable brass, but they are broken and riven into fragments, and all the devils in hell are cowering back into the darkness, jibbering with craven fear as down in hell itself there stoops the strong Son of God, stretching down his arm to bring forth those whom he has rescued.
>
> (Gordon Rupp, *Principalities and Powers*, p. 61)

It cannot be emphasised too much that the only name which brings fear to Satan is the name of Jesus, and the only place that makes him give way is Calvary. There is power in the blood of Christ. There is nothing like it in all the world.

Then, second, they overcame by the word of their testimony. Each Christian saw himself commissioned as a witness, as an ambassador, as a mouthpiece for his risen and ascended Master. He knew that the Holy Spirit was given him for witness bearing. He recognised that Satan was driven back every time another person came to faith. That is why they all gave their testimony so fearlessly and continuously. Nothing could stop them. It was the Saviour's last command (Matt. 28:19). It was the purpose of the Spirit's coming upon them (Acts 1:8, Jn. 15:26, 27, Mk. 13:10, 11). It was the natural response of those who had found mercy (2 Cor. 4:1). It was in any case immensely rewarding. Anyone who has had the privilege of leading another to Christ will not need me to persuade him that this is the greatest joy on earth. That element of witness-bearing is an important part of what made the early church into overcomers.

And finally, they did not love their lives unto death. They were totally committed to the Lord who had totally committed himself for them. That commitment meant discipleship, hardship. It meant becoming a laughing-stock. It meant the willingness to be deprived of friends, home, money, career, liberty, life itself. And all in order to spread to captives the news of the Liberator. They loved not their lives unto death. What a testimony to the church which overcame! They had the right perspective. They knew that Satan was a defeated foe. They knew that the cause of Jesus Christ could not be stopped. They knew that whatever the reverses they encountered, whatever the sufferings they endured, whatever the death meted out to them, the Lord God omnipotent was reigning, the Lamb once slain was in the midst of the throne of God. And therefore they could rejoice. And therefore they could overcome. And so can we, if we are prepared to pay the price.

Let John Bunyan have the last word on Satan's downfall. This is the authentic attitude of the overcoming church throughout the ages.

But as God would have it, while Apollyon was fetching his last blow, thereby to make a full end of this good man, Christian nimbly stretched forth his hand for his sword, and caught it, saying, "Rejoice not against me, O mine enemy: when I fall I shall arise"; and with that gave him a deadly thrust, which made him give back, as one that had received his mortal wound. Christian, perceiving that, made at him again, saying, "Nay, in all these things we are more than conquerors through him that loved us." And with that Apollyon spread forth his dragon wings, and sped him away.